A TIME FOR TRUTH 2001

by Elliot M. Kramer

Acknowledgement Page

Thank you to:

Dr. Phyllis S. Kramer, Professor Gil Troy, Professor Shawn Aster, Simon Bensimon, Mordecai Kramer, Mark Bellows, Jay Rubin for their editorial comments,

Hillel Montreal for use of its offices and unparalleled resources, the Canadian Institute for Jewish Research (CIJR) for use of its archives,

Edward Shostak for help with research and strategy, Mimi and David for the graphics and artwork,

& Rabbi Michael Kramer, Baruch Cohen and Murray Goldstein for a steady supply of relevant articles.

About the Author

Elliot M. Kramer received his B.A. from McGill University in Political Science and his M.A. from Georgetown University in National Security Studies. He is a former editor of *Dateline: Middle East*. He was an accredited journalist in the Middle East during the Persian Gulf War.

TABLE OF CONTENTS

CHARTS/GRAPHS/TABLES

INTRODUCTION

Since September 1993, Israel has been under attack. The war against the Jewish State is being waged against all Jews in the cities and towns of Israel and also in the international media. It is the same anti-Western war that struck the United States on September 11, 2001. It is a war against democracy, freedom and human rights. Any person who believes in these principles needs to know the truth about the conflict and be able to recognize the lies that we are all being fed in the media.

A 'common misconception' about the Middle East, that may have been aired on the news or printed in a newspaper or magazine, is presented to you in **bold** with *italics*. This is immediately followed by a 'response' based on facts that most likely did not appear in the news.

In writing this book, every effort has been made to present facts that can be substantiated. When evidence was unavailable, quotations were used from regional personalities who play important roles in the events of the Middle East. I have also tried to present evidence for each topic in a concise and easy-to-read format.

I do not believe that there is a conspiracy to discredit Israel in the Western media. Rather, the coverage suffers from five ailments:
1. Journalistic sloppiness, i.e. journalists who do not verify whether their sources are telling the truth.
2. A lack of balance, i.e. Israeli society is accessible because it is free and democratic, whereas the Palestinian Authority and Arab countries are restricted and information fed to the media is carefully scripted.
3. The desire for sensationalism, i.e. Western media outlets search for news that it can sell to the public and the image of a Palestinian rock-thrower against a modern Israeli army makes for captivating footage, even if it is inaccurate.
4. Journalists not educating themselves about the history of the conflict, i.e. reports lack context.
5. An unchallenged acceptance by journalists that both sides of any case deserve equal time, i.e. since terrorists and murderers are given equal access to present their case in the media, it leaves Western audiences confused as to who the real victims are.

This book emphasizes events and declarations that have been made since the Oslo Process began in 1993. However, knowledge of history is paramount to understanding the conflict, so an attempt was made to integrate important historical facts with the current events in order to help the reader see a wider context.

6

I hope that *A Time for Truth* helps provide a counterbalance to the coverage that is given on television, radio and in newspapers. I also hope it allows readers to widen their perspective on the Middle East and gain more of a global understanding of what the Arab-Israel conflict is, and is not, all about.

I also hope that the information in this book is beneficial to people who believe in freedom, democracy and real peace. Those who stand firmly behind these principles that define Judeo-Christian civilization should know what is really happening in the Arab-Israel conflict and what the actual issues are. We have all been subjected for too much time to lies and distortions. It is definitely *A Time for Truth*.

[Events until October 16, 2001 are included in this book.]

Palestinian Authority

Area:	6,220 sq. km
Population:	2.9 Million
Chairman:	Yassir Arafat
GDP per capita:	$1,100
Military Manpower	35,000
Armed Fighting Vehicles:	45
Defense Budget	$500 Million

PALESTINIAN AUTHORITY

i. Statehood

The Palestinian Authority is the first true Arab democracy

Marwan Barghouti, the General-Secretary of Fatah in the West Bank and leader of the Tanzim, declared in July 2001 that "When we signed Oslo, we began a process of democratization." It has been more than eight years since Oslo. Is Barghouti's statement accurate?

Since the Israelis withdrew from large parts of the West Bank and Gaza, leaving the Palestinians under the rule of Yassir Arafat and the Palestinian Authority, the PA has routinely denied its people fair trial. Amnesty International reported in December 1996 that "The great majority of the more than 2,000 political detainees arrested and detained by the PA over the past two years have been held without charge or trial."

A national Palestinian election has not been held since 1993, Jewish sites of worship, such as Joseph's and Rachel's Tombs, have been repeatedly attacked and the Palestinian press has been restricted and censored. Amnesty quoted a journalist who wrote an article critical of the PA: "I was traveling to a meeting by car when three cars surrounded me and about 15 men with Kalashnikovs rushed forward shouting at me to raise my hands. They were in civilian dress and the cars were unmarked. They tied my hands, blind-folded me and took me to the Military Intelligence."

There is no due process for the accused. Human Rights Watch reported in 1999 that "Palestinian security forces continued to carry out arbitrary arrests and detentions, holding detainees for years without charge and without access to lawyers or family visits, sometimes even after the PA's Attorney General or courts had ordered access to lawyers or releases."

Financial accountability, freedom of speech, rights to own property and women's rights are almost non-existent. PA Justice Minister, Fraih Abu Meddain told Palestinian Radio in June 1999 that the Palestinian human rights organizations "are doing political work that does not serve the Palestinian people. We want to pass a law regarding these organiza-tions…The money these institutions receive is earmarked for the Palestinian people, and we can't allow a small group of people to spend millions of dol-lars without supervision" *(Ha'aretz,* June 13, 1999). When Abdel Ghanem, one of Arafat's senior advisers, complained about Arafat's handling of the refugee issue, he was arrested and detained for over a month. Arafat has ruled for over eight years without consensus, parliamentary approval or checks and balances (*US Department of State, Country Reports on Human*

Rights Practices). Hussam Khadr, a member of the Palestinian Legislative Council, said of his council on February 4, 2001 that they "missed a true opportunity to establish a respectable regime that would be different from the various regimes that do not recognize human rights in our society" (*MEMRI*, February 13, 2001). A State of Palestine would fit right into the Arab world where monarchies, theocracies and military dictatorships abound.

Once a Palestinian state is established, the Western world will have a new friend and ally

During the height of the terror-filled 1970s, Arafat was closest to the USSR, East Germany, Libya and post-Revolution Iran. The PLO also trained together with the Italian Red Brigades, the Baader-Meinhoff Gang and the Japanese Red Army. Two of the modern world's most ruthless killers, Uganda's Idi Amin and Equitorial Guinea's Macias Nguema Biyago, both employed PLO bodyguards and PLO-trained internal security forces. Ayatollah Khomeini's personal bodyguards were PLO personnel. Arafat remains closely linked with Cuba and North Korea to this day. The Black September Organization that carried out the 1972 Munich Olympics massacre of Israeli athletes and the 1973 Khartoum murder of American and Belgian diplomats, operated under Arafat's personal command. The Chief of Operations for Black September was Ali Hassan Salameh, who Arafat referred to then as "my adopted son."

Arafat's closest ally has always been Saddam Hussein of Iraq. For many years, Arafat had an Iraqi airliner for personal use that was a gift from Saddam. According to the February 21, 2001 *Jane's Weekly*, Arafat has an emergency escape plan to be effected if Israel ever forces him into exile, which has him running a government-in-exile from Baghdad. During the Gulf War, he resided for some time in Baghdad and was an unqualified supporter of Iraq against the US-led coalition defending Kuwait.

Arafat currently gives personal shelter to Hamas' Muhammad Def, who is #1 on Israel's Most Wanted List. Def is the mastermind of several kidnappings and killings of IDF soldiers, a bus bombing in Jerusalem and the bombing of a shopping center in Tel Aviv in 1996. Arafat refers to *Sheikh* Yassin, the spiritual leader of Hamas, as "my brother" and has released all Hamas murderers of Israelis from prison.

He was banned from entering the US for years until the peace process began because of his lengthy record of killing American civilians and diplomats.

Nowhere is the American flag burned more frequently than in the streets of Palestinian cities, towns and villages. Following the September 11, 2001 attack on the World Trade Center and Pentagon, Palestinians danced, celebrated and passed out candies in the streets of Lebanon, Gaza and the West Bank. When US Secretary of State Colin Powell met Arafat in Gaza in May 2000, an anti-American demonstration was held outside the meeting place immediately after he departed. *Al-Hayat Al-Jedida* reported on November 11, 2000 that 73% of Palestinians support attacks against the US.

How does the PA treat the Western World in public?

The official PA press, *Al-Hayat Al-Jedida*: "The suicide bombers of today are the noble successors of their noble predecessors...the Lebanese suicide bombers, who taught the US Marines a tough lesson in [Lebanon]...and then, with no preconditions, they threw the last of the remaining enemy [Israel] out of the [security] zone. These suicide bombers are the salt of the earth, the engines of history...They are the most honorable [people] among us..." (*Palestinian Media Watch*, September 11, 2001).

Al-Hayat Al-Jedida, November 24, 1997: "They [the Americans and the British] are war merchants and oil and blood suckers who do not strive for peace and stability. This is the Colonialist mentality which still leads Britain and the US to a single [path]."

Al-Hayat Al-Jedida, November 15, 1997: "History does not remember the United States...the murderers of humanity, the creators of the barbaric culture and the bloodsuckers of the nations, are doomed to death and destined to shrink to a microscopic size, like Micronesia."

Al-Hayat Al-Jedida, November 11, 1997: "Immediately following the Gulf War, James Baker spied on the Arab countries in order to bring the Arab capitals - which transformed into obedient females - under Israeli protection, after they had already been put under American protection during the Gulf War."

Al-Ayyam, August 10, 1999: "You are not the only one persecuted, Osama Bin Laden. You are not the only one harassed by American terrorism, after the [American] Cowboy took over the world in this century's dark final decade."

Communiqué issued by Fatah and other PLO factions in 1998: "The purpose of the American provocations against the Iraqi government and its people is to humiliate the Arab nation and harm Iraq" (*Al-Quds*, January 19, 1998).

What about the Palestinian popular feeling? Does Arafat's camaraderie with the despots of the world deviate from the sentiment of his people? A Bir Zeit University survey that ran in the July 21, 1997 *Al-Ayyam* showed that Palestinians rank Saddam Hussein first among Arab leaders in popularity.

The Palestinian-Israeli conflict will end as soon as the Palestinians get a state in the West Bank and Gaza

In 1964, the PLO approved its charter calling for the destruction of the State of Israel (See Appendix I). The PLO Charter remains the official guide for

Yassir Arafat and the Palestinian Authority. Israel only took control of the West Bank and Gaza in 1967, three years *after* the charter was approved by the Palestine National Convention (PNC).

The 12th session of the PNC in June 1974 approved a program of stages, i.e. to establish a state in as much territory as possible and then use it as a springboard to conquer the rest. Here are four of the decisions enacted by the PNC that remain its stated objective:

Decision #2. The PLO uses all means, the most important of which is armed struggle, in its fight to liberate the Palestinian land and establish the national independent Palestinian authority, on every liberated part from the Palestinian land. Achieving this requires creating a change in the power balance in our nation's favor.

Decision #3. The PLO struggles against any design to create a Palestinian entity in return for recognizing and normalizing relations with Israel and its safe borders, and leads to giving up the Palestinian national rights and depriving our people from their right to return and self-determination on our land.

Decision #4. Any partial liberation is just one part of the realization of the PLO's strategy to establish the democratic Palestinian State as decided by the PNC.

Decision #8. After establishing the Palestinian authority, it should struggle for unity between conflict-involved countries, as a step towards a complete liberation of the Palestinian land as part of the complete unity.

Following the Six-Day and Yom Kippur Wars, the Israelis were ready to sign a peace agreement with any of the Arab countries that lost land to them on the principle of land-for-peace. Autonomy was offered to the Palestinians. In the Camp David Peace Accords of 1978, the Egyptians and Israelis adopted the same formula. Fatah and the PLO were opposed to Palestinian autonomy. Had autonomy been accepted, Arafat would have been rendered useless and replaced by indigenous leadership. The Palestinians would also have accepted Israel and agreed to peace with them. This was also anathema to Fatah and the PLO.

Does the PLO still support these statements with its actions and words, or has there been a change since the Oslo process began?

On September 13, 1995, the same day that the Palestinian-Israeli peace agreement ceremony was held at the White House, Arafat told *Jordanian Television*: "Since we cannot defeat Israel in war we do this in stages. We take any and every territory that we can of Palestine, and establish sovereignty there, and we use it as a springboard to take more. When the time comes, we can get the Arab nations to join us for the final blow against Israel."

If the PA only wanted a state in the West Bank and Gaza, Yassir Arafat would have accepted Israeli Prime Minister Ehud Barak's proposal to end the Israeli-Palestinian conflict once and for all. Barak, under intense pressure from President Clinton to offer a maximal Israeli position, offered unparalleled concessions. His offer was printed in *Al-Ayyam* just before the Israeli public went to the polls on February 6, 2001. It included an independent Palestinian state in 95% of the West Bank, all of East Jerusalem, the entire Gaza Strip, elimination of nearly all settlements, full sovereignty over the visible Temple Mount and complete recognition from Israel.

After eight years of living under PA rule, the Palestinians still seek out Israelis, no longer patrolling their town centers, but in Oslo-sanctioned military posts that are outside Arab city limits. Palestinian suicide bombers attack civilians in Hadera, Tel Aviv, Ashkelon, and Kfar Saba, all situated in Israel's heartland. Why? Arafat's organization, Fatah, placed its constitution on its Internet web site in 1998, and answered this question in stating its main goal: "The complete liberation of Palestine and eradication of Zionist economic, political, military and cultural existence."

The PA only wants the West Bank and Gaza as its state

Al-Hayat Al-Jedida, the official newspaper of the PA, stated in July 2001, that: "We must transfer the war to the lands of the enemy -- if we may use this phrase, with the knowledge that all of Palestine is conquered, and the time has come for us to wake up and fight them on every centimeter -- let's move the fight to the land that has been conquered since 1948."

The Palestinians do not have a homeland

Jordan was created for the Arabs of Palestine in 1921. The British divided the territory of its Mandate in Palestine to accommodate the Arabs and the Jews by giving Transjordan, which comprised 80% of the territory, to the Arabs and the western side of the Jordan River, which comprised 20% of the land, to the Jews. There were never two peoples known as Jordanians and Palestinians; Arabs from this area were from the same families and tribes. Today, the population of Jordan is over 70% Palestinian.

A Time for Truth: In 1970, Yassir Arafat said, "What you call Jordan is actually Palestine." King Hussein of Jordan commented in 1981: "The truth is that Jordan is Palestine and Palestine is Jordan." With a population that is more than two-thirds Palestinian, the State of Jordan always has trouble not far from the surface.

The PA only wants East Jerusalem as its capital

Ikrimi Sabri, the *Mufti* of Jerusalem, appointed by Arafat, states the PA position on Jerusalem: "There is no room for compromising solutions with regard to occupied Jerusalem. Israeli citizenship is forbidden for Palestinians according to *Shari'a* [Islamic law]. Those who have already acquired it should give it up because it does not honor them particularly, since Israel's days are numbered" (*Al-Hayat Al-Jedida*, October 5, 2000).

ii. Freedom

The PA has established a judicial process and a Western court system

The PA established a system of courts upon its arrival in the territories. Many judges were appointed because of their affiliation with Fatah. Fayez al-Quidrah, President of the High Court of Justice in Gaza, said that "New judges need to be trained, especially because the way in which they are appointed has become unacceptable."[1] Mohammad Ayoub, a defense attorney from Ramallah, said that: "Judges do not have the necessary knowledge to exercise their functions."[2] "We are not calling this martial law, but we are in a transitional period," said Attiyah Abu Moor, Head of the Legal Development Program of the Palestinian Authority's Ministry of Justice, on the PA's failure to implement High Court decisions.[3] The Palestine Human Rights Monitoring Group (PHRMG) reported that of 73 High Court orders for release of prisoners, Arafat agreed to release only 4 of them.

Many of the cases heard are brought into court only because the accused has done something to personally anger Yassir Arafat. Maher Alami, editor of the *Al-Quds* daily, was arrested and detained for six days because he placed an interview between the Greek Orthodox Patriarch of Jerusalem and Arafat on page 8 instead of on the front page of his paper, as Arafat requested.

Iyad al-Sarraj, the Commissioner General of the Palestinian Independent Commission for Citizens' Rights and the Director of the Gaza Community Mental Health Program, was detained for 9 hours in December 1995 for criticizing the PA for its record on human rights. In May 1996, he was held for 8 days on similar charges. On June 10, he was arrested for a third time, beaten and kicked by the police. He was charged with possession of drugs and assaulting the police. After local and international groups began a campaign for his release, Arafat eventually agreed to release him. He was set free after 17 days in prison. The Palestinian Legislative Council passed a law guaranteeing freedom of expression, but Arafat has yet to ratify it.

---

[1] Detainees Denied Justice, Gerard Simpson, Kluwer Law International, Page 241.
[2] ibid. p.250.
[3] ibid. p.2.

Unlike a Western system, the PA has legislation that is racist. The penalty for selling land to Jews is death, whereas killing them does not merit capital punishment. In practice, killing Jews does not meet with punishment on any level in the vast majority of cases.

Vigilante justice is rampant in the streets of the West Bank and Gaza, with PA policemen, Force 17 and Tanzim members carrying out assassinations and personal retribution. Amnesty International reported that there were 50 civilians killed and over 100 wounded by Palestinian police between 1994-1996. The security forces take the law into their own hands because they are mostly granted immunity. Of all the illegal detentions by the Executive Authority and the security forces, not one has been convicted by the High Court. One interesting case involved a member of the Abu Sultan family killing two members of the Khalidi family over a 'Peeping Tom' incident. The Abu Sultans were all members of Palestinian Security. However, the Khalidi family belonged to Palestinian Security and Fatah. A quick military trial found the Abu Sultans guilty and they were executed the next day by firing squad (*www.miftah.org*).

There have been several sensational murders where Israeli and American public pressure mounted on the PA for arrests. The murderers were arrested by Arafat's police, brought before courts and found guilty. After serving short jail terms, Arafat commuted their sentences and they were released back to freedom. Amnesty reports that "the scale and arbitrary nature of the arrests has frequently suggested that attempts were being made simply to round up large numbers of suspected sympathizers of opposition parties, without any relation to whether or not they had committed or were suspected of having committed any criminal offense."

The Palestinian Human Rights Monitoring Group (PHRMG) has collected testimony from 36 Palestinians about the PA's Preventive Security Apparatus (PSA) apprehending successful local businessmen, torturing and imprisoning them until they agreed to pay "taxes" as high as $50,000 for their release.

There are over 200 people suspected of collaborating with Israel in Palestinian prisons, many on death row. Many others are brought before kangaroo courts and executed. The executioners are members of Arafat's Fatah. One group with close ties to Arafat, Asfah 77, stormed into the shop of a Tulkarm shopkeeper and murdered him for "spying" on April 9, 2001. Many others are given speedy kangaroo-style military trials with no defense or evidence, followed by a public execution. *Arutz 7* reported on August 7, 2001 that 3 Arabs were arrested for "collaborating with Israel" and taken to the jail in Nablus. A mob of people broke into the jail at 3 AM and threatened "We'll kill them on our own if you won't do it." A 10-minute trial was held and the 3 men were shot. The execution of Allan Bani Oudeh in Nablus was attended by a cheering mass of well over 100 people, including his young daughter and wife, who were forced to attend. *The Palestine Broadcast Association* secretly filmed an execution in Gaza City, which it sold to Israeli television. The following week, the head of the station, Hisham Maki, was gunned down in the street. Arafat was a pallbearer at the funeral, then, a few days later, he seized all of Maki's property, assets and bank accounts, worth over $17 million.

Unlike Israel, the PA is religiously tolerant

Since Israel declared independence, Arabs have lived in Israel as citizens. There are now more than 1,000,000 Christian and Moslem Arabs with Israeli citizenship. They vote, own land, worship their religion and form their own political parties. They participate in just about all areas of life in Israel.

There is a track record on the PA treatment of Jews and Judaism since 1993, when the PA began ruling in the West Bank and Gaza. On an official PA religious program of February 16, 1999, *Sheikh* Yussef Abu Snineh was quoted as saying: "...they changed this Torah to an expression of the History of the Jews, and their history is full of guilt and crimes...they changed the grace of Allah into heresy and they faked this Torah..." On February 18, 1999, *Al-Hayat Al-Jedida*, the official PA newspaper, referred to Yad Vashem, the Holocaust Memorial in Jerusalem, as the "Jewish center for eternalizing the Holocaust and the lies."

Joseph's Tomb has served as a memorial to the ancient Jewish leader for centuries. Since the early 1980s it has served as a yeshiva (religious school) and synagogue. Before this shrine was handed over to the Palestinians as part of the peace agreement, an Israeli Border Guard was shot and Palestinian police barred the Israeli evacuation team from entering the area for 4 hours. During this delay, the man bled to death. Joseph's Tomb in Shechem (Nablus) was overrun by a mob of Palestinians on October 7, 2000, the second week of the Intifada. The mob murdered Hillel Lieberman, an Israeli who was trying to save a Torah scroll inside the compound, and burnt the Tomb to the ground. Palestinian police, guarding the shrine, turned their guns on it and participated in the massacre. All Jewish holy articles were destroyed and the tomb was completely dismantled. Now there are no traces left of a Jewish presence. The Tomb now functions only as a mosque.

In Jericho, a Palestinian mob razed an ancient synagogue to the ground on October 9, 2000. PA police prevented a firetruck from reaching the site while it still could have been saved. The '*Shalom Al Yisrael*' (Peace for Israel) synagogue was not in use, but was an important archaeological site. It was renowned for a unique Byzantine mosaic floor that was in exceptional condition. The mosaic had a *Torah* ark, *shofar*, *lulav*, *menorah* and an inscription with a quotation from the Book of Psalms. Under the conditions of the

Oslo accords, Jericho was ceded to the Palestinians on the assurance that this ancient site be preserved and protected.

Near Shfaram, a town in the Galilee, the grave of Rabbi Yehuda Ben Baba, a Talmudic-era sage, was desecrated on October 26, 2000. Palestinians piled holy Jewish books on the grave and lit a bonfire.

The Temple Mount has been repeatedly violated by Palestinian acts. Solomon's Stables, dating from the First Temple Period, has been rebuilt as a mosque. This is the third mosque on the mount, and the first to be constructed in over 1,000 years. Because of this construction, the southern wall of the Temple Mount is in danger of possible collapse. The *Waqf*, the Moslem body that administers the site, dug up over 6,000 tons of earth and dumped it into garbage heaps and rivers. A 16' x 6' wall thought to be part of the Herodian Temple courtyard wall foundation was demolished before archaeologists could study it. Dozens of trucks have been entering the Temple Mount and removing archaeological material on a regular basis. A 24' x 12' stonecutter sits atop the Temple Mount for the purpose of removing massive limestone blocks from the remains of ancient Temple buildings. Antiquities from the periods of the First and Second Temples have been dumped onto garbage heaps. The *Waqf* has been cited for 35 different violations of Israeli Antiquities Law. Moshe Katsav, the President of Israel, said in July 2001 that the *Waqf* is trying "to erase every Jewish trace" on the Mount as part of their campaign to deny that there was ever a Jewish presence on this, the holiest site in Judaism.[4]

Beit Jala is a Palestinian Christian town on the outskirts of Jerusalem, next to Gilo, a Jewish neighborhood. Palestinian snipers repeatedly use local residents' homes for the purpose of shooting at Israelis in the neighboring community. These snipers are not residents of the town and are Moslems. There have been numerous reports of Arab Christians who say that the snipers are unwanted and operate in their town only because the local population is under the threat of violence if they try to prevent the Moslem-dominated PA from attacking Israel from their homes. *Arutz 7* reported on September 2, 2001 that Farid Aziza, a Christian leader from Beit Jala, was attacked by Moslems and seriously wounded because of his good relations with Israel.

Arafat came to power through free elections and governs democratically

When the PA first entered the West Bank and Gaza, it held an election where European observers and a team led by former American President Jimmy

---

[4] No reports of these violations appeared in the international media. When the Israelis opened a gate to the ancient tunnel running outside the Mount on the Via Dolorosa, reports appeared all over the world that Israel had violated the *al-Aqsa* mosque. The subsequent bloodshed that occurred because of the ensuing organized Arab riots was immense.

Carter were called upon to monitor the process. There were many violations, including rampant intimidation of alternative, non-Fatah candidates. There were numerous cases of coercion at voting stations as well. Bassem Eid, the director of PHRMG (Palestine Human Rights Monitoring Group), spent Election Day in Hebron and said that of the 15 polling stations that he visited, only 3 reported visits from European monitors. None of these observers spoke any Arabic and subsequently were not capable of detecting irregularities or violations. Because the Carter Center only had 40 representatives, there was only so much it could do.

There has not been a follow-up election, nor are there plans for one. It is unclear whether Arafat could win another election because of widespread Palestinian disenchantment due to PA nepotism and corruption. Arafat's regime has been termed a 'kleptocracy' because of his propensity for funneling international funds earmarked for development into personal Swiss bank accounts.

Over 70% of Palestinians feel that the PA is corrupt, according to an April 2000 poll by the Center for Palestine Research and Studies (CPRS). Only 22% feel that the PA is doing a good or very good job with regard to democracy and human rights.

The population has become more radicalized and could possibly support Hamas, an organization that overtly calls for armed conflict in order to eradicate Israel. The CPRS found that only 38.6% would vote for Arafat in an election. The Israeli daily *Ha'aretz* reported in August 2001 that because of waning popular support, Arafat is considering a 'national unity' government with Islamic Jihad and Hamas, two groups on the US State Department list of terrorist organizations.

Under the PA there is full freedom of the press

To date, there have been over 30 Palestinian journalists arrested and imprisoned without charge because of articles they wrote. The most prominent Palestinian journalist, Daoud Kuttab, was held for over a week without charge. The editor of *Al-Hayat Al-Jedida* was beaten up by Palestinian policemen for attempting to attend a military tribunal hearing in Gaza against two Palestinians who made anti-Arafat statements. He and two of his colleagues who reported on the trial were arrested and detained without charge. *Al-Jezira*, the CNN of the Arab World, had its broadcasts in PA-controlled areas terminated when it ran a report critical of Arafat. Maher Alami, a columnist for *Al Istiqlal*, was jailed without charge after he wrote an editorial about Arafat and the PA's rampant corruption. Private TV stations and radio stations (*Al Nasser*, *Al Mahed* and *Al Menara*) were shut after being critical of Arafat's policies on statehood. The owner of one of these stations was jailed as well. The News Director of the *Voice of Palestine* was arrested for similar reasons. A popular Palestinian talk show host, Maher Dasuki, was arrested, jailed for 20 days and tortured. When he was released, he reported that he had witnessed numerous other human rights violations in this Palestinian prison.

Israeli journalists have been warned that setting foot in the PA areas would be done at risk to their own lives. When a Polish TV crew filmed the lynching of two Israeli reservists in Ramallah, Palestinian security agents surrounded them, beat them and seized their videotapes. A British photographer, who also witnessed the lynchings, was punched in the face and had his camera smashed. An Italian TV crew captured the only video footage of this event. The station head must have received some serious threats to his life because several days later, he issued an apology to the PA for broadcasting this footage and professed solidarity to the Palestinian cause.[5] Even *CBS* was given sanctions and slapped with moving restrictions in the PA-controlled areas after a report on Arafat's corruption aired on *60 Minutes*.

On 29 May 2001, Arafat's Fatah Hawks kidnapped two *Newsweek* correspondents, one American and one Brit. They were held for about 5 hours, then released. However, the Hawks issued a warning that all American and British journalists operating in the PA areas are at risk because of the foreign policies of their countries.

All I see on the news are clips of Palestinians throwing stones and Israelis firing on unarmed defenseless civilians; hence Israel is really the oppressor because pictures and film do not lie.

The Palestinians have become very sophisticated when it comes to the media. Following the terrorist attacks on the World Trade Center and Pentagon on September 11, 2001, Palestinians took to the streets to dance and celebrate. Reporters in Shechem (Nablus) were immediately detained by armed Palestinians, who kept them under guard in a hotel until the celebrations were finished. One journalist who succeeded in photographing some of the festivities was told that if he published the photos, his life would be in danger (*Jerusalem Post*, September 12, 2001). When pro-Bin Laden demonstrations were held throughout the West Bank in late-September and October 2001, the PA realized the danger of having the world see overwhelming Palestinian support for Al Qaeda, and Palestinian cameramen were phoned and instructed not to send their footage to their agencies. PA Cabinet Secretary Ahmed Abdel Rahman phoned the *Associated Press* and *Reuters* bureaus and warned them not to broadcast the footage (*Jerusalem Report*, October 8, 2001). The Foreign Press Association in Israel filed a compaint against the PA because of the threats that members of the international press corps received (*Jerusalem Post*, September 14, 2001).

---

[5] He was removed from the Jerusalem bureau days later.

When two Israelis were lynched in Ramallah and the murderers bathed their hands in the blood of the two murdered men, there were reporters present. The Palestinians, who repeatedly choreograph scenes of violence for the media, mostly in the hopes that young Palestinians will be injured or killed on camera, threatened and beat up reporters who took photographs and video tapes. Cameras were smashed because a core group of Palestinians knew how damaging such footage would be to their cause and they prevented all but one cameraman from escaping intact.

Arafat has established a system whereby he controls nearly all of the images and reports coming out of the PA areas. Israeli journalists have been told that if they enter these areas, they do so at risk to their lives. A Fatah announcement on February 13, 2001 was carried in the *Jerusalem Post*, reading: "Fatah is warning that any Israeli, even a journalist, is barred from entering Bethlehem and anyone who does so won't get out alive." Foreign journalists are increasingly less comfortable about working in the West Bank and Gaza, so they opt for Arab stringers to find news stories and provide them with photos of what is occurring. Most bylines of coverage from the West Bank and Gaza Strip have Arab names. The *Jerusalem Report* (June 7, 2001) estimates that Palestinian film crews shoot 95% of all video footage emanating from the PA areas. The two major agencies, *Reuters TV* and *APTN*, run an entire network of Palestinian stringers, freelancers and fixers. These Palestinian stringers all answer to the PA. For those foreign journalists who venture into the PA-controlled areas, most are always accompanied by Palestinians who know what to show them and what not to show them.

A Time for Truth: The foregoing explains why the images you see on the news present a very skewed picture of the conflict and makes the Israelis out to be using "excessive force." The journalists, even while fearing for their lives and not entering the PA-controlled areas, still know what sells newspapers, so they print articles, oftentimes without verifying the veracity of a story. A poignant example of this lack of professionalism is the picture of a bleeding youth with an Israeli soldier standing above him, an angry look on his face, holding a police baton. The caption that was printed the world over was that the Israeli soldier had just beaten this Arab youth on the Temple Mount. The truth was that Arabs had pulled this American Jewish boy from a taxi in a Jerusalem neighborhood and beaten him bloody until the IDF soldier had arrived and scared off the Arabs, preventing the murder of an American civilian.

Now that Palestinians run their own jails, there are no longer any human rights abuses against prisoners

Amnesty International has highlighted the use of torture on prisoners of conscience in Palestinian prisons. They have accused the PA of many violations and abuses. Subhiyye Jumaa, a defense lawyer at the Palestinian

Independent Commission for Citizens Rights, said: "Before the coming of the Palestinian Authority I was able to visit Palestinian prisoners in Israeli prisons. Now I am not able to visit Palestinian prisoners in Palestinian prisons."[6] Amnesty reported in December 1996 that "the majority of more than 800 detainees arrested in Gaza since February 1996 have been tortured and at least a quarter of detainees arrested from the West Bank."

In the territories, Amnesty has to rely on personal accounts from released prisoners, since it is not granted freedom of access to these sites. Since most of these people were imprisoned for speaking out against Arafat, they are usually unwilling to talk to groups like Amnesty. The Palestinian Human Rights Monitoring Group reported on 7 Palestinians dying from torture while in custody in 1997, up from 4 in 1996. It also reports that "torture is frequent and routine in the Palestinian Authority." 24 people have died in Palestinian prisons since the Oslo Accords; 42 have received death sentences since 1995. A Palestinian human rights organization called *Al-Damir* accused the PA of detaining dissidents. As of May 1999, it listed 181 political detainees.

The PA is dealing with extremists by arresting and imprisoning them

According to a July 13, 2001 statement by Fatah leader Marwan Barghouti "We have stopped extremists. We have arrested them." Jibril Rajoub, Chief of the PA Preventive Security, told the Islamic Association for Palestine on June 9, 2001: "This is an Israeli dream. We will not arrest the sons of our people in order to appease Israel, let our people be assured that this won't happen." Who is right? Over 250 Palestinians have been released from PA prisons in the last year alone. All of these prisoners were serving time for their involvement in attacking Israeli civilians. They are back on the streets and participating in anti-Israel activity once again.

Even those terrorists who are convicted and imprisoned are not subjected to the kind of prisons common in the West. Firstly, they are really acting in concert with the PA, so they are not treated as felons and murderers by the prison staff. Secondly, they are not confined to cells under the PA. They are in prison on the "honor system." *Middle East News Line* reported in February 1999 that "...the PA has allowed dozens of Hamas members detained last year to leave prison every morning on condition that they return that night." The *Jerusalem Post* reported on April 22, 1998 that two Hamas terrorists were given permission "to leave their cells for studies at Bir Zeit University." The *Jerusalem Report*, in their March 5, 1998 edition quoted Palestinian eyewitnesses who saw two men who murdered Israelis and who were supposed to be in a Jericho jail, at coffee shops and markets with

---

[6] Detainees, Simpson, p.2.

family in Jericho. *Peace Watch* reported in May 1996 that one of the masterminds of the 1996 Jerusalem bus bombing that killed 4 was hired as a guard in the PA's Jericho jail, even though he was convicted to a 12-year prison sentence. *The Associated Press* quoted a PA security official who reported that 4 Hamas bombers who killed 20 Israelis were given day passes to leave Nablus prison whenever they desired. Eventually, they never came back. On a trip to the Juneid prison in Nablus, an *AP* correspondent reported in September 1997 that: "The prison door was wide open. So was the barred door leading to the small cellblock. So was each cell door. Mingling with their captors or chatting among themselves were 15 members of the Islamic group Hamas...The Hamas detainees said they had been told their detention was temporary, and meant to shield them from covert Israeli action." More than 50 of these prisoners were released in October 2000, when Arafat launched the recent campaign of violence. Many of these released convicts hired Force 17 guards, who were their former jailers, for their new clandestine bomb shops (*Ha'aretz*, July 27, 2001).

On August 22, 1997, the *New York Times* quoted an Israeli government spokesman: "Rather than arrest the militants named on the lists provided by Israel, the Palestinian Authority appears in some cases to have provided them with bodyguards to protect them from a possible Israeli snatch."

At the Wye Conference of October 1998, Israel presented the PA with a list of people responsible for the murder of over 100 Israelis. The PA agreed to apprehend them as part of the agreement. On this list was a Palestinian who opened fire on Yoel Solomon Street in Jerusalem, killing 2 and wounding 8 in 1993. He planned a bombing at the Jerusalem Convention Center in 1994 that injured 13. He took part in the murder of 3 IDF soldiers. Following his arrest he was drafted into Jibril Rajoub's Preventive Security Service. Another member of this list planned 2 Jerusalem suicide bombings for Hamas in February and March 1996 and another in Ashkelon in February 1996 that left 45 dead. He was hired by the Palestinian security forces in lieu of imprisonment. Of the 30 people on the Israeli list, 12 are now members of the PA's police and security forces.

Here is a partial list of terrorists (name, political affiliation, place of residence) who have been released from prison by the PA:

Abdallah Abu Sakran, Hamas, Gaza: trained to carry out suicide attacks
Hamad Hamad, Hamas, Khan Yunis: helped prepare explosives for suicide attacks
Ayman Abu Hin, Hamas, Gaza: recruited men for suicide attacks
Salah Tilahme, Hamas, Hebron: involved in planning terrorist attacks
Wael Naser, Hamas: participated in shooting attacks against IDF forces in the Gaza Strip
Sharif Tahayna, Islamic Jihad, Jenin: planned mass-killing attacks

Naser Sama'ane, Hamas, Jabalia: helped 2 Hamas members infiltrate into Israel in order to carry out a suicide attack

Muhammed Mousa Hasan Gadalah, Hamas, Gaza: funded and operated a terrorist cell in Ramallah which planned to carry out attacks and to kidnap soldiers

Ibrahim a-Karim Bani-Uda: participated in bombings in public park in Afula and Netanya (Feb-Mar 1998), in which 2 Israeli civilians were injured

Hashem Ashur a-Malek Dib, Islamic Jihad, Gaza: in charge of the suicide bombing at the Tel Aviv Dizengoff Center in March 1996, in which 13 were killed and 125 injured

Mohammed Zakar Rageb Zatma, Islamic Jihad, Rafiah: involved in planning suicide attacks, including the suicide bombing at the Beit Lid junction, in which 22 Israeli soldiers were killed and 59 wounded

Adnan Mahmus Jabber Awul: prepared explosive charges for the suicide attacks carried out by Hamas and the Islamic Jihad in Feb-March 1996, two attacks against the No. 18 bus in Jerusalem, the attack at the Ashkelon junction, and the attack at the Dizengoff Center in Tel Aviv

The PA has good relations with its own minorities

The PA has been launching attacks at Israel from unwilling Christian communities. Beit Jala, a Christian town, has been repeatedly used by the Tanzim to snipe at Israeli homes in Gilo, a Jerusalem neighborhood, resulting in many exchanges of live-fire. According to the May 20, 2001 *Arutz 7*, the Tanzim raped a local girl at its newly founded Beit Jala club. No action was taken against the perpetrators. The Tanzim has extorted many Christian-run businesses in Bethlehem and Beit Jala for protection money as well. On May 12, 2001 *Israel Radio* reported that the Christian Arabs of Bethlehem and Beit Jala had grown so frustrated with the PA's reign of terror in their communities that they began feeding the Israelis the names of the Tanzim snipers so that the attacks from their communities will cease.

Under the PA, there has been a covert campaign to take over churches in the territories. The PA now has control of the churches of Bethlehem, including the Church of the Nativity, and Jerusalem churches such as the Latin Patriarchate, the Anglican, Greek Catholic and Lutheran Bishoprics as well. There are reports that the PA is trying to gain control over the Greek Orthodox establishment and the Church of the Holy Sepulchre.

In Bethlehem, Elias Freij, the Greek Orthodox mayor of 25 years suddenly retired. This happened shortly after the PA started ruling the city. Freij was renowned for having his own opinions on issues, which caused numerous clashes with the PLO over the years. He was one of the first Palestinians to meet with Israelis despite threats that he would be treated as a "collaborator," i.e. a traitor.

A Time for Truth: Since ancient times, the city of Bethlehem has had a Christian majority. The Christian population was estimated at nearly 80% until the early 1970s. They now constitute approximately 35% of the population. Christians are continuing an exodus that began under Israeli rule because of economic concerns. Now they are leaving because the Moslem-dominated PA has brought the local economy to a standstill. Because of incessant campaigns of anti-Israeli violence and religious persecution by the PA, this campaign has had a visible effect on the quality of life as the city's buildings and surroundings deteriorate.

Women are given equal rights under the PA

The Working Woman Group, a Palestinian organization, claims that women lack equal rights under the PA. It unsuccessfully attempted to convince Arafat to enact a law that would change current laws preventing women of any age from marrying without parental consent, from divorcing, and that would enforce alimony payments. In Israel, 45% of the work force is female; only 12% of women work in the PA-controlled areas. Their average monthly salary is a meager $60. Out of 26 ministers in local councils, only one is a woman.

In Beit Jala, members of the Tanzim were accused of raping a local girl. Because of the 'shame' that this girl brought to her family, her family put her to death (*Arutz 7*, May 20, 2001).

The PA has used international funds to better the lives of its people

Arafat and his senior hierarchy have subverted millions of dollars, earmarked for development in the PA areas, for personal use. Arafat has been using a personal bank account in Tel Aviv's Bank Leumi to deposit funds, which he then uses for a host of non-developmental projects. Some of these funds have been transferred to terrorist training camps in Lebanon. This has occurred throughout the peace process. On February 4, 2001, Hussam Khadr of the PA Legislative Council spoke about the PA officials regarding "...the millions that they robbed from the money of the people, and which they gained by subordinating our national economy to the occupation. They have taken concessions, brokerage fees and easy profits for themselves, at the expense of our people and our national economic independence."

The Palestine Investment Fund, run by Arafat and his adviser, Muhammad Rashid, has holdings in excess of $345 million, including equity stakes in 36 companies, most of which are PA-protected monopolies. The company was the direct recipient of Israeli sales taxes from the territories and amassed over $500 million in tax receipts in 1998-99.

PADICO, the Palestine Development and Investment Company, is the holding company for Arafat's interests. It has monopolies over nearly all the key industries under the PA's rule, including cement, flour, oil and cigarettes. It controls much of the tourism industry, 70% of the stock market, has exclusive rights for all telecommunications and holds a 30% stake in the Jericho casino. If you were to start a business, you would apply for your license from PADICO, then get space in its industrial zone, pay it rent, install a phone using its telecommunications company, pay development taxes to it, and finally use its stock market to go public.

Not all the profits go to Arafat and Rashid. A Palestinian American businessman, Hani al-Masri, is a key beneficiary. He was given a $10 million contract to rebuild the central bus station of the West Bank town of Al-Bira without either external evaluations or competing bids. Suha Arafat, Yassir's wife, and the two security heads, Jibril Rajoub and Mohammed Dahlan, also receive large shares of PADICO profits.

In Gaza, the PA hierarchy has created an oasis of wealth that sits on the edge of the squalid Shati refugee camp. Arafat's seafront mansion and office have every conceivable Western comfort. Not far from his home is a cabaret. An exclusive French seafood restaurant is nearby, as is the hotel district. Abu Mazen, the chief negotiator of the Oslo Accords, lives in a $2 million villa on the sea. The Minister of Civil Affairs, Jamil Tarifi, earns additional money as a building contractor for Israeli settlements. Despite all this wealth, *Jane's Weekly* reported (February 2001) that Arafat did not pay his staff or followers for two months.

Next door to the PA wealth lie the open sewers of Shati. The PA has made no effort to transform the refugee camps into normal cities with permanent houses, infrastructure and urban services. The PA now controls 26 refugee camps in the West Bank and Gaza. Conditions have grown far worse since the peace process and PA rule. *Per capita* income has fallen somewhere between 40-75% in these few years. A UN report has cited an alarming increase in child labor. A Palestinian legislative panel from Nablus claims that of the $1.1 billion annual PA budget, $456 million has been squandered through corruption and mismanagement. Of the 20 legislators who signed this petition, 11 were incarcerated or placed under house arrest.

iii. Coexistence

PA is committed to conflict resolution through peaceful negotiation

Arafat accepted a cease-fire with Israel on June 13, 2001. This came after three weeks of a self-imposed unilateral Israeli cease-fire. No sooner did Arafat air his acceptance, than Fatah leader Marwan Barghouti indicated that this CIA-sponsored agreement would not hold, charging the US with trying "to end our Intifada without any political achievements." This statement, in and of itself, confirms that the PA sees violence as a political tool.

Palestinian Armed Forces

Pro-PLO forces:
*Palestinian National Liberation Army/Al-Fatah: 5,000-8,000 active and semi-active soldiers, most of whom were the core fighters in Lebanon before the PLO was expelled by Israel in 1982. They currently reside in numerous countries such as Algeria, Egypt, Iraq, Jordan, Lebanon, Sudan, Syria and Yemen
*Palestine Liberation Front, Abu Abbas Faction: 300-400 soldiers, based in Syria
*Arab Liberation Front: Iraqi-based group, 300-500 members
*Democratic Front for the Liberation of Palestine: Led by Naif Hawatmeh, 400-600 men based in Lebanon and Syria
*Popular Front for the Liberation of Palestine: Led by Ahmad Sa'adat, 800 men, based in Syria, Lebanon, West Bank and Gaza
*Palestine Popular Struggle Front: Led by Samir Ghawsha and Bahjat Abu Gharbiya, 600-700 men, based in Syria

Non-PLO Islamic Forces:
*Hamas: Based in West Bank and Gaza, led by Ahmed Yassin, 300 men in the military wing, growing popularity, tens of thousands of supporters
*Islamic Jihad: Based in the West Bank and Gaza, led by Asad Bayud al-Tamimi, Fathi Shakaki, Ahmad Muhana and Ibrahim Odeh, 350 in the core group, hundreds of supporters
*Hezbollah: 3,000 men, but the core group is only 300 men, based in Lebanon

Anti-PLO forces:
*As-Saiqa: 600-1,000 men, led by Issam al-Qadi, based in Syria
*Fatah Revolutionary Council, Abu Nidal: 300 men led by Abu Nidal (Sabri al-Bana) based in Lebanon, Syria and Iraq
*Popular Front for the Liberation of Palestine-Special Command: 50-100 men, led by Abu Mohammed (Salim Abu Salem)
*Popular Front for the Liberation of Palestine-General Command: 600 men, led by Ahmed Jibril, based in Syria, Lebanon
*Palestine Liberation Army: 4,500 men based in Syria
*Palestine Revolutionary Army: 24-48 men based in Lebanon
*Fatah Intifada: 400 men led by Abu Musa (Said Musa Muragha)
        Source: CSIS

Gaza Refugee Camps

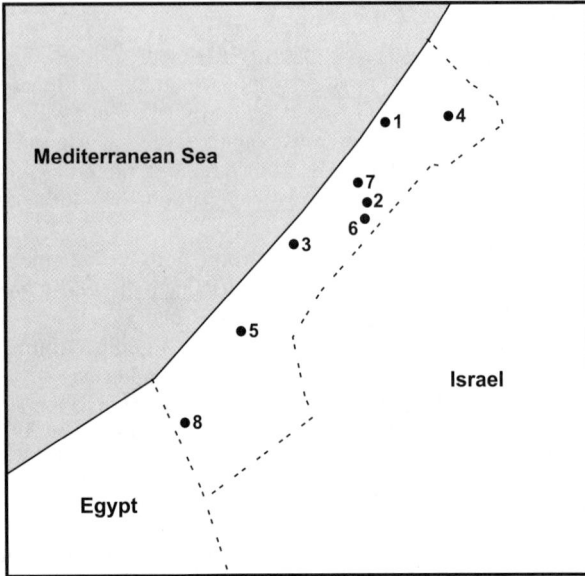

Population:

- **1** Beach (74,464)
- **2** Bureij (28,946)
- **3** Deir el-Balah (19,093)
- **4** Jabalia (99,039)
- **5** Khan Yunis (58,891)
- **6** Maghazi (21,559)
- **7** Nuseirat (59,969)
- **8** Rafiah (86,934)

Source: UNRWA

West Bank Refugee Camps

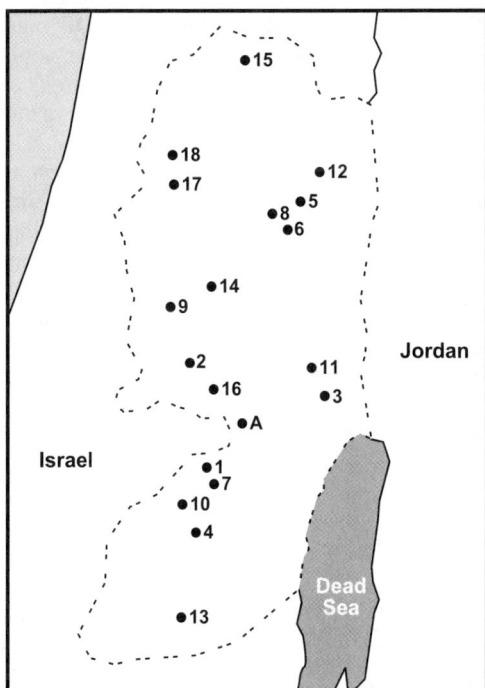

Population:

- **1** Aida (3,785)
- **2** Am'ari (7,273)
- **3** Aqabat Jabr (4,637)
- **4** Arroub (8,184)
- **5** Askar (12,311)
- **6** Balata (18,672)
- **7** Beit Jibrin (1,681)
- **8** Camp #1 (5,678)
- **9** Deir Ammar (2,038)
- **10** Dheisheh (9,624)
- **11** Ein el-Sultan (2,145)
- **12** Far'a (6,178)
- **13** Fawwar (6,178)
- **14** Jalazone (8,040)
- **15** Jenin (13,055)
- **16** Kalandia (7,964)
- **17** Nur Shams (7,429)
- **18** Tulkarm (14,328)

Israeli administered refugee camp:
- **A** Shuafat (8,684)

Source: UNRWA

In the Oslo Accords, the PLO agreed to locate illegal weapons, confiscate mortars, locate bomb factories and refrain from participating in planning attacks against Israel. More than 400 Israelis, mostly civilians, have been killed since the 1993 Oslo Accords. According to the IDF Chief of General Staff Shaul Mofaz, in the first 11 months of the recent campaign of violence, "At least 61 (Israelis) were killed and murdered in operations carried out by the Palestinian security apparatus and the Fatah-Tanzim organization."

The PA also committed to abstaining from using the Palestinian press for incitement against Israel when it accepted the Tenet cease-fire plan. It had already violated Oslo by allowing these conditions to develop. During the previous cease-fire in November, Arafat was quoted telling Barghouti: "Every time that you hear me declare a cease-fire and a halt to the violence, ignore these declarations. You know that I am under heavy pressure from the United States and Europe. You should ignore this and continue...Our only hope for getting money is from the Arab states. But the Arab states will not give money if there is not blood. Therefore, press, press, press" (*bridgesforpeace.com*, Nov. 8, 2000). The day after this cease-fire began, the front page of the PA newspaper *Al-Hayat Al-Jedida* condemned the suicide bombing in Tel Aviv that killed 21 youngsters, while on page 2 it ran an ad from the "National and Islamic Forces" (a pseudonym for Fatah, Hamas and Force 17) saying that the Intifada will "continue until victory."

When Israel seized Orient House, the PA's Jerusalem headquarters, on August 9, 2001, weapons, files detailing an offensive military strategy against the Jewish communities of the West Bank and Gaza and photographs of Israeli police and security forces were found (*Arutz 7*, August 10, 12).

The Palestinian suicide bomber who attacked the Sbarro pizzeria in Jerusalem on August 9, 2001 was run by a Hamas cell that included at least two members of Arafat's Force 17 group (*Jerusalem Post*, September 17, 2001). In June 1997, Israel arrested Colonel Masimi, the Head of the Criminal Department of the Nablus Police, after a shootout with his men who were leading an attack against an Israeli community, Har Bracha.

Rashid Abu Shabbak, the deputy of Mohammed Dahlan, the head of the PA's Preventive Security Apparatus in Gaza, was caught on CIA tapes ordering a bombing of a schoolbus near Kfar Darom in November 2000 (*Arutz 7*, April 15, 2001). Two Israelis were killed and several children maimed for life as a result of the attack. Ziad Abu Ain, a Fatah leader, said in the aftermath of the cease-fire declaration that "We said from the beginning that there is no cease-fire for the settlers" (*International Herald Tribune*, June 20, 2001). *Ma'ariv* quoted Yassir Arafat giving orders to his militants on July 11, 2001: "Pay no attention to what I say in the media, on television or in public appearances...Kill a settler every day...Kill settlers in every place."

The PLO has based its existence on armed struggle against Israel. It has never waived the article advocating armed struggle from the PLO charter. Between 1994-97, Fatah was largely uninvolved in anti-Israel violence, but has returned to the fore in activity against Israel in the West Bank and Gaza and in Israel-proper. The armed struggle is still alive. The official Fatah Website echoes this emphasis: "Only when Israeli soldiers and Israeli settlers have sustained heavy casualties will the Israeli government decide it cannot, after all, afford the price of continuing the oppression of the Palestinian people."

Police and Security Forces

1) National Security Forces: This should be the only security apparatus necessary for the PA

2) Civil Police: For law-enforcement, headed by Ghazi Jabali in Gaza. 10,000 members; 4,000 in Gaza and 6,000 in the West Bank

3) Public Security: General security service. Headed by Naser Yusef in Gaza. 14,000 members; 6,000 in Gaza and 8,000 in the West Bank

4) Palestinian Preventive Security Service: Supposed to coordinate with Israeli security services. Headed by Mohammad Dahlan in Gaza and Jibril Rajoub in the West Bank. 1,200 in Gaza and 1,800 in the West Bank

5) Criminal Investigation Department: Deals with investigating crimes already committed

6) Intelligence: Arrests political detainees. 3,000 members

7) Military Intelligence: Supposed to oversee security services. 500 members

8) Force 17: The Presidential Guard. Answers directly to Arafat. Formed in Lebanon to guard Arafat and other PLO VIPs. 3,500 activists are enlisted to protect Yassir Arafat and provide internal stability within the PA. Faisal Abu-Sharch is the head of this group. They travel in BRDM-2 armored vehicles and possess light weapons. They are responsible for numerous shootings against Israeli civilians including mortar launching against Israeli cities and towns on both sides of the Green Line. Force 17 members are employed to guard Hamas and Islamic Jihad terrorists who plan suicide bombing missions

9) Naval Police: Used to detain civilians

10) Special Forces: Oversees other branches

11) Civil Defence: Emergency services and rescue

12) Republican Guard: May exist separate from Force 17

13) University Security: Created in August 1996 to prevent student uprisings, put them down, monitor on-campus politics and arrest students who oppose the PA

PA television broadcast a sermon by Dr. Ahmad Abu Halabiya, member of the PA "*Fatwa* Council" in a Gaza mosque (October 13, 2000), in which he said: "Have no mercy on the Jews, no matter where they are, in any country. Fight them wherever you are. Wherever you meet them, kill them."

Asad Abd-al Rahman, the PA representative for Refugee Affairs was quoted on October 7, 2000 in the PA newspaper *Al-Hayat Al-Jedida* on his opinion of the negotiations with Israel: "The negotiations that are being conducted between the Palestinians and Israeli sides are negotiations of blood. Despite the many casualties, the Palestinian people are inclined to continue the confrontation because it is beginning to bear fruit."

A June 2001 poll conducted by Rassan al-Hatib's *Jerusalem Media Center* found that 53.9% of Palestinians are opposed to the Oslo Accords, 79% support the *al-Aqsa* Intifada, and 41.2% of all Palestinians feel that the goal of the Intifada is the complete liberation of Palestine, i.e. the destruction of Israel. Only 9.2% believe the aforementioned statement of Abd-al Rahman, that the Intifada is being carried out to improve the Palestinian negotiating position.

Faisal Husseini was a proponent of coexistence with Israel

The *Washington Post* wrote an obituary for Husseini, the PA Minister for Jerusalem, in which it wrote that he "adapted his prominent family's bitter multi-generational struggle against Zionism to what he imagined would be a new era of diplomacy and pragmatism." He was the grandson of Hajj Amin al-Husseini, the *Mufti* of Jerusalem, who allied himself with Hitler and collaborated with the Nazis throughout World War II, and cried in 1948: "I declare a holy war, my Moslem brothers! Murder the Jews! Murder them all!" His father was killed in the 1948 war against Israel. Faisal cannot be faulted for his grandfather's anti-Semitic past, but has he earned the accolades of peacemaker and visionary bestowed upon him by the *Washington Post*?

He told the *Bulletin of the Jerusalem Institute for Western Defense* in June 1994, just after the Oslo Accords: "Peace for us means the destruction of Israel. We are preparing for an all-out war...we have become the most dangerous enemy that Israel has. We shall not rest...until we destroy Israel."

Although someone who negotiated with the Israelis, he saw it as a means to a very limited end, saying: "I may be obliged to have contacts with Sharon's government in order to achieve the vital needs of our people, but this does not justify establishing relations with Israel..."

Two months before his death in May 2001, Husseini was still an adherent to the maximalist Palestinian position. Quoted as praising Hezbollah for defeating Israel in Lebanon, he further stated: "...our eyes will continue to aspire to the strategic goal, namely, to Palestine from the river to the sea." Arafat claimed that Israel was responsible for causing his heart attack in Kuwait because he was tear-gassed by Israeli troops two weeks earlier while rioting in Jerusalem. He was in Kuwait to attend a conference on resisting normalizing relations with Israel.

In April 2000, while speaking to the Center for Policy Analysis on Palestine, Husseini said: "There will be violent confrontation and death, but this time on both sides. Are the Israelis more numerous and better equipped? Yes, but the superiority of us Palestinians lies in the fact that we are willing to lay down our lives, whereas for them every death is a tragedy that society cannot bear."

A Time for Truth: The PA is a despotic anti-Western regime that never committed to the peace process; rather, it used the timeout from hostilities created by the peace process to arm, as if preparing for all-out war. Instead of using international aid to better the lives of its people, the PA established a nepotistic system that created a small elite group around Yassir Arafat that benefits from the aid money, while the common resident of the PA-controlled areas sees only continued destitution.

YASSIR ARAFAT

Arafat, a Nobel Peace Prize Laureate, is a man of peace

In 1973, Israeli and American intelligence taped Arafat and his Black September organization plotting a terrorist operation against international diplomats in Khartoum, Sudan. The National Security Agency attempted to warn the US Embassy in Sudan, but the alert was delayed due to a transmission problem. During this delay, 8 terrorists stormed the Saudi Arabian Embassy and took several hostages, including American Ambassador Cleo Noel and Chargé d'Affaires George Moore. When President Nixon would not negotiate with the hostage takers, Arafat gave the order for Noel, Moore and a Belgian diplomat to be killed, which was what occurred. American tapes again recorded Arafat giving the order.

Arafat has been directly responsible for murdering other American civilians and diplomats. Has Arafat suddenly turned into a man of peace? When offered a chance at history, to put a peaceful end to the Middle East conflict, Arafat unleashed the fighters he was allowed to train and arm under the Oslo Accords against Israel. Arafat and his planners orchestrate many of the clashes. Arafat's group, Fatah, was created to pursue an armed struggle against Israel and has never annulled this part of its covenant, nor deviated from it in practice.

In 1972, when Arafat was asked if he would stop fighting Israel if everyone else (including the Palestinians) made peace with Israel, he responded: "No! We don't want peace. We want war, victory. Peace for us means the destruction of Israel and nothing else."

Egypt expelled Arafat in the 1950s because of subversive activities. After he murdered several Syrian military officers in 1966, he was banished from Syria. In 1970, Arafat tried to overthrow King Hussein in Jordan. The Jordanians expelled him from the country. He moved the PLO to Lebanon where he began a decade-long campaign of violence against Israel, which ended in his being expelled from Lebanon in 1982. He was thrown out of Syria again in 1983 for subversion. Since 1993, when Prime Minister Yitzchak Rabin allowed Arafat and the PLO to enter the West Bank and Gaza as a ruling body over 98% of the Palestinian people and to arm a 35,000-man police and security force, Arafat has prepared for an all-out war against Israel.

US Middle East Special Envoy Dennis Ross told the *Jerusalem Post* on June 20, 2001: "Chairman Arafat could not accept Camp David. It was too hard for him to make this decision [because] when the conflict ends, the cause that defines Arafat also ends." Former US Ambassador to Israel, Martin

Indyk, said of Arafat: "He has not forsworn violence, as he agreed to do back in September 1993, as a tool for achieving his objectives." Former Israeli Prime Minister Ehud Barak told the *Associated Press* in July 2001 that "The Intifada of 2000 started because Yassir Arafat decided to turn to violence. Arafat understood he could no longer fool Israel with generalities in English about peaceful intentions, and in Arabic to continue inflaming the hopes for the destruction of Israel in phases."

Arafat can be trusted to keep his word once he signs an agreement

Arafat violated 72 cease-fires with Lebanon in 1975-76. Prior to that, Arafat signed the Cairo Agreement promising that Lebanese territory would not be used to shell Israel. The deal also prevented the PLO and Fatah from operating bases in southern Lebanon and providing military training in the refugee camps. The Lebanese army had enough of Arafat's violations in 1973 and moved against him. The Malkert Agreement ended the fighting and concluded that the PLO would remove heavy weapons from refugee camps, end terrorism and cease using refugee camps as training bases. The Shtaura Agreement in 1977 reiterated all these PLO promises after it violated them again. By 1982, because Arafat continued to ignore all the agreements he signed, he ruled without checks in southern Lebanon, attacking Israel at will, eventually compelling the IDF to invade. Some of the weapons that the PLO army possessed in Lebanon were T-55, T-54 and T-34 tanks, 130 mm, 150 mm and 57 mm cannons, armored personnel carriers, SAM-7 and SAM-9 anti-aircraft missiles, 40 and 20 barrel Katyusha rockets with a range of 18 miles and heavy mortars.

Under Prime Minister Barak, the Israelis accumulated an extensive list of PA violations of the Oslo Accords. Dr. Abdel-Aziz Rantisi, the Hamas spokesman, told *Jerusalem Post Radio* (June 5, 2001) that immediately after Arafat agreed to the June cease-fire, he never once ordered Hamas to stop attacking Israel.

Arafat signed the Wye document in which he promised to confiscate all illegal weapons. He committed to apprehend all terrorists and vowed to stop incitement, especially in the PA press. None of this was done. The PA continues to arm as if it is preparing for all-out war, releases convicted terrorists and mass murderers to the streets of the West Bank and Gaza and incites the Palestinian population to hatred and violence. When Arafat accepted the US-sponsored Mitchell Report and the Tenet cease-fire, he immediately contravened the agreement by pronouncing that the cease-fire did not apply to Israeli residents of the West Bank and Gaza.

Arafat says he has no control over the mortar fire into Israeli communities on both sides of the Green Line. However, it was revealed in the June 18, 2001 *Jerusalem Report* that the same Gaza office complex where Arafat sat while denying involvement to the foreign press, was the actual building that housed the apparatus in charge of mortar production; and, the person in charge of the operation was Arafat's Chief of Police, Ghazi Jabali.

Arafat's Unkept Commitments

* Renunciation of the use of terrorism and other acts of violence (Arafat's Letter to Rabin, September 9, 1993).

* Recognition of the right of Israel to exist in peace and security (Arafat's Letter to Rabin, September 9, 1993).

* Commitment to the peaceful resolution of the conflict and that outstanding permanent status issues will be resolved through negotiations (Arafat's Letter to Rabin, September 9, 1993).

* Adoption of all necessary measures to prevent acts of terrorism, crime and hostilities and taking of legal measures against offenders (Gaza-Jericho Agreement, Article XVIII; Interim Agreement, Article XV).

* Establishment of a strong police force in order to guarantee public order and internal security for Palestinians (Declaration of Principles, Article VIII; Gaza-Jericho Agreement, Article VIII; Annex I, Article III; Interim Agreement, Article XII, Article XIV).

* The Palestinian Police will act systematically against all expressions of violence and terror (Interim Agreement, Annex I, Article 11.1).

* The Palestinian Police will arrest and prosecute individuals who are suspected of perpetrating acts of violence or terror (Interim Agreement, Annex I, Article 11.1).

* Immediate, efficient and effective handling of any incident involving a threat or act of violence or incitement (Interim Agreement, Annex I, Article 11.2).

* Apprehension, investigation and prosecution of those directly or indirectly involved in acts of terrorism, violence and incitement (Interim Agreement, Annex I, Article 11.3).

* Security arrangements concerning planning, building and zoning (Gaza-Jericho Agreement, Annex I, Article VI; Interim Agreement, Annex I, Article XII).

* Reaffirmation of commitment to fight terror and violence (Note for the Record on Hebron - January 1997).

* Reaffirmation of commitment to systematically and effectively combat terrorist organizations and infrastructure (Note for the Record on Hebron - January 1997).

* Reaffirmation of commitment to apprehend, prosecute and punish terrorists (Note for the Record on Hebron - 1997).

* Recognition that it is in their vital interests to combat terrorism and fight violence (Wye River Memorandum, Article II).

* Israeli-Palestinian cooperation to combat violence and terror (Wye River Memorandum, Article II).

* Comprehensive, continuous and long-term struggle against terror and

violence with respect to terrorists, terror support structure and environment conducive to the support of terror (Wye River Memorandum, Article II).

* Palestinian side will make known its policy of zero tolerance for terror and violence against both sides (Wye River Memorandum, Article II.A.Ia).

A Time for Truth: Yassir Arafat has proven that a leopard cannot change its spots. He has not changed. The terrorist who addressed the UN with a pistol in his belt remains as committed to violence as ever. Arafat has passed on numerous opportunities to make peace and history. Arafat's diplomatic track record of promises is perfect -- he has broken all of them. There is no record of his ever having kept his word on any agreement.

State of Israel

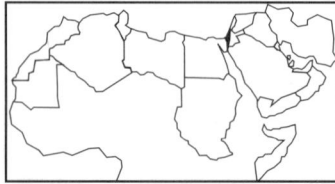

Area:	20,770 sq. km
Population:	6.5 Million
Date of Independence:	May 14, 1948
Head of State:	Ariel Sharon
GDP per capita:	$18,300
Defense Budget:	$7.0 Billion
Active Military:	172,500
Tanks:	3,900
Combat Aircraft:	446
Artillery:	1,537

ISRAEL

Ariel Sharon's visit to the Temple Mount triggered the latest wave of Arab violence

Current Israeli Prime Minister Ariel Sharon visited the Temple Mount on September 28, 2000. This visit was used by the PA as a pretext for a wave of violence that has already lasted one year. The Temple Mount is the holiest site to Jews, but the Moslem *Waqf* administers the upper portion of the site where two major mosques are situated. Prior to his visit, Sharon received security clearance from the Palestinian Chief of Security, Jibril Rajoub. In the days of violence that ensued, Palestinians stockpiled bricks and stones on the Mount that they then dumped down onto Jews praying below at the Western Wall on the eve of Rosh Hashanah, the Jewish New Year. Because of the danger to the worshippers, the area had to be closed, despite its being one of the holiest days on the Jewish calendar.

Since they had lost significant international sympathy for their cause when Arafat rejected then-Prime Minister Barak's compromises at Camp David, the Palestinians used this event as a pretext for a pre-planned campaign of violence. However, the wave of violence that occurred was already underway before Sharon's visit. This visit was then conveniently used by the PA as "the cause of Arab outrage."

Palestinian Minister of Communications, Imad Faluji, confirmed, in *Al-Ayyam* of December 6, 2000 "that the Palestinian Authority had begun preparations for the outbreak of the current Intifada from the moment the Camp David talks concluded." In fact, several major incidents had already taken place. The IDF outpost at Netzarim Junction had been firebombed and Molotov cocktails were thrown at it. On September 27, David Biri, an Israeli policeman, was killed when a roadside bomb detonated in this same area. A new wave of violence against Israel had already begun and the PA used the Sharon visit to the Temple Mount as an excuse to justify it.

Jews stole the land from the Arabs

On January 18, 2001, *The Connection, WBUR*, quoted Hanan Ashrawi saying: "[In] 1947 -- Jews owned 7% of the land, Palestinians owned 93% of the land." In actuality, the local Arabs owned very little of the land. Less than 20% of the land belonged to local Arabs, according to British Mandate statistics. People who resided outside of Palestine or left before the war accounted for more than 4/5 of this percentage. This means that Arab residents of Palestine owned less than 4% of the land. The government owned about 70% of the land and Jews owned 8.6% at the dawn of the 1948 War of Independence.

Israel is a Western colonialist imperialist creation

If Israel had Western support when it was trying to establish a state, it most likely would have ended up with more than 17.5% of the British Mandate's territory in Palestine. The Jewish State faced an uphill battle because Western countries were against it from the outset. US support for Israel did not begin until the thick of the Cold War with the Soviet Union. The British limited Jewish settlement of Palestine with pro-Arab policies for imperialist reasons. The British ignored Arab riots against the Jewish *Yishuv*, and the *Haganah* and *Irgun* were prevented from reacting by the British on numerous occasions. The creation of Israel was a Jewish affair only, there was no external support, certainly not from any Western imperial countries.

Guilt over the Holocaust caused the West to allow Jews into Palestine in order to found their own state

Modern Jewish immigration into Palestine began in the 19th century, half a century before the Holocaust. The First and Second *Aliyahs* began in 1882 and 1904 respectively. The *Yishuv* was an autonomous entity before World War II started. The British were reducing quotas on Jewish immigration through the 1920s, and reduced the quota in 1939, when more Jews were trying to flee Europe. British quotas were responsible for untold numbers of Jewish deaths in Nazi concentration camps.

The British White Paper of 1939 limited Jewish immigration to Palestine to 75,000 people from 1939-1944, at a time when Jews were applying by the thousands for sanctuary from certain death by the Nazis. The White Paper also promised the Arabs independence in all of Palestine by 1949. Jews would have "special minority rights" in this Arab State. A ban on the sale of land to Jews was imposed by the British. Both the Arabs and the Jews rejected the White Paper. The British adhered to the White Paper for three years, despite the Arab leadership in Palestine being pro-Nazi and the Jews fighting with the Allies.

The Jewish community in Palestine grew anyway, despite British limitations. However, because the *Yishuv* was creating greater economic opportunity in the area, Arabs flocked to Palestine. Unrestricted Arab immigration allowed its community to grow at an even greater rate than the Jews. Between the two World Wars, 380,000 Arabs immigrated to Palestine, slightly more than the 375,000 Jews. But no Arabs were turned away. This contrasts sharply with the thousands of Jews who ended up perishing at the hands of the Nazis. When the British finally left Palestine, they turned over their strategic positions and military materiel to the Arabs, not the Jews.

Zionism is a modern day political movement that was created to legitimize stealing a foreign land

Israel became a nation in 1312 BCE. For more than 3,000 years Jerusalem has been the capital of the Jewish nation. Zionism is the title of the modern day nationalist movement, but it is only an extension of three millennia of Jewish history. Zionism, by definition, has been around since the Jewish people were forcefully exiled from the Land of Israel with the destruction of the Second Temple in 70 CE. Zionism is the love of the land of Israel and the aspiration to live there. From this perspective, modern day Zionism is merely a renewal of the very dimension of Judaism that has abided in every Jewish community throughout history. Jews have prayed for the return of all Jews to Israel for 2,000 years while facing in the direction of Jerusalem. When the Jewish people returned to the land in large numbers starting in the late 19th century, they found dozens of ancient synagogues, tombs of patriarchs, matriarchs and leading scholars from every period of the Jewish nation's history.

Most of the Arabs fled their homes in 1948 because the Jews evicted them

The Arab population of British Mandate Palestine was leaving by the thousands before Israel declared independence in June 1948. The Arab Higher Committee, led by Hajj Amin al-Husseini, was run from Cairo and Damascus. Husseini, the *Mufti* of Jerusalem, was residing in Cairo well before Israel's 1948 War of Independence. British intelligence supports the claim that one third of Haifa's Arab population had evacuated by December 1947, well before the fighting began. In March 1948, the AHC ordered an evacuation of all women and children in Palestine. By April 1948, one month before the war began, 100,00 Arabs had left and 390,000 by early June, according to a *Haganah* report.

The *Research Group for European Migration Problems* reported in March 1957: "As early as the first months of 1948 the Arab League issued orders exhorting the people to seek temporary refuge in neighboring countries, later to return to their abodes in the wake of victorious Arab armies and obtain their share of abandoned Jewish property." On August 16, 1948, the Greek Catholic Archbishop of Galilee was quoted in *Sada al-Janub*, a Lebanese newspaper: "Their (Arab) leaders had promised them that the Arab armies would crush the 'Zionist gangs' very quickly and that there was no need for panic or fear of a long exile." On April 27, 1948, Jamal Husseini, the Arabs' chief representative at the UN spoke extensively in the General Assembly. He did not mention refugees. *The London Times*, known for its hostility to Zionism, ran 11 lead articles in April, May and June 1948 on the war in Israel and did not mention a Jewish campaign to drive out the Arabs from their homes. Jordanian newspaper *Ad-Difaa* wrote in September 1954: "The

Arab government told us: 'Get out so that we can get in.' So we got out but they did not get in." Glubb Pasha, the former commander of the Arab Legion, was quoted in the *London Daily* Mail in August 1948, saying that "villages were frequently abandoned even before they were threatened by the progress of war."

Israel is an apartheid state

Israel is the only democracy in the Middle East. It is home to people of all colors and races. All its citizens are given full and equal rights. Arab contentions of Israel as an apartheid state have, ironically, often come from Arab Israeli Knesset members. Three Arab parties presently hold seats in the Knesset, Israel's parliament. In all, there are 9 Israeli Arabs who serve as Members of Knesset in the Sharon Government.

Another non-Jewish community in Israel is the Moslem Druse. There are 100,000 Druse citizens of Israel. Salah Tarif, a Druse member of Knesset, was appointed as a Cabinet Minister in the Sharon Government. He is a Minister Without Portfolio and serves on several prestigious committees, including the Foreign Affairs and Defense Committee. He also is the Chairperson of the Knesset Committee. Yusuf Mishlev was the first Druse to climb to the senior ranks of the IDF, attaining the rank of major general in May 2001. Of Israel's nearly 6 million citizens, 1.2 million are not Jewish. In fact, Azmi Bishara of the Israeli Arab Balad National Democratic Assembly Party had submitted his candidacy for the position of Prime Minister of Israel in the February 2001 election before Arafat pressured him to drop out of the race.

A Time for Truth: From the start, David Ben Gurion, Israel's first Prime Minister, instituted a policy of integrating the Arab population into the country. His government involved Arabs in government, the police force, the Ministry of Education and created an Arab press. The fruits of this policy show today, where Israel has evolved into a country where its 1.2 million non-Jewish citizens participate in all areas of society.

From the outset, the Arabs were hostile to Jews coming to Palestine

The Jews, despite being promised the entire British Mandate of Palestine under the Balfour Declaration, were relegated to accepting less than 20% of the area. But they did accept a two-state solution, (which really meant a three-state solution, since Transjordan was carved out of British Mandate Palestine as well). Interestingly, the only residents of the region who advocated the creation of a state for the Arabs of Palestine were the Jews, through their acceptance of the UN Partition Resolution. Every Arab country rejected this opportunity to establish an independent state for the Arabs of Palestine outright.

The Arabs felt that they would wipe out the Jews as soon as the British left. The British abandoned the Mandate in 1947. But in the 30 years prior to that, when Jews immigrated to Palestine from Eastern Europe, North Africa and Arab Middle East countries, establishing communities in mostly uninhabited areas such as the Negev, Galilee and Sharon Valley, they were subjected to numerous Arab attacks.

Most Arab leaders initially accepted the appearance of European Jews in Palestine as a good sign for the region. Hussein, *Sharif* of Mecca, extolled the Balfour Declaration of 1917 as an achievement for the region since "these regions represent a sanctified homeland, beloved by its ancient sons and their various communal groups." The Syrian delegation to the 1919 peace conference said "we have suffered too much from suffering resembling theirs [the Zionists] not to throw open wide to them the doors of Palestine." Palestine was then considered all of what is today Israel and Jordan. In 1919, the Feisal-Weizmann Agreement called for the rights of both communities to be recognized and developed side-by-side. Emir Feisal, who represented the Arab Hedjaz Kingdom, wrote to Felix Frankfurter, a Chief American Zionist: "We feel that the Arabs and Jews are cousins in race, suffering similar oppressions at the hands of powers stronger than themselves, and by a happy coincidence have been able to take the first step towards the attainment of their national ideals together. We Arabs, especially the educated among us, look with the deepest sympathy on the Zionist movement…We are working together for a reformed and revived Near East, and our two movements complete one another."

Israel is the international pariah of the world, as evidenced by dozens of condemnatory resolutions taken by the UN over the decades

The role of the UN in the Arab-Israel conflict has never been impartial. The Third World and Arab countries use the UN to repeatedly lambaste Israel. Committees having nothing to do with Israel or the Middle East adopt resolutions that condemn Israel for "abuses." Arab members use every opportunity to cast Israel as the pariah of the international community. The US is the only nation that (sometimes) uses its veto power in the Security Council to provide a counterweight to the Arab votes.

According to Israeli sources, the UN spent $10 million in 1986-87 just to finance activities and projects related to the Palestinians. UNRWA, the United Nations Relief and Works Agency, was created for the Palestinians. It spends more than $300 million annually on the Palestinian cause.

Comparative Scale

(Israel shown in black)

France

California

Lake Michigan

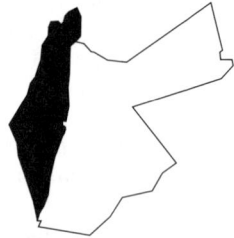

Jordan

Iraq

Saudi Arabia

Ariel Sharon is directly responsible for the massacres at Sabra and Shatilla

The PLO operated in Lebanon in much the same way that it does today in the West Bank and Gaza, hiding behind women and children when it shoots at Israelis. It knows that if there is a response, it is likely that civilians will be injured or killed. In Lebanon, the PLO set up shop in civilian centers, primarily refugee camps, and put the inhabitants in tremendous danger. Today, the Hezbollah has adopted the same approach.

Not only was the PLO operating out of these camps against Israel, but it was using them as training centers for European recruits and sympathetic terrorist organizations from Algeria, Britain, Germany, Iran, Ireland, Italy, Japan and Pakistan.

The 1982 Sabra and Shatilla refugee camp massacres should be put into context of what was occurring in Lebanon at that time. The Lebanese civil war had just terminated, but without achieving results for a peaceful future. Bashir Gemayel, the Christian Maronite President of the country, had just been assassinated along with 25 other Christian leaders. Such massacres had become commonplace in Lebanon. Israeli objectives were to rid Lebanon of the PLO, not to rule or administer Beirut. Thus, when Israel, working with the Christian Phalange, secured West Beirut, it opted to transfer authority to its allies. When the Phalange entered the Sabra and Shatilla camps, killing 460, including 15 women and 20 children, the Israeli army took responsibility even though it did not participate in any way. While the Phalange got the upper hand, it is important to note that it was engaged in hand-to-hand combat with armed terrorists who were hiding among civilians. Among the dead were Pakistanis, Iranians, Syrians and Algerians -- all of whom were trainees at these terrorist camps.

A commission was established to look into possible Israeli violations because of protests in the streets of Tel Aviv (the only place in the region that had protests). The Kahan Commission dismissed Chief of Staff Raphael Eitan and Defense Minister Ariel Sharon, not for having any complicity in the massacre, but for not anticipating the Phalange intent and preventing it. When Shiite Moslems attacked the very same Shatilla and Burj el-Barajneh refugee camps in 1985, there was not even a whisper about 635 killed and 2,500 injured.

The Head of Security and the Commander of the Lebanese forces were the actual leaders of the massacres. Neither has ever been tried because they are under the protection of the Syrians. On June 22, 2001, a senior commentator for the *Hamas Weekly*, Saleh Al-Na'ami, wrote that the Syrians and Christian Phalange should be tried for the massacres, not Ariel Sharon. Eli Hobeika, the former Head of Security for the Phalange, was made a minister in the Lebanese Parliament by the Syrians as a reward for his role in the massacre. Na'ami wrote: "Israel has established an investigation committee headed by a judge in order to investigate the Sabra and Shatilla massacres. This committee forced the Begin government to fire Sharon from the Ministry of Defense. Israel has also discharged many of its army commanders. However, we have not seen the Lebanese government doing [what Israel did] even though one would expect them to do it. When such a committee was, finally, established by the Lebanese government, it acquitted Hobeika of any responsibility for committing the massacres and unloaded all the responsibility on Israel, even though the court established that it was Hobeika's soldiers who committed the massacres."

Bibi Netanyahu was voted out of office because he is an extremist

In the 2000 race for Prime Minister of Israel, the Israeli public voted for Ariel Sharon over Ehud Barak because Barak failed to produce results with the Palestinians, despite making concessions that the Israeli public felt went too far. In the previous election, it was felt that Netanyahu was not offering enough and so he was voted out of office. In actuality, Netanyahu lost the election by creating conditions whereby Israelis felt they could afford to take new risks. Netanyahu was voted in to stop Palestinian terrorism. He did. Under Prime Minister Yitzhak Rabin, suicide bombings had voters gravely concerned. When Netanyahu came into power, Israelis who felt security was the foremost concern of the nation fell from 73% to 39%, a clear sign that his "stop Arafat" policy was effective. Netanyahu combated Arafat's terrorism by holding him personally accountable for each and every act. While the international media called his policies "obstructionism," Netanyahu called it "reciprocity," demanding that Arafat "give" in order to "get." Clearly terrorism abated during Netanyahu's tenure as Israeli Prime Minister, so much so, that when it came time for a new election, the Israeli public decided to take a chance on Barak, who promised to use a terrorism-free Israel as a stepping stone to ending the conflict.

A Time for Truth: The modern State of Israel is an extension and fulfillment of Jewish history. Jewish life has existed in the Land of Israel since the time of Joshua. Israel is the only democracy in the Middle East and protects the rights of all its citizens. The constant threat of war makes all these features very difficult to maintain. A continuous effort by the press to catch Israel violating its democratic principles has resulted in lead stories in newspapers across the globe that were later revealed to be erroneous. Israel set a high ethical standard for itself from the outset, and it has sustained that standard despite threats, attacks and wars.

Lebanese Republic

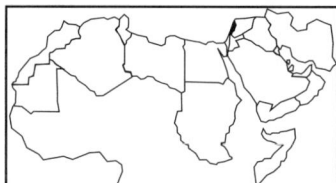

Area:	10,400 sq. km
Population:	3.6 Million
Date of Independence:	Nov. 22, 1943
Head of State:	Emile Lahad
GDP per capita:	$4,400
Defense Budget:	$846 Million
Active Military:	63,750
Tanks:	327
Combat Aircraft:	3
Artillery:	174

LEBANON

Israel's withdrawal from Lebanon was done in fear

There is a belief in the Arab World that Hezbollah chased Israel out of Lebanon. Among many of the Arab leaders there is hope that, because of this achievement, Israel can now be defeated. Because the PA subscribed to this conclusion, it eschewed the peace process in favor of violence against Israel. The IDF withdrew from Lebanon, no longer able to sustain casualties to its soldiers. Is this perception correct?

Upon leaving Lebanon, the IDF left behind armored personnel carriers, a small number of South Lebanese Army (SLA) tanks, trucks and cannons, according to the May 30, 2000 *Ha'aretz*. All this materiel was found by Hezbollah. Why was Israel in a rush? On the political front, the Government of Israel had committed to a withdrawal and fulfilled this commitment according to a strict timetable established months before. Ehud Barak was elected Prime Minister of the country on a platform that called for unilateral withdrawal of IDF troops from Lebanon, a feeling that was shared by a majority of Israelis. As the IDF withdrew, events occurred that could have thrown off the timetable for departing, but the Government of Israel decided to adhere to the political timetable for leaving, deeming it more important than adjusting for minor troubleshooting.

A majority of Israelis felt that its army was no longer achieving objectives by staying in Lebanon. Soldiers' lives were endangered for no overt political or military objective, thus they were pulled out and returned home. Israel also found that the longer it stayed in the security zone, the more the local population supported the legitimacy of attacks on the IDF. Additionally, the playing field was not level due to Hezbollah's tactic of hiding from Israeli army reprisals in civilian areas. The ongoing attrition led to an IDF policy that reacted to the tactics of Hezbollah and the dictates of Iran and Syria.

As a democracy, the Israeli public had spoken in a loud and clear voice, prevailing upon its leaders to end the Israeli presence in Lebanon. The public no longer accepted that its soldiers were needed across its northern border for maintaining its security. At no point does fear or weakness enter into this formula.

Israel and its army can be defeated as shown by the recent withdrawal from Lebanon

The withdrawal has left many Arabs with the impression that Israel can be defeated through protracted campaigns of hit-and-run terrorism. And while terrorism can exact a price -- even an expensive one, it cannot threaten the existence of a country. Thus, the campaign of terror against Israel, carried out by suicide bombers, snipers and Molotov cocktail throwers can only achieve limited results. The same can be said for the repeated Hezbollah ambushes of the IDF in Lebanon. The psychological impact of these incessant campaigns on a country is still immense, but will never cause Israelis to abandon their State.

The balance of power in the Middle East remains the same as it has been since 1967. Israel maintains a strategic military edge over its collective Arab neighbors. The conventional wisdom has always been that the moment the balance would tilt back to the Arabs' favor, they would not hesitate to launch an all-out war against Israel. If the IDF withdrawal from Lebanon proved that the Arabs now have the means to destroy Israel, it is likely that a war would have been waged already.

A Time for Truth: IDF soldiers remain better equipped, trained and motivated than any army in the Middle East. Were this to ever change, Israel could suffer disastrous existential consequences.

Israel's withdrawal from Lebanon was a publicity stunt since it did not withdraw from all Lebanese territory

Israel established a security zone in southern Lebanon in 1982 during the war against the PLO, who had established a mini-state in the south. Israel occupied this area until it withdrew in 2000. When Israel withdrew, it did so completely. Even the United Nations, typically hostile to Israel because of the significant Arab and Moslem voting block, agreed that Israel's withdrawal was complete according to UN Security Council Resolution 425. So too did Fatah leader Marwan Barghouti in an interview with *Jewish Week* on July 13, 2001: "Israel has to return to its 1967 borders. They did that with Egypt...with Lebanon."

Syria controlled the Har Dov region (Shebaa Farms) from 1948-67, an area at the base of the Golan Heights, and lost it to Israel in the 1967 Six-Day War. Israel, under the terms of UN resolutions regarding Lebanon, did not have to withdraw from Syrian territory, only from Lebanese.

It is only because of Syria's support and control of Hezbollah that the Har Dov region is used as a pretext to continued assault on Israel. It is extremely unlikely that Syria would ever agree to Lebanese sovereignty over this small portion of land.

Israel's withdrawal from Lebanon has at least reduced Israeli casualties

The number of Israeli casualties and hostages has increased since the IDF withdrew from Lebanon. As of August 2001, Israel had been attacked 8

Har Dov (Shebaa Farms)

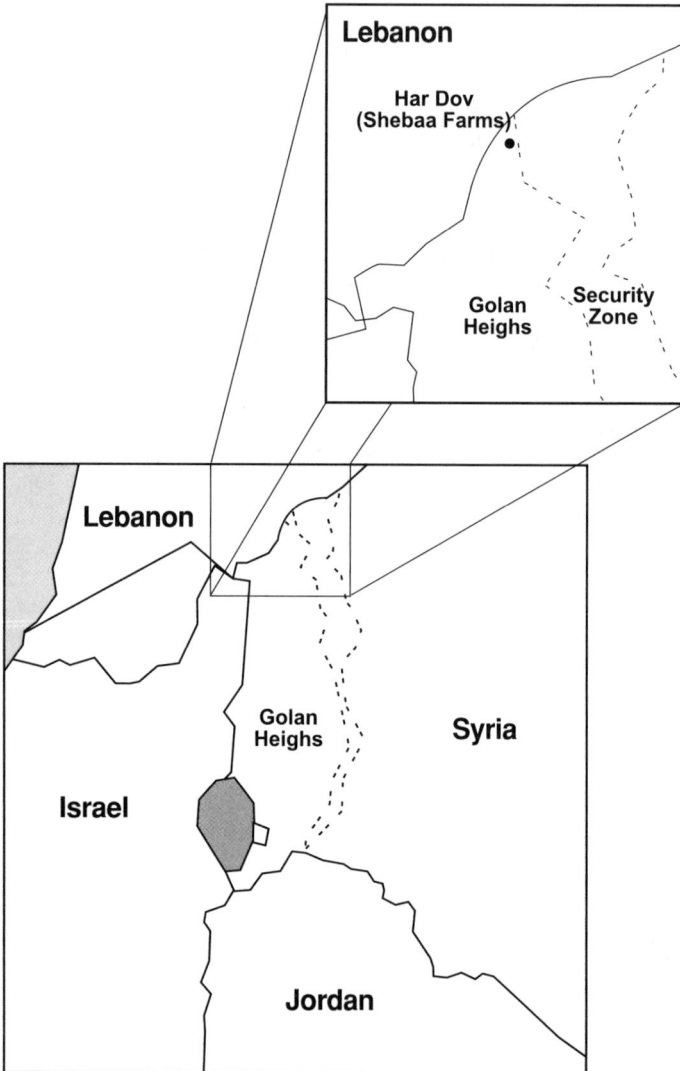

times, numerous infiltrations have been attempted, 2 soldiers were killed and 4 Israelis abducted, 3 of whom were patrolling near the border.

The Palestinians watched Hezbollah achieve all its demands without ever having to sit across a negotiating table from Israel because of the one tool at its disposal -- violence. Arafat's latest campaign of violence was calculated from the conclusions drawn about Lebanon -- that Israel, because of its weakness for public support, can be beaten militarily if enough hit-and-run violence is employed against it.

With the withdrawal of Israeli forces, Israel will have a quiet border

When the IDF withdrew on May 24, 2000, Hezbollah, whose overt *raison d'être* has been to repatriate all Lebanese territory, should have claimed a victory and disbanded. This did not occur. During a speech to his partisans, Hezbollah Secretary General Hassan Nasrallah was asked if he would end the fight with Israel if it also withdrew from Har Dov (Shebaa Farms). He said that he would not "because Israel wants to take our water and there is a need for the resistance to stay and defend our resources." Hezbollah's present demands are for the total liberation of Lebanon and the release of all Lebanese prisoners in Israel.

The real reason for Hezbollah's existence is the destruction of the State of Israel. Lebanese land and the Lebanese people mean very little to Hezbollah. After all, it is funded and trained by Iran, and claims allegiance to the Palestinian cause. It is only in Lebanon because no other state bordering Israel will permit it to operate against Israel from its country. Ironically, it is Syria who allows and encourages hostility against Israel, but only from Lebanon, because of Syrian hegemony over its western neighbor. Hezbollah has never attacked Israel from Syrian territory.

Hezbollah entered the political scene with a series of kidnappings of Western hostages in the 1980s. This was followed by its blowing up several heavily occupied buildings in Buenos Aires, Argentina. Since then, it has been ambushing, booby-trapping, rocket-launching and shooting at Israeli troops in southern Lebanon and northern Israel. Nasrallah insists that the Jews "go back to where they came from" and on continuing the fight until Israel has disappeared off the map. Despite these remarks, Syria decides whether or not Hezbollah has a free hand to attack Israel. Right now, Syria is opposed to peaceful accommodation with Israel; thus it gives a green light to terror attacks against Israel over the Lebanese-Israeli border. Even the Lebanese government goes along with this plan. Lebanese Prime Minister Rafiq Hariri recently made claims on Har Dov and supports Hezbollah activity against Israel. The Lebanese Army has sent only a few hundred of its 65,000 troops to southern Lebanon, and they are instructed to stay as far away from the border as possible. This means that Hezbollah's activity in southern

Lebanon is unchecked. In fact, recent shelling of Har Dov shows that Hezbollah has free reign right now from Syria. The lack of incidents in other areas of the border seems to indicate that Hezbollah's orders are to concentrate, for the time being, on this region only.

Until a massive economic development plan is put in place in southern Lebanon, Israel expects continued activity from Hezbollah. Currently, Hezbollah has stepped into the void of Israel's departure to run hospitals Israel had operated, and provide a host of other services to the local population. This endears its combatants to the residents, gives it greater access to areas close to the border and areas with civilian population, where it can hide from Israeli reprisals. Since the withdrawal of Israeli forces, there have been 8 Hezbollah attacks on the northern border, killing 3 IDF soldiers. Three Israeli hostages were taken during a cross-border incursion. The UN has a videotape of the hostage-taking that shows the Hezbollah captors wearing UN Peacekeeper uniforms. The border has not grown quiet because of the Israeli withdrawal and shows no signs of becoming quieter in the foreseeable future.

Israel's withdrawal has allowed Lebanon to regain its independence

In the Taif Accords of 1993, Syria committed to evacuating its military from Lebanon. Syria maintains a ubiquitous control of Lebanon. 35,000 Syrian soldiers are permanently stationed in Lebanon, controlling the arms flow in and out of the country. Hezbollah must have at least tacit consent from Syria before launching operations against Israel. Syria has recently imported radar stations into Lebanon to provide greater coverage of Israeli terrain. When Hezbollah launched a Sagger anti-tank missile into Israeli territory, killing one Israeli soldier, Israel responded with an air attack against one of these radar stations situated on Mount Lebanon on April 15, 2001. The radar was destroyed and 3 Syrian soldiers were killed. This was the first time since 1996 that Israel struck at Syrian targets in Lebanon. On July 1, 2001, Israel struck back again, destroying another radar system in Riak.

Lebanese Christian Maronite Patriarch Nasrallah Sfeir led a demonstration in Beirut against the Syrian occupation in May 2001. Walid Jumblatt, the Lebanese Druse leader, called for implementation of the Taif Accords. Because the Lebanese government and army are not in control of its country and have not prevented terrorism being carried out from its land, the US put a $20 million aid package to Lebanon on hold. The World Bank and the IMF subsequently froze its projects for Lebanon as well.

Lebanon has yet to regain its independence and this has nothing to do with the presence or absence of Israeli forces. Lebanon has not had full sovereignty over its country since the PLO started using it as a base for terrorism and launching attacks at Israel in the early 1970s. This is what prompted

Israel to launch Operation Peace for the Galilee in 1982. Lebanon did not have sufficient control to prevent the PLO from repeatedly attacking Israel, which is why Israel entered the country and established its security zone in conjunction with the South Lebanese Army (SLA). With the IDF departure, Lebanon still remains powerless to control its own affairs -- because of Syria.

Israel abandoned its allies from the South Lebanese Army and left them to die

More than 7,000 Lebanese, 80% of them Christian, fled their homes when Israel withdrew its armed forces from Lebanon. Israel, sensing an impending bloodbath of its SLA allies, opened its border as an act of compassion to all those who needed sanctuary. This new class of Middle East refugees ran for their lives, being certain that UN Peacekeepers would not prevent Hezbollah from coming into their towns and villages to settle scores. Everyone who had a close association with Israel felt vulnerable to Hezbollah retribution. Israel felt it could not turn its back on these people because it provided 6,000 families with their livelihoods. Israel created jobs in Lebanese hospitals, clinics, civil service and in Israel. It opened its doors to these refugees, while Israeli Arabs have been hostile to them, labeling them as "collaborators" and barring the refugees from their neighborhoods.

Since the IDF withdrew from southern Lebanon in May 2000, more than 2,600 cases of "collaboration" have been tried in Lebanese military courts, according to the April 5, 2001 *New York Times*. The top brass of the SLA fled the country, but many of the senior officers were convicted *in absentia*. SLA Commander General Antoine Lahad was given a death sentence while Nabih Abou Rafei, the third most senior member of the SLA, was convicted and sentenced to 15 years in prison.

By unilaterally withdrawing from Lebanon, Israel has put the Arabs on the defensive

David Levy, Israel's Foreign Minister during the Barak Administration, conveyed the Israeli government's reasons for the IDF withdrawal on May 23, 2000: first, it would end the dispute with Lebanon; second, it would eliminate Hezbollah as a regional player; third, it would gain Israel international support; fourth, it would bring Syria back to the negotiating table; and last, it would enhance the deterrence and morale of the army to no longer be at the mercy of a guerrilla hit-and-run campaign.

Lebanon surprised Israel by demanding territory it had never owned before -- Har Dov (Shebaa Farms). This area has never been part of sovereign Lebanon. Hezbollah decided to maintain its campaign against Israel so it arbitrarily challenged the Israeli withdrawal by claiming land Syria had lost in the Six-Day War. The Government of Lebanon then began demanding this piece of land too.

In the first year since the pullback, there have been as many Israeli casualties as a result of attacks from southern Lebanon than in Israel's last four years in the Security Zone. International support was strong for a very short time. The UN certified Israel's withdrawal from Lebanon as complete, according to UN Security Council Resolution 425. The international community even agreed to Israel's one demand -- that the Lebanese army deploy in southern Lebanon to prevent Hezbollah from carrying out hostilities against Israel. This has yet to occur and the international community has been silent about it.

The international media now calls Har Dov "disputed territory" giving claim to the Lebanese assertion that it may belong to them. Syria, now under the rule of Bashar Assad, did not budge an inch when Israel withdrew its forces. Shlomo Ben-Ami, Israel's then Minister of Internal Security, said that Assad, "was very stressed by Israel's decision to withdraw from Lebanon." One year later, it does not look like it mattered to him, other than the fact that he could get his proxy army, Hezbollah, that much closer to Israel's border. Lastly, Israel's deterrence has suffered immeasurably because the withdrawal was met with the Arab conclusion that violence pays. If a small gang of terrorists can drive Israel out of Lebanon through a slow war of attrition, then psychologically, the impact of thousands of Palestinians using stones, knives, guns, mortar fire and Katyusha rockets could be even greater. The morale of the army is even lower because the average soldier sees that he must now be embroiled in an even larger conflict that shows no visible end.

There is no connection between the case of Lebanon and the case of the Palestinians

A symbiotic relationship exists between Hezbollah and the PA. This relationship is growing closer every day. Hezbollah has agreed to train fighters and provide the PA with anti-tank and anti-aircraft weapons. Arafat's personal bank account in Bank Leumi Tel Aviv shows a direct flow of millions of dollars to Hezbollah for the purpose of training Palestinians for future violence against Israel (*Washington Times*, February 22, 2001). The Palestinians have learned much more from Hezbollah than how to acquire weapons. They watched very carefully as Hezbollah achieved all its goals in Lebanon without ever having to sit across a table from Israelis and negotiate an IDF withdrawal.

Hezbollah was faced with an existential problem once the Israelis withdrew from Lebanon. Rather than claim victory over Israel and disband into a political organization in Lebanon, it chose to direct its efforts towards building the Palestinian struggle within Israel. Hezbollah has been creating cells in the West Bank and Gaza, and also in Israeli Arab communities. In March 2001, a cell of Israeli Arabs operated by Hezbollah was uncovered in the Galilee. It has attempted to attack Israel by importing terrorists from abroad. A tourist from Britain working for Hezbollah was apprehended by the IDF when he tried to slip into Israel to carry out a terrorist attack in a civilian area in January 2001. Within the territories, Hezbollah is tied most closely to Islamic Jihad because of the close association of both groups with Iran. Iran is where both groups receive their training.

On February 13, 2001, Israeli helicopters attacked a Hezbollah operative who was running a cell in Gaza. This cell carried out several terrorist operations against Israel including mortar attacks against Netzarim, an Israeli town. On January 29, 2001, Hezbollah was caught trying to smuggle arms into Gaza by boat.

When Israel departed from Lebanon, many rallies were held in the West Bank and Gaza where the Hezbollah yellow flag was waved. This flag has become a prominent symbol in the streets of the PA-controlled areas during the 2000-01 Intifada. The Palestinian admiration for Hezbollah has grown since it abducted 4 Israelis in October 2000. The Palestinian people increasingly see Hezbollah achieving results against Israel. Marwan Barghouti, leader of the Tanzim, told *Al-Hayat Al-Jedida* (January 31, 2001): "I think that the experience of our Hezbollah brothers, in Lebanon as well, has changed our approach and that of the new Palestinian generation."

Since it has Israeli hostages, Hezbollah now has the ability to free Palestinian prisoners from Israeli jails, a feat that the PA has yet to manage. The PA, under Hisham Abdel-Razaq, its official in charge of prisoners, submitted a list to Hezbollah of which prisoners to demand in exchange for the release of the IDF soldiers. The Israeli Foreign Ministry reports that Hezbollah sent mail to Palestinian prisoners in Israel promising to free them. Some of these prisoners are responsible for some of the bloodiest attacks on Israelis in the past year, such as planning suicide bombings.

| Adi Avitan | Binyamin Avraham | Omer Souad |

The Palestinians have also adopted Hezbollah tactics, such as the suicide bomber. In Lebanon, it was not uncommon for Hezbollah to attack Israel using roadside bombs detonated by a cell phone and by an individual carrying powerful explosives that would be detonated on impact.

Lebanon has always considered Israel its enemy, thus the PLO really was representing the popular sentiment when it started attacking Israel in the 1970s

Between 160,000 and 180,000 people came to Lebanon from Palestine in 1948 during the Arab war waged on Israel. To this day, Lebanon keeps them in refugee camps with squalid conditions. While Lebanon still technically remains at war with Israel to this day, the Lebanese border was quiet until the aftermath of the Six-Day War.

Due to Syrian assistance, Palestinian terrorist organizations were implanted in Lebanon. Lebanon was fertile territory for terrorist camps because its civil war did not allow for policing its population, implementing policy and punishing anti-governmental activity. It was into this vacuum that the PLO moved. When the PLO was evicted from Jordan, the radicalization of Lebanese Palestinians began because the PLO pursued its own agenda. Although this agenda was anti-Israel, it ended up damaging the Lebanese political infrastructure. These negative implications continue to affect the country.

A Time for Truth: Israel mounted Operation Peace for the Galilee in 1982 for only one reason – to allow its northern citizens to live a normal life. No sovereign state would allow its border to become a shooting gallery. Once Israel thought that the presence of the IDF was no longer needed, it withdrew. The situation in Lebanon has shown how die-hard the Arabs are in their hatred of Israel because Israel's departure from Lebanon has not produced a peaceful border; rather Arab attacks into northern Israel have been renewed and intensified.

Syrian Arab Republic

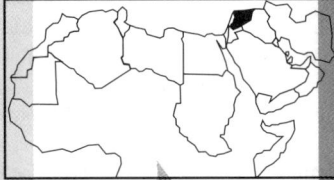

Area:	185,180 sq. km
Population:	16.3 Million
Date of Independence:	April 17, 1946
Head of State:	Bashar Assad
GDP per capita:	$6,600
Defense Budget:	$1.8 Billion
Active Military:	316,000
Tanks:	3,650
CombatAircraft:	589
Artillery:	2,530

SYRIA

Syrian President Bashar Assad is a voice of moderation

Since Hafez Assad died and his son Bashar came to power in June 2000, there has been no radical change in Syrian policy, domestically or internationally. Vis-à-vis Israel and the Jews, Bashar has the same approach as his father. He insists on full Israeli withdrawal from the Golan Heights as a precondition to peace talks. Syria maintains a steady stream of anti-Semitism in its media and from its public figures. During a Papal visit to Damascus, Bashar denounced Jews as betrayers of Jesus and Mohammed.

After many public statements, it is clear that Assad, like his father, does not recognize the PLO as the legitimate representative of the Palestinian people. It is likely that Syria would vehemently oppose any deal reached between the PLO and Israel and attempt to use the Arab masses to counter the effectiveness of such an agreement.

The Taif Accords, meant to restore sovereignty to Lebanon, are used instead to justify a continued Syrian presence across its western border. Syria now says that a joint decision, only after civil peace has been achieved, would allow it to withdraw its armed forces back to Syria.

Domestically, Bashar has been heralded in the international press as a reformer. Up to now, he has opposed reform in his country. He has prevented decentralization of the government and participation of any non-governmental elements in the development of society. His Ministry of Information continues to censor all newspapers.

One area that has seen change is Bashar's courting a warmer relationship with Saddam Hussein of Iraq. Trade has resumed between the two countries and the Syrian-Iraqi pipeline now flows with more than $1 billion of oil each year.

Syria has become less militaristic since Bashar Assad took power

Syria is still on the United States list of states that sponsor terrorism. Syria maintains a paternal relationship with Hezbollah, promotes anti-Israel activity in Lebanon, arms terrorist groups and helps train them. It has helped Iranian surface-to-surface missiles reach Hezbollah, giving them a much-enhanced capability against Israel. As a result, the potential for conflagration between the Arabs and Israel in Lebanon is rising daily.

Not only has the military *status quo* remained in Lebanon since Bashar began to rule, but Syria has become more daring. In May 2001, according to military sources in Beirut, Syria replaced its regular troops in Lebanon with more able and better-trained fighters. According to the June 4, 2001 *Jerusalem Report*, five new sophisticated radar systems were imported into Lebanon to give Syria deep monitoring penetration into Israel. The first system was deployed in Deir al-Ashayer, on the Syrian-Lebanese border, and includes a state of the art anti-aircraft guidance system that covers most of northern Israel. The second was stationed in the Biqa Valley to monitor ground and air movements in that region. The third was set up in northern Akkar to monitor the sea all the way to Cyprus. The fourth is a mobile system that is the most sophisticated and hardest to hit. It has been kept in the middle of Lebanon and gives improved coverage of Israel's north. A fifth system was obliterated by Israel as a reprisal to a Hezbollah attack on the Har Dov region that killed an IDF soldier on patrol.

A Time for Truth: Under Bashar Assad, Syria has not strayed from the path that his father walked. Syria is still a force to be reckoned with in the region and its renewed relationship with Iraq has the potential to stoke the Middle East fire even more. Syria controls anti-Israel operations in Lebanon through Hezbollah and is responsible for the rise in tension on the Lebanese-Israeli border since the IDF withdrew.

Republic of Iraq

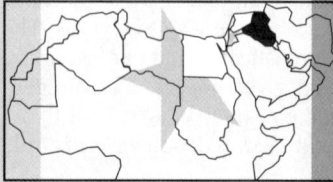

Area:	437, 072 sq. km
Population:	22.7 Million
Date of Independence:	October 3, 1932
Head of State:	Saddam Hussein
GDP per capita:	$2,000
Defense Budget:	$1.4 Billion
Active Military:	387,500
Tanks:	2,700
CombatAircraft:	353
Artillery:	2,200

IRAQ

Because of the Gulf War and internal problems, Iraq has been diverted from its anti-Israel role

It was reported in the *Khaleej Times* on February 8, 2001 that Saddam Hussein has reactivated the Arab Liberation Front, a group established in the 1940s to fight the Jews in Palestine, in order to liberate Jerusalem. He is calling for the expulsion of all Jews who have immigrated to Israel since 1948. According to *UPI* (February 9, 2001), because of the loosening of sanctions on Iraq, and the recovery of its oil industry, Iraq was able to donate $1 billion to the Palestinians. Saddam has smuggled rocket-propelled grenades, anti-tank missile launchers and anti-aircraft guns to the PA. He has been trying to build an anti-Israel coalition with Syria and Iran. *UPI* further reports (February 9, 2001) that Bashar Assad has agreed to join him for military planning, ending well over a decade of icy relations with Syria. Despite a population that lacks many basic necessities, Saddam gives $10,000 to each Palestinian family with a member who dies in the fight against Israel. He also provides $1,000 to those who receive serious injuries and $500 to those incurring less serious wounds.

The Gulf War destroyed the Iraqi military, therefore Iraq no longer constitutes a threat to Israel

Iraq's revenue from oil sales is now at about the same level it was before the Gulf War. Since the early 1990s, Iraq has been buying components for the development of nuclear and long-range missiles from Russia, Ukraine, Belarus and Romania. Iraq has been trading its oil to Jordan, Syria and, recently, Lebanon at cut-rates in exchange for assistance in circumventing the international arms embargo still in effect. The free-trade port in Aqaba, Jordan has been the main terminal for Saddam's nuclear, biological and chemical weapons programs. Iraqi purchases arrive in Jordan, are loaded onto trucks and driven across the desert, where the equipment crosses the Iraqi border unchecked. In return, Jordan receives approximately $300 million in Iraqi oil, all of which is in violation of the UN oil-for-food program that was imposed to control Iraq's arms industry. Iraq also repaired the oil pipeline to Syria, where another $1 billion in oil flows annually. Lebanon is rumored to have just begun a similar program for importing oil from Iraq over and above the UN quotas (*Commentary*, July-August 2001).

Even when Iraq was pledging to disarm and being subjected to intense inspection by the UN, it learned to avoid detection and kept developing its arms industry. The UN discovered many complex clandestine sites, which contained biological and chemical weapons that could be used on warheads. Saddam was importing weapons and weapons components from at least 20 different countries while the inspection teams were in Iraq. One area of grave concern for the international community is Russia's assistance to Iraq in developing the Soviet SS-N-18 missile, which can be launched from a submarine at targets more than 4,000 miles away.

In 1998, the UN inspection team was forced out of the country. For three years, Iraq has now been developing and producing weapons unfettered, with billions of petro-dollars at its disposal. The *New York Times* reported on July 1, 2001 that Iraq restarted its missile program and flight-tested a liquid-fueled, short-range ballistic missile capable of carrying conventional, chemcial or biological warheads. This capability can be adapted to missiles with a longer range, such as the 1,800-mile range missiles the Germans report the Iraqis are working on. Iraq definitely constitutes a threat to Israel and all its neighbors.

Not only is Iraq capable of inflicting greater damage on Israel than the 39 SCUD missiles it hit the Jewish State with during the Gulf War, but in July 2001, the IDF captured an Iraqi-trained Palestinian terror cell that planned to carry out an attack at Israel's Ben-Gurion airport, showing that Iraq is reducing its distance from the conflict.

Israel's attack against Iraq's nuclear facility at Osirak had no military significance

Twenty years later, it is clear that Iraq was preparing its French-supplied nuclear reactor to produce plutonium for warheads. It is also evident that had Israel not destroyed the reactor, the soldiers of the US-led coalition in the Gulf War would have been vulnerable to atomic attacks. The 39 SCUDs fired at Israel might also have been equipped with atomic warheads, causing much more damage than the 300 injured and 4,000 homeless.

Israel's attack on Iraq's nuclear reactor in 1981 shows how readily Israel violates international law

After Israel destroyed the Iraqi nuclear reactor in 1981, UN Security Council Resolution 487 "strongly condemned" Israel for its actions and said that "Iraq is entitled to appropriate redress for the destruction it has suffered." The US joined in this criticism.

According to international law, nations are permitted to carry out anticipatory self-defense. The conditions for striking first are when danger posed is "instant, overwhelming, leaving no choice of means and no moment for deliberation." Iraq has maintained an official state of war against Israel since 1948. When Israel attacked the Iraqi nuclear facility, no civilian casualties were caused, and no radiation danger existed at the time. In hindsight, had Israel allowed Iraq to develop a nuclear capability, it is possible that Saddam Hussein would have introduced nuclear weapons to the region, either against US forces in the Gulf War or against Israel via the SCUDs that he fired at it. Therefore, the IDF attack constituted an act of anticipatory self-defense that not only saved Israeli lives but likely American-led Gulf War coalition forces as well.

A Time for Truth: Iraq has picked up the pieces of its military program as if there never was a Gulf War. Saddam Hussein continues to call for war against Israel and is developing an enhanced capacity to strike at it with more than conventional weapons, as he did in 1991. Saddam's military is very much intact and since the Iraqi economy is booming and the UN embargo has proven to be completely ineffective, it will only become more potent.

ARAB NATIONS

The Arab and Moslem World is just anti-Israel, not anti-Semitic

Syrian Defense Minister Mustafa Talas penned a book, called *The Matzo of Zion*, in which he claims that Jews use the blood of Gentiles in their Passover flatbread. The plot invokes the infamous 1840 Damascus blood libel. The book has achieved so much domestic success that it is being made into a movie. Syrian state-controlled newspapers vie with each other to see who can print more astonishing stories about Jews and Israelis committing heinous anti-human acts. Newspapers in Lebanon, Syria, the PA and Egypt routinely deny the historical veracity of the Holocaust. One Egyptian newspaper editorial, written by Ahmad Ragab, on April 18, 2001 stated that "Thanks to Hitler, of blessed memory, who on behalf of the Palestinians, revenged in advance against the most vile criminals on the face of the earth. Although we do have a complaint against him for his revenge was not enough." PA newspaper *Al-Hayat Al-Jedida* wrote on April 13, 2001: "The figure of 6,000,000 Jews cremated in the Nazi Auschwitz camps is a lie for propaganda."

A new book called the *New History of the Arabs and the World*, put out by the PA, pretends to quote the Jewish Talmud: "Non Jews are pigs who God created in the shape of man in order that they be fit for service for the Jews, and God created the world for them."

Syrian leader Bashar Assad, in an audience with the Pope, said Israel "tried to kill the principles of all religions with the same mentality which they betrayed Jesus Christ and the same way they tried to betray and kill Prophet Mohammed." Assad was also quoted in the March 29, 2001 *Syria Times* as saying "[Israel] is a racist society, a society more racist than the Nazis." The Editor of *Tishreen* wrote: "Zionism created the Holocaust myth to blackmail and terrorize the world's intellectuals and politicians."

On April 24, 2001 the leading Moslem cleric in Iran, Ayatollah Khamenei, speaking at a pro-Intifada gathering in Teheran, said "There is evidence which shows that Zionists had close relations with the German Nazis and exaggerated statistics on Jewish killings."

In Jordan, Arafat Hijazi wrote at the Jordanian Writers' Union conference in May 2001 that "The number of Jews then [in World War II] did not exceed 3 million...and the number of available gas chambers then could not burn more than half the bodies."

A song entitled "I Hate Israel" made it to the top of the Egyptian pop charts in spring 2001. In 1996, an Egyptian tabloid reported that an Israeli-made chewing gum contained an aphrodisiac that caused women to sexually assault men. (The gum was made in Germany). Libyan leader, Moammmar Qaddaffi, accused Israel of infecting Palestinian children with AIDS (*Al-Ahram*, April 29, 2001).

Israeli Arab Knesset Member Azmi Bishara (July 30, 2001): "[Israel] was born illegitimately. But this illegitimately established state created a nationality of Hebrew Jews."

All these statements occurred a few weeks *after* Israeli Prime Minister Ehud Barak offered the PA more than 95% of the West Bank and Gaza, to dismantle nearly all the settlements and create a Palestinian state with East Jerusalem as its capital.

Martin Luther King once stated, "When people criticize Zionism, they mean the Jews. You're talking anti-Semitism."

The Arab economic boycott of Israel is over

Officially, the boycott against the Jews that began in 1946 -- two years before the State of Israel was declared, was ended a short time after the Oslo process began. However, in the past few years Arab nations have renewed the boycott against Israel. It is not yet as cohesive as it used to be, coming from all sorts of different sources. Benetton was put under pressure by the American Arab Anti-Discrimination Committee for stating plans to build a factory in the West Bank. The Arab League threatened Walt Disney Co. because of an exhibit at Epcot Center that included an Israeli pavilion that had references to Jerusalem as Israel's capital. Ben & Jerry's, Burger King and Sprint have come under pressure for operating in the West Bank. The *Chicago Tribune* reported on January 9, 2001 that Pizza Hut, McDonald's, Marlboro, Procter & Gamble, Hostess, Gillette, Coca-Cola, Pepsi, Heinz and Nike have also been subjected to boycotts because they conduct business with Israel. Egyptian Moslem clerics have issued a decree stating that importing Israeli and American products is "religiously forbidden" and that the importers are committing "a great sin." Some of the high profile Moslem clerics that have endorsed the boycott are Egypt's Grand *Mufti* Nasser Farid Wassel, *Sheikh* Yousef al-Qaradawi and Lebanon's highest Shiite cleric, *Sheikh* Mohammed Hussein Fadlallah.

At the June 2001 meeting of Arab Foreign Ministers, an affirmation of the previous meeting's decision to break off all contacts with Israel and to reinstitute the Arab economic boycott of Israel was passed.

Jews are no longer persecuted in Islamic countries

Thirteen Jews from the Iranian city of Shiraz were arrested and held for 19 months on charges of spying for Israel. The Revolutionary Court claimed that their years of religious service and devotion to their Jewish faith was in fact a cover for illegal aid to and espionage for Israel.

Of these 13 men, 10 of whom were convicted, there were shopkeepers, rabbis, Hebrew teachers, a shoe salesman and a civil servant. The trial was closed to the public and the public defender was not given the case file until just days before the trial. In the 19 months without seeing their families or receiving legal counsel, confessions were forced from 8 of the men. According to the defense attorney, the court did not prove, or even claim, that these men had access to classified information. In the verdict, the judge said the men operated an extensive network for over 20 years that "was founded on the basis of Judaism and its success was due to the fact it tried to keep religion alive."

Immense international pressure was put on Iran to release these men from custody. Death sentences were probably waived and sentences reduced from 2-6 years from the original terms of 4-13 years to placate the plethora of international human rights groups who mounted a campaign against this trial. Yet, the "Iran 10" were jailed and punished for their religious beliefs and nothing more.

In Egypt, a country without a Jewish population, the Egyptian Press Syndicate presented the top honor in Egyptian journalism to a columnist who wrote an editorial praising Hitler. Another editorial in *Al-Ahram*, the government-run newspaper, was entitled "Israel -- The Plague of our Time and a Terrorist State." This article was replete with citations from the *Protocols of the Elders of Zion*.

A soldier from Jordan, another country without a Jewish population, opened fire on Israeli schoolgirls at the Israeli-Jordanian border in 1997, killing 7. His mother said on a May 23, 2001 call-in show on *Al-Jezira TV*: "My son did a heroic deed and has pleased Allah and his own conscience. My son lifts my head and the head of the entire Arab and Islamic nation. I am proud of any Moslem who does what [my son] did."

The Arab nations see the Arab-Israel conflict as a regional problem

An editorial in the Egyptian daily, *Al-Ahram*, in late August 2001, outlines a popular Arab perspective on the Arab-Israel conflict: "The conflict that we call the Arab-Israeli conflict is, in truth, an Arab conflict with Western, and particularly American, colonialism. The US treats [the Arabs] as it treated the slaves inside the American continent. To this end, [the US] is helped by the smaller enemy, and I mean Israel" (*Wall Street Journal*, September 20, 2001).

Islamic Republic of Iran

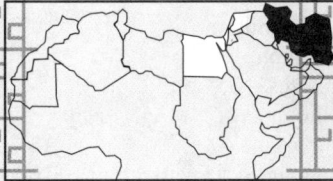

Area:	1.648 Million sq. km
Population:	65.6 Million
Date of Independence:	April 1, 1979
Head of State:	Mohammad Khatami
GDP per capita:	$5,300
Defense Budget:	$5.7 Billion
Active Military:	513,000
Tanks:	1,410
Combat Aircraft:	304
Artillery:	3,224

The Arab nations help push the Palestinians towards resolving the conflict peacefully

The Islamic Development Bank reported on August 19, 2001 that Arab States have given nearly half a billion dollars to the Palestinians in support of the Intifada.

Saudi Arabia - $210 million
Kuwait - $57.5 million
United Arab Emirates – $57.5 million
Egypt - $7.5 million
Yemen - $8 million
Qatar, Algeria, Oman, Syria & Bahrain - $100 million
Jordan - $1.5 million
Sudan - $.5 million

According to Israeli intelligence sources, Hamas receives tens of millions of dollars from the princes of Saudi Arabia.[7]

Iran does not have the capability to destroy Israel

US officials believe that Iran may have acquired nuclear technology from the former Soviet Union on the black market. Iran has been testing intermediate range missiles that could reach Israel. Until 2000, the US did not think that Iran possessed nuclear capability, but that opinion has changed. In Bushehr, Iran, the Russians are helping build a 1,000 megawatt nuclear reactor that they say is only for civilian use. The power station is part of a $300 million annual arms package with Russia (*Washington Post*, October 2, 2001).

Israel possesses a nuclear deterrent that prevents the Arabs from waging war against the Jewish State

During the Gulf War, Iraq hit Israel with 39 SCUD missiles. The Iraqis were not deterred by the IDF might or reputation. It did not even fear nuclear retaliation.

A Time for Truth: The Islamic World is seething with hatred for Jews, the traditional scapegoat for all its societal ills. The Islamic World does not seem to miss an opportunity to try to strike at Israel and Judaism, which are treated synonymously, be it through economic boycott, military threats, or Holocaust denial. Its anti-Semitism is so strong that even countries without Jewish populations participate in the hatred.

---

[7]Islamic Aid, a London-Based organization run by Youssef Islam, formerly known as Cat Stevens, also is a heavy contributor to Hamas.

PALESTINIANS

i. History

Palestine was an Arab country

Throughout history, there was never an independent autonomous Arab country in Palestine. Since the destruction of the second Temple in 70 CE, numerous countries conquered Palestine. The Romans, Greeks, Turks, Syrians, Egyptians and British have taken turns ruling the land. There was never a separate identifiable Palestinian nation until very recently.

Throughout the centuries, there was always a Jewish presence in the country. Jerusalem and the Galilee had longstanding communities that numbered in the thousands. The landowners of Palestine were predominantly absentee owners who lived in more affluent areas such as Damascus or Cairo. Palestine was devoid of population for most of recent history. Carl Hermann Voss, an American pastor, wrote in his book on Palestine that "In the twelve and a half centuries between the Arab conquest in the seventh century and the beginnings of the Jewish return in the 1880s, Palestine was laid waste. Its ancient canals and irrigation systems were destroyed and the wondrous fertility of which the Bible spoke vanished into desert and desolation." Thomas Shaw, an 18th Century British archaeologist, noted that Palestine was "lacking in people to till its fertile soil." Mark Twain, on a visit to Palestine's Jezreel Valley in 1867, wrote: "There is not a solitary village throughout its whole extent -- not for thirty miles in either direction. There are two or three small clusters of Bedouin tents, but not a single permanent habitation." In the Galilee, he wrote of "...these unpeopled deserts, these rusty mounds of barrenness...Nazareth is forlorn."

The Palestinian people have a lengthy history in the Promised Land

Count Bernadotte, UN Mediator for the Arab-Israel conflict in 1948, said: "The Palestinian Arabs have no will of their own. Neither have they ever developed any specifically Palestinian nationalism." The Arab office in Jerusalem submitted "The Case for Palestine" in March 1946 to the Anglo American Committee of Inquiry: "Geographically Palestine is part of Syria; its indigenous inhabitants belong to the Syrian branch of the Arab family of nations."

When the Arab war to destroy Israel in 1967 ended in an Arab defeat, none of the Arab nations offered citizenship to the people who had fled the war zone at the request of Arab leaders, but put them into tent camps. These camps all became hotbeds of hatred of Israel. Instead of developing humane living conditions for the refugees, the Arab countries pumped money into continuing the war against Israel. The Arab nations used the Palestinians to continue attacking Israel as its proxies. This campaign of violence was the origin of the Palestinian nation. Arafat related to his biographer, Alan Hart, that "it was only by fighting that we Palestinians could fix our identity." Thus, the Palestinian nation was born -- through Arab state-sponsored violence.

The PLO was created before the 1967 War, but it was run from Egypt, not from the Arab-controlled West Bank and Gaza. Gamal Abdel Nasser, the President of Egypt, ran the PLO as a proxy army with which to attack Israel while avoiding direct responsibility for the violence. Because Egypt had a proxy for fighting Israel, Jordan, Iraq, Syria and Lebanon also created terrorist forces to combat Israel. Although the world had never before heard of a Palestinian, Palestinian groups devoted to violence against Israel were appearing in Arab countries. The Popular Front for the Liberation of Palestine, Popular Front for the Liberation of Palestine-General Command, Democratic Front for the Liberation of Palestine, Abu Nidal, as-Saiqa and Fatah all cropped up for the same reason. "The PLO is a conglomeration of organizations that are a reflection of inter-Arab divisions," according to the *Islamic World Review* of 1983. In July 1968, the Palestine National Convention convened to approve its charter calling for the destruction of Israel through armed struggle. These are the roots of the Palestinian nation.

Of all the Palestinian leaders, George Habash of the PFLP was the only one born in what is today Israel. Neither Ahmed Jibril of the PFLP-GC nor Naif Hawatmeh of the DFLP was born in Palestine. The two leaders of as-Saiqa, once the second largest faction in the PLO, are both Jordanian Bedouins. Even Yassir Arafat is not Palestinian. He was born in Egypt, and only later in life did he move to Jerusalem. In truth, this is the case for most of the older generation of Arabs who identify themselves as Palestinian. Most of this group have Egyptian, Jordanian or Syrian citizenship because that is where their families were from and where they were born. The native Arab population of Palestine was minimal until Jewish immigration brought economic opportunity to the region from which neighboring Arabs wanted to profit.

Palestinians routinely deny Jewish history in order to try to gain legitimacy for their cause. On *Al-Jezira TV* on June 28, 1998, the PA stated that, "...until now, all the excavations that have been carried out have failed to prove the location of the Temple. It is 30 years since they [the Israelis] captured the city and they have not succeeded in even giving one proof as to the location of the Temple." *Newsweek* (June 27, 2001) reported that Arafat told President Clinton during a meeting that he doubts that a Jewish Temple ever existed on the Temple Mount. Palestinian leaders, especially Arafat, routinely borrow from Jewish and Christian history in order to convince their people (and themselves) of the righteousness of their cause. New Testament figures such as Jesus, Peter and Paul are referred to as "Palestinian Arabs."

Abraham is called a Semitic Aramean leader. A fifth-grade textbook put out by the PA reads: "Abraham was a Moslem monotheist." They say that Palestinian Jebusites founded Jerusalem. Even the Jewish resistance against the Romans was referred to by Arafat as the "Palestinian resistance" at a UNESCO conference in Belgrade, Yugoslavia in 1980.

Were it not for Israel, there would be a country called Palestine

Syria, once the controller of much of Palestine under the French colonial regime, always considered Palestine part of its country. It also considers Lebanon part of Greater Syria, which is why the Syrians have maintained a military presence there. Egypt, many times a ruler of Palestine over the millennia, was looking to extend its rule over more of Palestine than just Gaza. Had the invading Arab armies won in 1948, 1967 or 1973 there still would not have been a country called Palestine; they simply would have divided up the spoils.

The invading Arab armies conquered much of Palestine in the 1948 War, cutting the country in half. The Jordanians held the West Bank for 19 years. The Egyptians held on to Gaza for most of this time. Neither country offered to create an independent Arab state for a people calling themselves Palestinians; but both continued to call for Israel's liquidation. Palestinian nationalism technically began in 1964 with the founding of Fatah by Yassir Arafat, but this group did not become a force until it seized leadership of the PLO and began a massive campaign of international terrorism in the 1970s. This campaign was encouraged and funded by Israel's Arab neighbors as a means of continuing the war against Israel without having to do the dirty work.

The PLO would never have been allowed to grow in Jordan, Egypt or Syria. Arafat was expelled from Egypt in the 1950s and Syria in 1966. The PLO started a coup in Jordan in 1970, was put down ruthlessly and banished from the country. Dissident movements in Syria and Egypt have suffered similar fates. The PLO was able to find a home in Lebanon because the society was torn apart by its extended civil war and no central government could exert control over its population. Subsequently, the PLO came into southern Lebanon heavily armed and ran a state-within-a-state until Israel invaded to chase it out and quiet its border from its frequent attacks.

ii. Intentions

Leading Palestinians are trying to pave the way to peace with Israel

Hanan Ashrawi told *The Connection, WBUR* on July 28, 2000 that "Arafat was not only ready [to make a peace deal], but he actually prepared his constituency for peace." What are the leaders of the PA really saying to their people?

70

Yassir Arafat was the first to blame Israel for the death of Faisal Husseini when he died of a heart attack in a Kuwait City hotel room. Husseini had long suffered from asthma and high blood pressure; nevertheless, Arafat claimed that he died because he had been tear-gassed by Israel about 10 days earlier.

Following a Palestinian attack during February 2001, where an Arab driver intentionally plowed into a group of Israelis waiting for a bus, killing 8 and injuring 26, Arafat chose not to condemn the violence but told *AP* on February 15, 2001 that "[It] was a road accident."

In February 2001, Arafat, while on a visit to Turkey and Jordan, accused Israel of using "black gas" on residents of the Khan Yunis refugee camp in Gaza. The Palestinian media broadcast this libel widely.

On July 29, 1998, Arafat addressed the Organization of the Islamic Conference's Jerusalem Committee: "The Israeli policy of ethnic cleansing has taken on the ugliest of forms in recent months...Israel has started the war over Jerusalem...but with Arab and Islamic assistance, this shall be our faithful *jihad* (holy war) -- to defend Jerusalem from the danger of Judaization and the Zionist plot."

April 16, 1998 in *Al-Hayat Al-Jedida*: "My colleagues in struggle and in arms, my colleagues in struggle and in *jihad*...Intensify the revolution and the blessed Intifada. Reinforce the strong stance and strengthen the faith. We must burn the ground under the feet of the invaders."

April 18, 1998 on Egyptian *Orbit TV*: "The peace agreement which we signed is an "inferior peace"...We respect agreements the way that the prophet [Mohammed] and Salah a-Din respected the agreements which they signed." (They both used the peaceful conditions following their agreements to rearm and then both routed their enemies).

July 30, 1998 in *Al-Hayat Al-Jedida*: "We shall continue to save holy Jerusalem from the Judaizing monster and the despised settlements...they [Israelis] are determined to destroy the Dome of the Rock and *al-Aqsa* Mosque on the Temple Mount and to replace them by building Solomon's Temple."

Leading Palestinians

Many leading Palestinians are making inflammatory remarks. Suha Arafat, Yassir's wife, speaking to the media on November 11, 1999 in the presence of Hilary Clinton: "The Israeli occupying forces have poisoned our air with poisonous gases, and have destroyed 80% of our water resources, which have now become putrefied. Our lands are soaked with chemicals, inherited from the period of occupation, and this is increasing the rate of cancer and other horrible diseases, especially among women and children." When Mrs. Arafat was criticized for embarrassing Mrs. Clinton, she apologized but never recanted her statement.

Ambassador Nabil Ramlawi, the Permanent Observer of Palestine to the UN Commission on Human Rights told the Human Rights Conference in Geneva on March 11, 2001 that "the Israeli authorities have infected by injection 300 Palestinian children with the HIV virus during the years of the Intifada."

PA Health Minister Riyadh Al-Za'anoon told *Al-Ayyam* on July 25, 1998 that Israeli doctors "use Palestinian patients for experimental medicines and training new doctors."

PA Minister of Ecology Yousef Abu-Safiyyeh was quoted in the April 3, 1999 *Al-Hayat Al-Jedida* saying that Israel has been dumping liquid waste into the Palestinian areas of the West Bank and Gaza.

PA Information Minister Yasser Abed Rabbo, speaking on the *Voice of Palestine*, called on the Palestinians in June 2001, to "teach the settlers the lesson they deserve." This statement was made in the immediate aftermath of the cease-fire with Israel.

The PA press alleged that Israeli planes were dropping infected candies into Palestinian schoolyards in May 2001.

The most convincing lie propagated by the PA was that the Israelis were trying to destroy the *al-Aqsa* mosque, which was the means by which Arafat launched the latest campaign of violence against Israel. It did not even matter that no examples of how Israel was attempting this destruction were offered.

Marwan Barghouti, leader of Fatah and Tanzim in the West Bank, responding to a July 13, 2001 question by *Jewish Week* on Palestinian violence and gunmen shooting at civilians on the tunnel road to Efrat: "...it's self-defense...If there is occupation in your homeland and you have done everything possible to obtain peace and in return you have received 600 dead, 3,000 wounded, 3,000 prisoners and a closure for 10 months what do you expect? It is self-defense."

Abu Ali Shahin, PA Minister of Supplies, said on *Al-Jezira TV* (May 23, 2001): "Accepting the Oslo Accords was for the Palestinians, a betrayal of the historical legitimacy of the Arab right to Palestine." However, he added that it was done "in order to gain a better position and to continue in the liberation of the land."

PA Deputy Minister of Supplies Abd Al-Hamid Al-Qudsi claimed in the August 22, 1998 *Al-Hayat Al-Jedida* that "Israel carries out a clear policy of annihilating our people and destroying our national economy by smuggling spoiled foodstuff...not fit for human consumption, into PA territories."

Sheikh Ikrimi Sabri, the leading Moslem official in the PA, said in 1998: "The Moslem embraces death. Look at the society of the Israelis. It is a selfish society that loves life. These are not people who are eager to die for their country and their God. The Jews will leave this land rather than die, but the Moslem is happy to die" (*New Yorker*, July 9, 2001).

Dr. Musa Al-Zubut, the Chairman of the Palestinian Legislative Council Education Committee, said on February 21, 2001 that: "The Holocaust has been exaggerated in order to present the Jews as victims of a great crime, to justify that Palestine is necessary as a homeland for them, and to give them the right to demand compensation" (*MEMRI* Dispatch # 187).

Faisal Husseini, the PA Minister for Jerusalem, said in Beirut: "The current Intifada...must not be stopped until it reaches full Palestinian independence...I am maintaining contact [with Israelis] in order to put an end to the relationship...We will continue to aspire to the strategic goal, namely, to Palestine from the river to the sea. Whatever we can get now cannot make us forget this supreme truth" (*MEMRI*, March 22, 2001).

Azmi Bishara, Israeli Arab Member of Knesset (MK), while attending a memorial service for Hafez Assad in Syria in June 2001 with heads of Hamas, Hezbollah and the PFLP-GC: "The government of Israel is trying to shrink the realm [of resistance], by putting forth a choice: either accept Israel's dictates or face full-scale war. Thus, it is impossible to continue with a third way -- that of resistance -- without expanding this realm once again so that the people can struggle and resist. Nor is it possible to expand this realm without a unified and internationally effective Arab political position. This is precisely the time for such a stance."

Abdul Malik Dahamshe, Israeli Arab MK, while visiting Syria in January 1995: "Palestine and Syria are one homeland. The Arab people will win by the sword; the victory will be won by the *jihad* of the Arab world" (*Jerusalem Post*, January 24, 1995).

Abdul Darawshe, Israeli Arab MK, August 1997: "Haifa and Jaffa are calling us! With blood and fire we shall redeem Palestine. If even Israeli Arabs, who have lived under the flag and sovereignty of Israel for many years, are willing to thus express themselves, then what peace is possible with the Palestinians who nearly all dream of the day when Palestine in its entirety will be theirs, converted to a Moslem Palestinian State?" (*Ma'ariv*, August 11, 1997)

The Arab World feels that Israeli society has grown weak and it cannot absorb any more casualties, thus Israel is in a position where it can be defeated

Egyptian *Al-Usbu* columnist Amru Nasif wrote in his May 28, 2001 column that he is volunteering to become one of the next suicide bombers against Israel. "…With every blow struck by the *al-Aqsa* Intifada, my conviction grows stronger that I, and all those who are of the same mind, have been right all along and am still right in my belief that the despised racist Jewish entity will be annihilated…All that it requires is to concentrate on acts of martyrdom, or what is known as 'the strategy of the balance of fear.' Let us do some mathematical calculations: 250 Palestinians have signed up for martyrdom operations, and it is not impossible to raise this number to 1,000 throughout the Arab world, i.e. one *fedayi* (fighter) out of every 250,000 Arabs. The average harvest of each act of martyrdom is 10 dead and 50 wounded. Thus 1,000 acts of martyrdom would leave the Zionists with at least 10,000 dead and 50,000 wounded. This is double the number of Israeli casualties in all their wars with the Arabs since 1948."

Ziyyad Abu Ziyyad, a senior Palestinian cabinet member, explained that the Palestinians are escalating terror inside Israel in order to create a pervasive fear in Israel that cripples everyday living. On the present reaction of Israelis that shows a greater resilience against these attacks, he said: "It is only the first, natural reaction to a state of shock. But after they get over their shock they will be led to accepting our demands." In the Palestinian mind, Israel was forced out of Lebanon by a group of roughly 300 unorganized Hezbollah fighters, therefore the Palestinians feel that they can achieve the same results with their greater numbers, access to all of Israel and better weaponry.

According to Hamas Spokesman Hassan Yousuf: "This operation (suicide bombing at the Dolphinarium in Tel Aviv that killed 21 Jews) deeply disturbed the Israeli people and shook their sense of security. One million Israelis have left [Israel] since the start of the Intifada" (*Palestine Report*, June 6, 2001).

A Time for Truth: Israel does not find itself in a new situation, nor is its society weary to the point of being vulnerable to defeat. There has been no call of soldiers to reserves. Neither has there been a disabling of the Israeli economy. There is no great exodus of citizens. Only hours after bomb blasts, cafés, stores and malls are busy again. Israel's military and psychological readiness has not changed because of Palestinian violence. The population is not ready to create committees to alter the political and geographic landscape of the country, as it did for Lebanon. Israel suffered through six years of attrition, primarily in Gaza, between 1967-1973. Frequent terrorism over the Egyptian border and military clashes with Egypt cost Israel over 200 lives during this period.

iii. Education

Palestinian summer camps are recreational

Children are encouraged to attend summer camps run by Fatah and other extreme organizations such as Hezbollah in Lebanon and the Islamic Jihad. 27,000 children aged 8-18 attended PA summer camps in 2000 where they learned how to slit throats and participated in mock kidnappings. It is prestigious in Palestinian circles to be admitted to a Fatah camp, because the children are then seen as potential fighters who fill the ranks of the Shabiba, the youth group of the Tanzim, Fatah's militia. Weapons training is provided for these children and the military-style camps are filled with political sessions where the campers are indoctrinated with anti-Semitism. At Islamic Jihad's 'Paradise Camps', children 8-12 are put through similar programs and are taught how to become suicide bombers.

Palestinian children are being taught democratic values in schools and at home

The PA uses classrooms in its schools to help incite Palestinians of the younger generation against Israel. A lesson for fourth-grade students reads as follows: "I believe that the Jews are the enemies of the Prophets and the believers." A fifth-grade textbook describes Jews as cowards who will rot in Allah's hell. A sixth-grade text says: "The honorable soul has two objectives: Achieving death and honor." An eighth-grade reader refers to Jews as "the butchers of Jerusalem." Another preaches: "Mankind has suffered from this evil both in ancient as well as in modern times, for, indeed, Satan has, in the eyes of many people, made their evil actions appear beautiful until they thought that their race was the best of all, and their kind better than all others, and that other people are their slaves and do not reach their level. Such a people are the Jews." A tenth-grade schoolbook says "...Martyred *jihad* fighters are the most honored people, after the Prophets." Many other texts have stories of the worthiness of stone-throwing attacks against Israelis and the importance and holiness of martyrdom.

A Palestinian version of Sesame Street, called Children's Club, calls for the perpetration of *jihad* against the Jews. "We will settle our claims with stones and bullets," says one child participant, "When I wander into Jerusalem, I will become a suicide bomber." Another child says: "I come here to say that we will throw them to the quiet sea. Occupiers, your day is near, then we will settle our account. We will settle our claims with stones and bullets." A fourth-grade project in a Hamas-run school involved parents and children staging a suicide bombing and chanting: "We die for the sake of Allah." PA TV runs commercials with Mohammed Al-Dura, the 12-year old boy killed during Palestinian-Israeli crossfire at an Israeli military checkpoint in Gaza, beckoning from the grave, urging children to follow him into martyrdom. His desk in a Gaza school has become a shrine, where children pray with their teachers for the destruction of Israel. Another children's show, the *Bird's Garden*, says: "Today I chose a really nice drawing for you of the map of Palestine. Let us look at it together. A drawing of Palestine. There is Acre, Haifa, Jaffa, Tiberias, Nazareth, Jerusalem...Palestine is so beautiful."

iv. Succession

There is a Palestinian alternative to Arafat that is moderate and will negotiate with Israel in good faith

Hamas is the second most popular group in the West Bank and Gaza after Fatah. Hamas leader, *Sheikh* Ahmed Yassin, said in May 1998: "The first quarter of the next century will witness the elimination of the Zionist entity and the establishment of the Palestinian state over the whole of Palestine. The strong will not remain strong forever and the weak will not remain weak forever" (*ICEJ News*, May 27, 1998). The Charter of Hamas calls for the total elimination of Israel. "The Islamic Resistance Movement believes that the land of Palestine has been an Islamic *Waqf* throughout the generations and until the Day of Resurrection, no one can renounce it or part of it, or abandon any part of it."

The average Israeli no longer sees any difference between Hamas and Arafat. After all, Hamas perpetrators of violence against and murder of Israelis have been released from prisons and those who have been identified by Israel as potential threats remain untouched by the PA. Arafat admitted to the *New York Times* on June 29, 2001, that: "I am not looking for Hamas or Islamic Jihad because there is a union between us."

Hamas has developed a close bond with the leaders of the Tanzim and carry out joint operations with them. Hamas has begun purging "collaborators," which includes any Palestinian cooperating with Israel. Show trials and executions of "collaborators" have become commonplace in the PA-controlled areas. This is part of Hamas' campaign to take over the Intifada by not only terrorizing Israelis, but any Palestinian who wants to put an end to violence.

Arafat's eventual successor will be more prone to negotiate a deal with Israel

There is no clear candidate for replacing Arafat. There are those who feel that Marwan Barghouti, the leader of Fatah and the Tanzim, is the strongest candidate because of his leadership role on the streets. What does this mean for Israel?

Barghouti leads the Tanzim, one of the groups that Arafat unleashes on Israel to carry out drive-by shootings, bombings, mortar launchings and street riots against Israeli targets. There are many, including the Government of Israel, who believe that Barghouti is the director of the violence in the recent Intifada. On June 12, 2001 a drive-by shooting claimed the life of a Greek Orthodox monk who was driving alone near Jerusalem. Following the incident, two men were arrested by the IDF and they said that they approached Barghouti for guns and he referred them to one of his aides who supplied them with the murder weapons (*Jerusalem Post*, June 2, 2001).

On September 23, 2001, the Israeli Justice Ministry officially requested that the PA turn over Barghouti to Israel. The extradition request presented evidence of Barghouti's involvement in attempted murder, illegal possession of weapons, abetting murder, directing unlicensed military training exercises and belonging to and working with terrorist organizations.

Barghouti is said to carry out operations with units consisting of Hamas, Islamic Jihad and Tanzim members. On August 5, 2001 Barghouti said, "I think we need a new government which allows Hamas and others to participate...This will enhance Palestinian unity." While attending a meeting for Ahmed Jibril's Popular Front for the Liberation of Palestine-General Command, an avidly anti-Arafat group, he told a reporter for the *New Yorker* in July 2001 that, "we're all fighting together now."

During the 1980s Intifada, Barghouti was the head of Fatah's Shabiba at Bir Zeit University and was deported to Jordan in 1987. He was one of the group that was allowed to return in 1994 under the terms of the Oslo Accords.

The only other candidates come from Islamic parties, who have the potential to overthrow or kill Arafat if he continues to guide the Palestinians down a path where there are no benefits from fighting Israel. If an Islamic cleric were to replace Arafat, Israel would have another Iran inside its borders.

There are no leaders on the Palestinian horizon that will negotiate a peace with Israel, so Israel must wait for a new generation of Palestinians

A new generation of Palestinian children is learning about the conflict through three mediums: school, television and the street.

School

Here are some examples of how the PA is teaching its youth in classrooms:
"There is no alternative to destroying Jerusalem." -- Title page of *Our Country* textbook
"There will be a *jihad* and our country shall be freed. This is our story with the thieving conquerors." -- *Our Arabic Language*, 5th Grade Primer
"The honorable soul has two objectives: Achieving death and honor." -- *Song of the Martyr*, 6th Grade
"The Jews claim that this is one of the places belonging to them and call it 'The Western Wall,' but this is not so." -- Islamic Education class for 8th Grade
"Racism: Mankind has suffered from this evil both in ancient as well as in modern times, for, indeed, Satan has, in the eyes of many people, made their evil actions appear beautiful...Such a people are the Jews." -- Islamic Education class for 8th Grade
"...Martyred *jihad* fighters are the most honored people, after the Prophets." -- Reading and Literary texts for the 10th Grade

Television

Palestinian youth programs also provide political messages. Here are some quotations from PA TV:
"When I wander into Jerusalem, I will become a suicide bomber." -- The *Children's Club*, spoken by a 9 year old, July 2, 1998
"Israel's mean, brutal, immoral, inhuman, fascist, racist, genocidal, cleansing wars..." -- *The Bird's Garden*, May 14, 1998
"Jerusalem is a Palestinian Arab city, and it has no connection to Israel." -- *The Bird's Garden*, May 24, 1998
"I am not waving to you to say good-bye, but rather to tell you to follow me." -- PA TV commercial featuring Mohammed Al-Dura, the 12-year old who was killed during a Palestinian shooting attack on an IDF outpost in Gaza

Street

Because the youth are pushed into the streets to combat Israel at a very early age by political leaders, religious clerics and family heads, there is little hope that a new generation of Palestinians will be less extreme. The more that the Palestinians shun peace in favor of violence, the worse off their local conditions become. As well, the PA leadership commits its money to private use and armaments, so there is no program for improving the standard of living. Refugee camps have all remained intact under the PA and the quality of life is much worse than it was 10 years ago under Israeli rule. Ironically, the worse conditions get under Arafat, the more the people feel that anti-Israel violence is the answer.

78

A Time for Truth: The older Palestinian generation has taught hatred and violence to the younger generations so that hatred is ingrained and rooted. Unless a massive campaign of re-education is ever undertaken, there is little likelihood of there being a Palestinian leader in the next 50 years who speaks the language of peace.

v. Refugees

Israel stubbornly refuses to deal with millions of Palestinian refugees because it would involve acknowledging this massive human rights violation

Shortly after the 1948 war had ended, Israel acknowledged some responsibility for the refugee problem and offered to take back 100,000 Arabs who had fled the war zone. The Arab countries refused the offer. Nevertheless, Israel established a committee to deal with compensating Arabs who were forced out of Israel during any of the wars. Israel did not precondition its help to refugees on a peace agreement or on reciprocity for Jews forced out of Arab countries. By 1975, 11,000 claimants were paid more than 23 million shekels at a 6% annual added value, rather than a fixed price for 1948, and given 10,000 acres as alternative holdings. Jews who fled Arab countries for Israel were never compensated for lands and property valued at more than four times that of the Arab refugees. Under Israel's Family Reunification Plan, 50,000 Arab refugees have become residents in Israel and another 75,000 have returned to the West Bank and Gaza.

When the Arabs left Palestine before and during the war of 1948, they found their way to Egypt, Jordan, Syria and Lebanon. Arab governments placed them in refugee camps and did not contribute any money towards their welfare. Between 1950 and 1983, Israel contributed over $11 million to the United Nations Relief and Works Agency (UNRWA), which was more than any Arab state. The international community, through UNRWA, spent millions of dollars on these refugees, unprecedented for any group of refugees since the establishment of the UN. The Saudis only began contributing to UNRWA in 1973, Kuwait and Libya in 1980. Today, Arab contributions account for less than 6% of the UNRWA budget.

Israel should compensate Arab refugees just like Jewish refugees were compensated by Arab nations

During the middle of the 20th century, there was rampant anti-Semitism from Islamic governments and the Moslem masses. 850,000 Jewish refugees never received any form of compensation from Arab governments. Their homes and possessions were occupied in much the same way that the Poles snatched the Jewish spoils during World War II. Over $13 billion in Jewish

Syria Refugee Camps

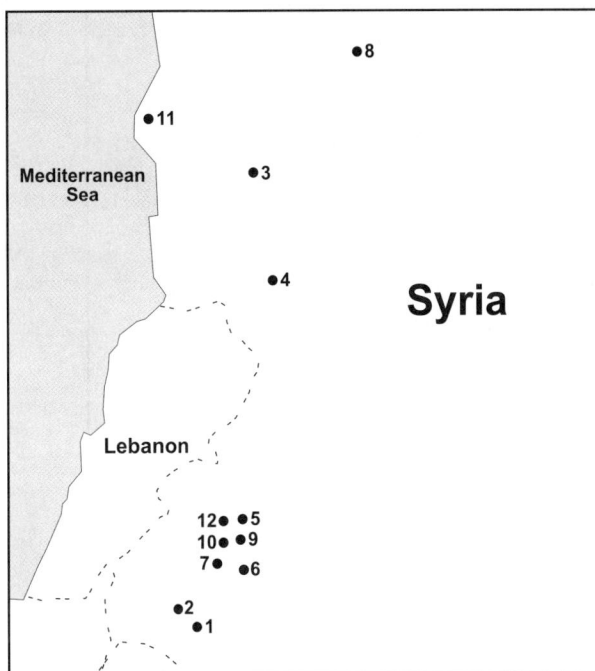

Population:

- **1** Dera'a (5,805)
- **2** Dera'a (Emergency) (5,380)
- **3** Hama (7,223)
- **4** Homs (13,349)
- **5** Aramana (8,950)
- **6** Khan Danoun (7,973)
- **7** Khan Eshieh (15,352)
- **8** Neirab (16,951)
- **9** Qabr Essit (13,066)
- **10** Sbeineh (15,857)
- **11** Latakia [unofficial camp] (2,500)
- **12** Yarmouk [unofficial camp] (103,000)

Source: UNRWA

Lebanon Refugee Camps

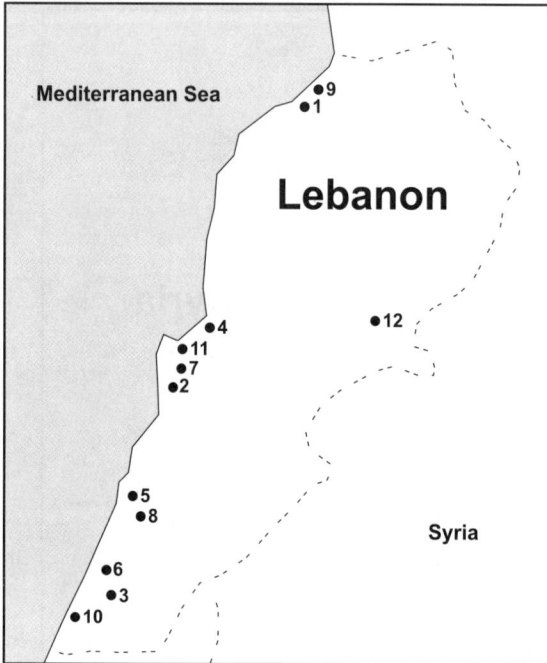

Population:

- **1** Beddawi (15,042)
- **2** Burj el-Barajneh (18,537)
- **3** Burj el-Shamali (17,605)
- **4** Dbayeh (4,717)
- **5** Ein el-Hilweh (42,754)
- **6** El-Buss (9,541)
- **7** Mar Elias (1,402)
- **8** Mieh Mieh (5,079)
- **9** Nahr el-Bared (26,941)
- **10** Rashidieh (24,009)
- **11** Shatilla (12,392)
- **12** Wavel (7,090)

Source: UNRWA

Jordan Refugee Camps

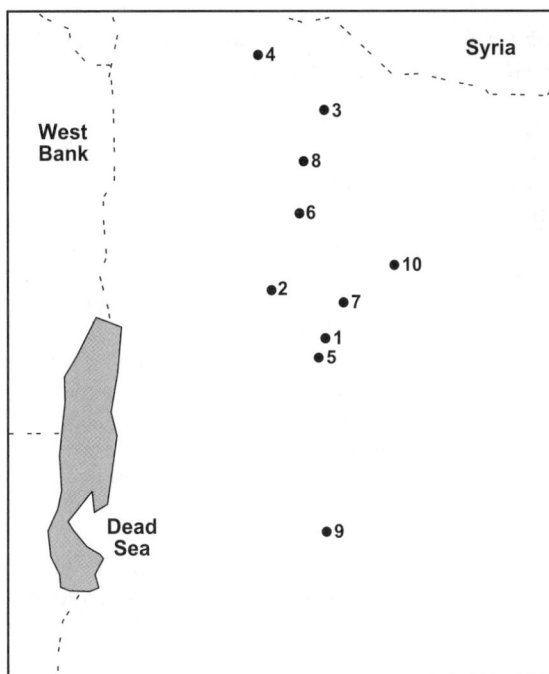

Population:

- **1** Amman New Camp (47,965)
- **2** Baqa'a (85,898)
- **3** Husn (25,579)
- **4** Irbid (22,546)
- **5** Jabal el-Hussein (27,624)
- **6** Jerash (25,980)
- **7** Marka (44,257)
- **8** Souf (15,000)
- **9** Talbieh (8,832)
- **10** Zarka (14,408)

Source: UNRWA

assets were confiscated throughout the Arab world. Israel absorbed and settled its group of displaced Jews, while the Arabs stuck their problems into refugee camps to fester there for more than 50 years.

The PA demands that millions of Palestinian refugees be allowed to return to an independent Palestine for humanitarian reasons

Amos Oz, the liberal Israeli writer, says: "implementing the 'right of return' means eradicating Israel." Why? Allowing over 5,000,000 refugees (by Arafat's count) to return to Israel would give the Palestinians a majority population in the democratic state and Israel would cease to exist. Thus, 'refugee return' has become a code word for eradicating Israel.

When Arafat refused Barak's offer at Camp David, one of his reasons was that Israel would not accept millions of Palestinian refugees as Israeli citizens. The PA does not want its own refugees as citizens of a nascent Palestinian State, but demands that they be returned to their original homes in Jaffa, Haifa and other Israeli cities in order to displace the Jewish population and create a Palestinian majority in Israel. These voters would then democratically vote Israel out of existence and combine with Palestine to create one large Arab State.

But will the refugees want to come back? *Per capita* income in Israel is 15 times higher than the Arab states in which the vast majority of the refugees live.

Israel has prevented the resolution of the refugee problem

Starting in 1993, when the Jericho region came under PA rule, Yassir Arafat has administered 18 refugee camps in the West Bank and 8 in Gaza. Rather than dismantle the shantytowns that are home to more than 800,000 refugees, Arafat has kept his people living in squalor.

In the early 1970s, the Israelis tried to resettle the Arab refugees in permanent dwellings under the "build your own home" program. In exchange for erecting your own home, Israel provided a host of services, including sewers and schools. More than 11,000 people moved into permanent residences as a result of this program. Because many more refugees wanted to build permanent homes in the Israeli program, the PLO, realizing that its political base would disappear without the poverty and destitution of the refugees in camps, began a successful campaign of intimidation against these Palestinians, which brought the program to an end.

The bulk of the refugee camps was established in the aftermath of the 1948 war. Egypt, Lebanon, Jordan and Syria placed the Arabs who fled the battlefields of Israel into these camps. In the immediate area, only Jordan granted the refugees citizenship. But even it did not provide them with permanent cities and towns. Not only did the Arab leaders not spend money to resettle the refugees, but they blocked international organizations from spending foreign money for this purpose. When UNRWA was first established, it suggested that 150,000 refugees be moved to Libya. Egypt blocked this plan. In 1951, a plan was proposed to move Arab refugees from Gaza into the Sinai, but Egypt said it would not allow water from the Nile to be used to irrigate these desert settlements, thus the plan was shelved. Another UNRWA initiative to resettle 85,000 Arabs into Syrian territory was blocked by Syria.

When Egypt called for the return of all captured territory from Israel in the Camp David Peace Accords in 1979, the Gaza Strip, which it possessed between 1948-1967, was excluded from this demand. Egypt did not want this heavily Palestinian area returned to it. Instead, it proposed autonomy for the 1,000,000 Palestinians in Gaza, half of whom live in Egyptian-founded refugee camps, something the Egyptians denied to them during the 19 years of its rule.

<u>vi. Sharing the land</u>

A binational secular democratic state is the solution to this conflict

On June 29, 2001, Palestinian professor Edward Sa'id was quoted in the *Khaleej Times* saying that this is "the only solution to the conflict between the two parties...It appears to me that a two-people state or a confederate union would be a reasonable solution for the Israelis, who would not be able to live in this land as an occupying force built on brute strength..." Potential heir to Arafat, Fatah and Tanzim leader Marwan Barghouti told *Jewish Week* on July 13, 2001: "Truthfully I think we should have one country for two nations." Are Sa'id and Barghouti right? Is this the best method to resolving this conflict?

The Palestinians do not offer to keep Jewish settlements intact or keep the residents of these communities as citizens of Palestine. Rather, they want them extricated from all of the West Bank and Gaza. Even when the PA agrees to a complete cease-fire, shooting at settlers continues.

If a binational state was founded without Palestinian refugees returning *en masse*, it would have a small Jewish majority. According to Professor Arnon Sofer of Haifa University, by the year 2020, this state would have a clear Arab majority even without refugee return because of the larger Arab birth rate. Jews would account for only 42% of the population of a binational state in the West Bank, Gaza and Israel-proper. The PLO says that only those Jews who were in Palestine before 1948 would be allowed to remain in a country under its rule. Since most of the immigration to Israel came after the War of Independence, Jews in a binational state would become a small minority.

How would the PA treat a Jewish minority? During the initial PLO negotiations with Israel in Oslo and Madrid, the PLO delegation employed a member of the fringe anti-Israel Nturei Karta Hasidic Jewish sect as its "Advisor on Jewish Affairs." This extreme right-wing sect of Hasidic Jews calls the Jewish State illegitimate and does not participate in any aspect of Israeli public life. They do not serve in the army. They do not speak Hebrew, the national language. They do not vote. Everything having to do with the State of Israel is anathema to them. Their agenda, while so far on the fringe that it is not considered on the political spectrum, is similar to the Palestinian one -- the demise of Israel.

There were Jewish leaders in the 1930s who advocated a secular democratic state for all inhabitants of the land, but no Arab leaders shared this hope. A spokesman for Fatah said in 1968 that each Jew from an Arab country would be able to go back as "a true Arab citizen, enjoying every right enjoyed by the Arab native, as he was before." It was on the basis of this opinion that the Arabs gathered in Lebanon in 1970 to discuss this approach. Rather than continue to call for "throwing the Jews into the sea," the Arabs became more sensitive to world public opinion and adopted the slogan of a binational state as a codeword for destroying Israel.

The PA wants over 5,000,000 Arab 'refugees' returned to the land. Most of these refugees have no legitimate claim since their ancestors were either from other areas and claimed refugee status with the UN to benefit from UNRWA relief packages, or left the country at the encouragement of Arab leaders. However, there were 600,000 Jews who fled from Arab State terror to Israel, who, according to the PA, would have to be evicted along with their families.

A secular democratic state would have two regional models for comparison: Lebanon and Israel. In Lebanon, there was a functional democracy until the PLO, under Arafat, came into the country in 1969 and ruined not only the democracy, but the entire political system. The PLO experience with democracy is that democracy is anathema. The second model is Israel, a multinational secular democratic state. Israel is home to Jews, Christians, Moslems and other religious groups from all across the globe. Non-Jews account for approximately 15% of the population. Israel has no official religion and all religious groups have total autonomy over their religious and political lives.

A Time for Truth: A binational democratic state with a Palestinian majority would be disastrous for Jews because the only thing that the PA knows about such a system of government is how to destroy it.

Jews would be well treated as a minority in a secular democratic state with an Arab majority.

There is a long history of hostility to Jews living under Islamic rule. It is true that thousands of Jews lived under Moslem rule, but so too did multitudes reside under Christian rule, despite massacres and pogroms. Even before Zionism, the local Jewish populations were subjected to anti-Semitism throughout the Islamic world. The first Moslem, Mohammed, wiped out the native Jews of Saudi Arabia when they would not convert to his new religion.

Jews were forced to live in '*mellahs*' (ghettoes) throughout the Arab world and never given equal rights. They were given the choice of conversion or paying a '*jizyah,*' an expensive protection tax. The Covenant of Omar, from 638 BCE, identified Jews as inferior to Moslems and denied them basic rights. These laws, '*dhimmi,*' were applied at various times throughout the centuries. But yet, the Jews lived in Arab countries from the time of the Babylonian and Assyrian exiles in the 8th century BCE, a century before the rise of Islam. Only Saudi Arabia and Jordan did not permit Jewish residents. Jordanian Civil Law No. 6 stipulates that "any man will be a Jordanian subject unless he is Jewish."

Starting in 1948, 850,000 Jews ran for their lives from Islamic countries. Orchestrated Arab riots forced this population to uproot itself without advance notice. 600,000 fled to Israel, the only open door of refuge.

Syria

Once a thriving Jewish population, Syria has 250 Jews today. In 1948, the population was 45,000. The community continues to face threats, governmental intimidation and blood libels. Syria's current Minister of Defense published a book that accuses Jews of using the blood of non-Jewish children for Passover matzos. In 1840, there was also a blood libel against the Jewish community that caused the murder of many Jews. Bashar Assad publicly accused the Jews of deicide during an audience with the Pope in 2001. The younger members of the community have managed to trickle out of the country, leaving an older population that is dying off. Emigrating usually entailed leaving a deposit of $2,000-$10,000, a sum most Syrian Jews could not afford. Until 1976, Jews were even forbidden to travel locally, were subjected to middle-of-the-night interrogations and arrest without charge. Their cemeteries and synagogues were repeatedly vandalized or destroyed.

Documented human rights abuses have included rape, arrest of juveniles and torture. Syria also attracted media attention for harboring Adolph Eichmann's chief aide, Alois Brunner, who advised Hafez Assad on 'security matters.' Brunner, in a 1987 interview with the *Chicago Sun-Times*, said that all Jews "deserved to die because they were the devil's agents and human garbage."

Iraq

125,000 Jews lived in Iraq in 1948. Today they number 120. Jews have been in Iraq, or Babylon, for nearly 3,000 years. In Baghdad, in 807 CE, Caliph Haroun al-Rashid ordered the Jews to wear yellow badges. In the 1940s, widespread pogroms left many Jews dead. Most of the Jewish population fled in 1951. In 1952, Jews were forbidden from emigrating and held hostage by the Iraqi Hashemite government. Two Jews were publicly hanged on fictitious charges of attacking the office of the US Information Agency. Jews were given yellow identity badges and freedom of movement was curtailed. After the Six-Day War, their property was seized, bank accounts were frozen, telephone lines were disconnected and businesses shut. Many Jews were placed under house arrest without charge. Others were brought into police stations, tortured and killed, and 19 more were charged with running 'spy rings' and publicly hanged. 500,000 Iraqis came to a parade in Baghdad and danced around the bodies of Jews who had been hanged. Another 18 Jews were hanged on similar charges between 1970 and 1972. In all, over $200 million in possessions was confiscated. Now the community, old and dying, signals that the rooted Jewish presence of three millennia is coming to an end.

Morocco

A community that numbered over 300,000 has been reduced to 7,500 because of emigration. Morocco was one of the more tolerant regimes under King Hassan, but emigrating, even to the West, was made difficult for Jews. Pogroms were carried out in the streets of Morocco on numerous occasions, causing many Jewish deaths. In 1033, 6,000 Jews were murdered. Between 1864-1880, more than 500 Jews were killed. In June 1948, a mass attack left more than 40 Jews dead. The Jews fled Morocco because of fear and intimidation.

However, despite the disappearing community, Morocco was at the forefront when the Madrid Conference led to Arab State recognition of Israel. King Hassan met with Prime Minister Shimon Peres as early as 1986.

Egypt

In Cairo, there was a pogrom against the Jews in June 1948. This led to the arrest of thousands of Jews and the annulment of their citizenship. Jews had been in Egypt since the destruction of the First Temple, 2,500 years ago. The 1948 population of 75,000 Jews in Egypt has dwindled to fewer than 100. In 1967, when the war with Israel began, the government seized all Jewish property and forcefully registered the 2,500 remaining Jews. Approximately 800 people were imprisoned at this time, including the Chief Rabbis of Cairo and Alexandria. Many of these prisoners were tortured. Today, Egypt is perhaps the most virulently anti-Semitic country in the world. The Egyptian press routinely depicts Israelis as Nazis, denies the Holocaust, charges Jews with deicide, creates blood libels and quotes the *Protocols of the Elders of Zion*.

Libya

Today there are no known Jews in Libya. In 1948, there were 40,000. Hundreds of Jews were murdered by Ali Burzi Pasha in Libya in 1785. In 1945, a wild pogrom occurred in which Jews were beaten, hurled from rooftops and their shops and homes burned. Synagogues were razed to the ground. In Tripoli, 120 Jews were killed, 500 more were wounded and 2,000 had their homes destroyed by arson. In 1946, close to 200 Jews were killed in Zanzur and several other smaller towns. In 1948, 14 Jews were murdered during an anti-Israel riot. One hundred more were killed during pogroms following the Arab armies' defeat in the Six-Day War of 1967. In 1970, Moammar Qaddafi confiscated all Jewish property and annulled all debts owed to Jews, costing the community millions of dollars.

Yemen

More than 60,000 Jews lived in Yemen in 1948. This Jewish community had roots in the country for thousands of years. Today, there are probably fewer than 800 Jews left in the country.[8] Jews were restricted in a myriad of ways throughout their lives in Yemen. They were treated as infidels and were not allowed to own property. In 1724, Jews were forbidden to observe their religion, had their synagogues destroyed and were forced into exile until 1781. Following the UN Partition Plan announcement in 1947, rioters in Aden killed 82 Jews. There was anti-Jewish activity in the country in 1948 and 1967, causing the evacuation of the native Jewish population to Israel in Operation Magic Carpet. In December 1947, dozens of Jews were murdered in three continuous days of anti-Jewish violence.

---

[8] It is impossible to ascertain because the country is one of the most undeveloped in the world and information and access to the population is still difficult.

Lebanon

Most of the 20,000 Jews in Lebanon immigrated to Israel in 1948. There were others who stayed until the civil war in the mid-1970s drove them out, leaving a handful remaining today.

Iran

Under the Shah, the Jewish population was not threatened and it remained in Iran until Ayatollah Khomeini seized power during the Islamic Revolution in 1979. Jewish emigration was forbidden as soon as the Islamic Regime began its rule. Anti-Jewish activity was rampant and remains so today. Jews have been in Iran for nearly 3,000 years. Before the revolution, there were 80,000 Jews in the country. Today, 25,000 remain. Despite restrictions, 55,000 managed to flee the country, leaving everything they owned behind. Close to 500 Jews have been detained and more than 10 have been executed by firing squads. The latest abuse of Iranian Jews involved a show trial that resulted in 10 Jews being found guilty of 'spying for Israel.' During the closed trial, no evidence was ever offered as to how they spied.

Algeria

Once 150,000 Jews lived in Algeria. Most emigrated to France and Israel. Less than 100 remain. During Algeria's War of Independence in the 1950s, Algeria's Jewish community was attacked repeatedly. A host of anti-Jewish legislation was passed and the Jews of the country were heavily taxed, forcing a mass exodus. All but one of Algeria's synagogues are now mosques.

Tunisia

Anti-Jewish riots broke out in June 1967, causing destruction to Jewish synagogues and shops. In 1985 a lone gunman opened fire on Jews in a Jerba synagogue. Historically, relations with the Tunisian government were mainly positive for the Jewish community. There are approximately 2,000 Jews left of the 110,000 who resided there in 1948.

A Time for Truth: The Palestinians continue to incite their people to violence against Israel. It is a campaign that is extremely thorough, targeting all ages and strata of society, including children in kindergarten. If the Palestinians stay on the path of hatred and intolerance, there is little hope that the next two generations of Palestinian leaders will ever be ready to negotiate a real peace treaty with Israel.

UNITED NATIONS

Zionism is racism

Zionism is the Jewish nationalist movement. While the modern movement has existed for only 120 years, Zionism began in 70 CE when the Second Temple in Jerusalem was destroyed and the Jewish People were forced into exile. Since this time, the Jewish People's love of the Land of Israel and its yearning to return there has been its continual focus. Despite an imposed exile and dispersion of its people, the Jews of the world preserved their unique culture through the *Torah* (the Bible) and the knowledge of a shared history in the ancient Land of Israel. For 2,000 years, Zionism has manifested itself through Jewish prayers and Bible study, making Zionism the oldest national movement in the world. Over the centuries, there has been an uninterrupted Jewish presence in the land of Israel, in cities like Hebron, Jerusalem and Safed.

Population in Thousands

	1949	1965	1980	1995	2005	2020
ISRAEL	1,173.9	2,598.4	3,921.7	5,612.3	6,930.0	8,672.9
Jewish & other	1,013.9	2,299.1	3,282.7	4,522.3	5,572.9	6,697.1
Arab	145.5	269.5	588.2	931.8	1,357.1	1,975.8

Source: Israel Central Bureau of Statistics; (Arab includes Moslem & Christian)

Of the 6,500,000 people living in Israel 1,200,000 are not Jewish. Israel is a diverse society with a range of people from over 100 different countries. There is no discrimination between black and white, as witnessed by Israel's repeated and ongoing rescue of Ethiopian Jews. Israeli law guarantees freedom of worship to all. The Old City of Jerusalem is brimming with churches of many different denominations and mosques, as well as synagogues.

A Time for Truth: When the UN passed a resolution equating Zionism with racism in 1975, it ignored the facts. The Zionist State is a tolerant, open-minded, free democratic society. It is also the culmination of 2,000 years of Jewish aspirations for a mass return to the land. It is ironic that the repressive Islamic regimes like Libya, Iran, Iraq, Saudi Arabia and Syria are the ones branding Zionism as racist in the world's legislative body.

The United Nations artificially created Israel for the Jews

Historically, there is no other people or nation in the world with a greater continuous, accepted, historic link to a land than the Jewish People. The Land of Israel was promised to the Jewish People in the Bible. It is the home of the Jewish nation despite persecution, war and imposed exile. The Jewish nation does not rely on the Balfour Declaration or a UN vote for recognition of this truth. Those who dispute this claim oppose both Jewish and Christian history. Palestinian declarations that the Temple never stood upon the Temple Mount is a denial of King Solomon, Isaiah, Jeremiah and Jesus, all of whom lived during the time when a Temple stood atop the Temple Mount and was the country's center of life. The UN's position on Israel is irrelevant to the relationship between the Jews and the Land of Israel.

The United Nations favored the Jews when it partitioned Palestine

Following World War II, the British were ready to abandon the Mandate for Palestine and turn it over to the United Nations. The UN Special Commission On Palestine (UNSCOP) was sent to the region to look for answers on how to treat this contentious peace of land. UNSCOP was comprised of representatives from Australia, Canada, Czechoslovakia, Guatemala, India, Iran, the Netherlands, Peru, Sweden, Uruguay and Yugoslavia. UNSCOP proposed dividing the country in the hopes of satisfying the aspirations of both the Arabs and the Jews. The leaders of the *Yishuv* accepted the terms of partition even though it further diminished the area of the nascent Jewish state and created narrow corridors that would make defending the country exceptionally difficult. Jerusalem was excluded from the Jewish National Home and was to be an international enclave. This was the second time that the Jews accepted a condensed version of a state. In 1921, Transjordan was created out of the Mandate territory; nearly 80% of the land was gifted to the Hashemite family. This second partition arbitrarily created an area called the West Bank; prior to this act it had always belonged to the Land of Israel. The Arabs all resoundingly rejected the Partition Plan, saying "no" to partition, "no" to Jewish immigration and "no" to a Jewish state. The UN Partition Resolution was passed, despite Arab objections, by a vote of 33-13 on November 29, 1947.

The United Nations has played an impartial role in the Arab-Israel conflict

The UN spends an inordinate amount of time discussing the Arab-Israel conflict. Of 175 Security Council Resolutions passed before 1990, 97 were directed against Israel. 429 out of 690 UN General Assembly (UNGA) resolutions condemned Israel on a wide range of topics. When the Jewish people and Israel have been maltreated, the UN has been eerily quiet. The around-the-clock diplomacy conducted by the UN to get European and American hostages released from Lebanon in the 1980s succeeded. The only hostages left behind were Israeli; more than 25 years later, the fate of Israelis Ron Arad, Zachary Baumel, Zvi Feldman and Yehuda Katz are still unknown.

1947 Partition Plan for Palestine

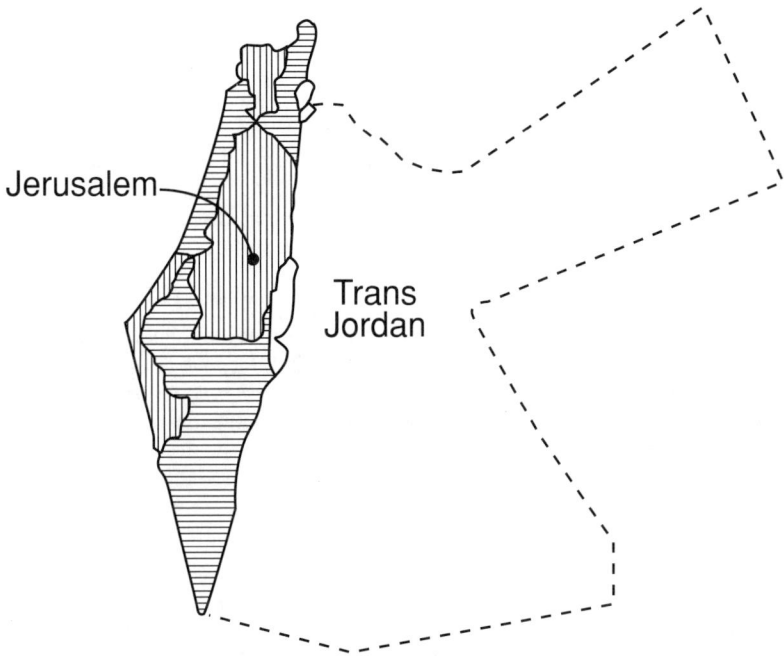

Jerusalem —

Trans
Jordan

▦ Jewish State
▥ Arab State
● International Zone

When Jordan was destroying Jewish synagogues (58) and desecrating cemeteries during its period of rule in the West Bank and Jerusalem between
1948-67, the UN never issued a condemnatory resolution; rather, it was
silent.

Middle East UN legislation is a byproduct of Arab hatred of Israel. In April
1983, Israel was accused of "mass poisoning" of Palestinians by the UNGA.
Israel invited the Red Cross and the World Health Organization to inspect
for poisoning and nothing was found to back up this allegation. The latest
piece of anti-Semitic UN legislation was proposed as a draft declaration at
the August 31, 2001 UN World Conference Against Racism, Racial
Discrimination, Xenophobia, and Related Intolerance: [Signifies an alter-
nate version]

> We express our deep concern about practices of racial discrimination
> against the Palestinians as well as other inhabitants of the Arab occu-
> pied territories, which have an impact on all aspects of their daily exis-
> tence such that they prevent the enjoyment of fundamental rights, and
> call for the cessation of all the practices of racial discrimination to
> which the Palestinians and the other inhabitants of the Arab territories
> occupied by Israel are subjected.
>
> We are convinced that combating anti-Semitism, Islamophobia, and
> Zionist practices against Semitism is integral and intrinsic to opposing
> all forms of racism and stress the necessity for effective measures to
> address the issue of anti-Semitism, Islamophobia, and Zionist practices
> against Semitism today in order to counter all manifestations of these
> phenomena.
>
> We recognize with deep concern the increase in anti-Semitism and hos-
> tile acts against Jews in various parts of the world, as well as the emer-
> gence of racial and violent movements based on racism and discrimi-
> natory ideas concerning the Jewish community.
>
> [The World Conference recognizes with deep concern the increase of
> racist practices of Zionism and anti-Semitism in various parts of the
> world, as well as the emergence of racial and violent movements based
> on racism and discriminatory ideas, in particular the Zionist movement,
> which is based on racial superiority.]
>
> We also recognize with deep concern the increased negative stereotyp-
> ing of and hostility expressed against Muslims in various parts of the
> world, and express concern with regard to any overt manifestations of
> Islamophobia.

[We also recognize with deep concern the increased negative stereo-typing of and hostility expressed against Muslims, the existence of Islamophobia and hostile acts and violence against Muslims which are evidenced in various parts of the world.]

We take note of and express our determination to eradicate any and all manifestations of anti-Arab bias and discrimination and, in particular, recognize that negative stereotyping contributes to racism, racial discrimination, xenophobia and related intolerance.

There is a continuous Arab use of the UN to delegitimize Israel by linking it in UN legislation and forums to colonialism, racism, oppression and aggression.

In July 2001, 9 months after 3 Israelis were taken hostage during a cross-border incursion by Hezbollah, the UN admitted it had a videotape of the incident. Israel demanded to see the tape but the UN would only permit a viewing once it edited the tape to obscure the faces of the Hezbollah abductors, who are identifiable on the film.

The UN has helped Arab and Jewish refugees

The United Nations Relief and Works Agency (UNRWA) was established by the international community to help Arab refugees from the Arab-initiated 1948 war against Israel. UNRWA was turned into a propaganda arm of the PLO in Lebanon, when the PLO established a mini-state in the southern portion of the country. *Faces Magazine* reported a conversation with a PLO information officer in 1975 in Lebanon: "Jada said he was an employee of the United Nations Relief and Works Agency and took much pride in claiming that almost the entire agency had been proliferated by 'soldiers of the revolution.' He escorted me to the agency's printing and graphics shop in Beirut where it appeared to me that dozens of people drawing UN salaries were pumping out PLO propaganda, posters and pamphlets, books and pictures, portraits of Yassir Arafat. I surmise that all this was being produced and paid for by the United Nations and perhaps in the ultimate analysis, being largely financed by the United States."

The Arabs claim that 630,000 refugees were created by the 1948 war. In 50 years, they and their descendants have grown to 5,000,000 people according to the PA. 850,0000 more refugees were forced to flee from Arab countries. These refugees were compelled to leave countries that they had inhabited for up to 3,000 years. These refugees were Jews.

The UN never provided any kind of assistance to these Jewish refugees. However, billions of dollars have been committed to Palestinian refugees since 1948. The UNRWA budget for 2000-01, all of which goes to the

Palestinian cause, is more than $600 million. The UN has been spending more than $300 million every year on the Palestinian refugees since the 1990s. In addition to that sum, three emergency appeals, in November 2000, February and June 2001, amassed nearly $80 million more for Palestinian refugees.

The UN took a tough stance on PLO terrorism in the 1970s

The PLO was granted observer status in the UN in the 1970s despite the fact that its only acclaim was hijacking airplanes, taking hostages and killing diplomats. Yet, because the Arab-Soviet-Third World bloc accounted for two-thirds of the UN vote, it determined the agenda of the UN. Arafat was invited in 1974 to address the UN while brandishing a pistol in his belt. Such a thing has never been allowed -- before or since. The PLO had just been expelled from Jordan following a failed coup that left more than 5,000 dead. Its fighters escaped to Lebanon where it began attacking Israel with whatever weapons it could acquire while launching a campaign of international terror that included the murder of Israeli athletes at the Munich Olympics. The PLO was given permanent representation in the UN in 1975, the same year that the infamous 'Zionism is Racism' Resolution was passed. In 1976, the Committee on the Inalienable Rights of the Palestinian People issued a report that recommended the establishment of an independent Palestinian state, which included the right of return to Israeli land as well.

When Kurt Waldheim, a World War II German army officer, was elected Secretary General of the UN in December 1971, the PLO became even more influential in UN committees. A former UN assistant to Waldheim recalled that during the Yom Kippur War, when the Arab side looked like it might emerge victorious, Waldheim showed no interest in mediating an end to the war, but as soon as the Israelis gained the upper hand, the UN began pressuring for cease-fires.[9]

International observers prevent the Israel-Lebanon border from being hostile

The UN Interim Force in Lebanon (UNIFIL) was formed because of Arab requests to prevent Israeli hostilities against the PLO following Operation Litani of 1978. With the breakdown of the country during its civil war, Lebanon became home to an inestimable number of gangs of terrorists. Due to the violent nature of these unstructured groups, UNIFIL never tried to apprehend or control continuous rocket launchings and violence directed at Israel. UNIFIL quickly established a reputation for one-sided reporting, condemning Israeli reprisals without mentioning the Arab attacks that laid way to Israeli reactions.

---

[9] In retrospect, had the UN exerted pressure on the Arabs to end the war when they were winning, they could have won the war.

When Israel withdrew from Lebanon, it fulfilled the terms of UN Security Council Resolution 425. However, the terms of the resolution called for immediate deployment of Lebanese Army troops into the former Security Zone in order not to allow Hezbollah freedom of access to this volatile region. The Lebanese army has yet to fulfill its obligation on this matter. That means it is up to UNIFIL to contain Hezbollah. To date, it has not.

When Hezbollah took 3 IDF soldiers hostage in a cross-border incursion on October 7, 2000, a UN Peacekeeper videotaped the event. The tape shows that the Hezbollah terrorists were wearing UNIFIL uniforms. Not only did UNIFIL not do anything to stop this violation, as it was supposed to, but it kept quiet about the tape for nearly 9 months. Ephraim Sneh, Israel's Transportation Minister, expressed his consternation on this issue: "Why are these UN forces sitting there? To shoot a video? They ought to have prevented the abduction." Israel demanded the release of the tape, but the UN refused because it wanted to edit the tape so the identity of the kidnappers was not shown. Israeli Defense Minister Binyamin Ben-Eliezer said: "The UN is cooperating or operating under the threatening hand of the Hezbollah and that's just not right." Israeli daily *Ma'ariv* alleges that Hezbollah bribed the UN peacekeepers before mounting its operation into Israel. Hezbollah chief, Hassan Nasrallah, warned the UN that it will be dealt with as enemies if it hands over this tape to Israel (*AFP*, July 12, 2001).

An international observer presence in the West Bank and Gaza would cause both sides to be accountable and more responsible, ultimately lowering fatalities

At the June 2001 Arab Foreign Ministers' meeting in Amman, Yassir Arafat called for an international observer force to be sent to the PA areas. The Arab FMs all agreed that an international presence would benefit the region. The US had already vetoed the Arab effort to railroad this objective through the UN.

In 1994, the Temporary International Presence in Hebron (TIPH) was established due to Arab pleas to stop "violent crimes" being committed against them. This followed Israeli Baruch Goldstein's murderous rampage near the Tomb of the Patriarchs in Hebron. Despite the presence of the TIPH, Hebron remains the most violent city in the ongoing conflict. TIPH has not managed to create any sort of role for itself in controlling or preventing violence.

When Israel surrounded the PLO in Beirut in 1982, Arafat appealed to the international community for help. American, Italian and French forces were dispatched to the region to help evacuate Arafat to Tunisia. When the Christian Phalange forces entered the Sabra and Shatilla refugee camps and killed over 400 people, the international community was called in again. Hezbollah then sent suicide bombers to attack the US embassy, killing 49, and to the joint US-French military barracks, where 58 French and 241 American peacekeepers were killed in 1983.

UNIFIL, the UN Interim Force in Lebanon, was established in 1978 because of Arab demands to the UN to stop 'Israeli aggression' following Operation Litani. Israel responded to continuous PLO shelling of its northern towns by mounting an operation into Lebanon to put an end to the rocket launching. UNIFIL then entered the scene, but has not had any success in preventing the Arabs from initiating violence against Israel. For this ineffective operation, the UN pays 4,500 soldiers $106.2 million per year. The most recent proof of UN impotence in Lebanon is the participation of the UNIFIL peacekeeping team in a Hezbollah abduction of 3 IDF soldiers on the Israeli side of the border. Hezbollah was attired in UNIFIL uniforms and had the operation videotaped by the 'peacekeepers.' UN Secretary General Kofi Annan, the Secretary General of the UN, approved a Security Council decision to modify UNIFIL because of the outcry against its role in the abduction of Israeli soldiers. Hezbollah responded to this decision by saying that any changes to UNIFIL will mean that it will be dealt with as a "conquering force."

Following the Sinai War in 1956, a UN Emergency Force was set up to patrol Sinai and prevent hostility on the border between Egypt and Israel. When President Gamal Abdel Nasser of Egypt closed the Straits of Tiran, mobilized his army in 1967 and ordered UNEF out of the Sinai, the agency obliged and left immediately.

UNESCO has helped finance the Palestinian Ministry of Education's brand new textbooks for its school system. UNRWA certified that there were over 140 anti-Semitic references in these books, paid for in part by the international community.

The Arabs are now calling for an international observer force to challenge Israel's sovereignty and use the presence of these forces to carry out its arms accumulation and terrorist operations unhindered by Israeli countermeasures. Secretary General Annan called on the Israelis to help preserve the June cease-fire by making unilateral concessions such as a settlement freeze. A few months earlier, when Israel offered to dismantle the vast majority of its West Bank and Gaza settlements, its offer was rejected by the PA in favor of a new Palestinian campaign of violence, that has lasted since September 2000 and cost hundreds of lives.

The issue of an international force is a timeworn Arab smokescreen for creating an anti-Israel presence within the Jewish State that would allow Arabs freedom of action while criticizing Israel for maintaining its security. UNIFIL, UNEF and TIPH have done nothing to create more responsibility and accountability because its soldiers do not confront Arab violations.

The United Nations' famous "Zionism is Racism" Resolution is dead

In 1975, the countries of the world branded the Jewish nationalist movement as racist by a vote of 75-35 with 35 abstentions. Zionism was condemned "as a threat to world peace and security," stamped as "a form of racism and racial discrimination" by the nations of the world. In December 1991, this scar on Jewish history was deleted by an overwhelming vote of 111-25 with only 13 abstentions. Saudi Arabia, Jordan, Lebanon and Syria voted against repealing the resolution, while Egypt, Bahrain, Oman, Morocco, Tunisia and Kuwait abstained because of intense diplomatic pressure exerted by the Americans. Resolution 3379 was thus erased from the books, ending an ugly chapter of UN anti-Semitism.

An increase of violence and tension in the Middle East always brings a corollary increase in anti-Israel rhetoric from the Islamic nations of the world. Its favorite forum for this is the UN, especially the General Assembly. In March 2001, the Human Rights Commission, sitting in Teheran (of all places), adopted a resolution with familiar language, accusing Israel of "racist laws," "genocidal" behavior and "crimes against humanity."

In Durban, South Africa, the Arabs wrote a draft declaration in September 2001 at the UN World Conference Against Racism, Racial Discrimination, Xenophobia, and Related Intolerance. In this draft, Israel was accused of "racial discrimination" and "racial superiority."

The Durban Conference ended with the Arabs losing out. Now the momentum lies with Israel

With Syria assuming a role on the Security Council as of October 2001, it is unlikely that there will be any changes in the UN approach towards Israel.

A Time for Truth: The UN role in the Arab-Israel conflict has been severely one-sided. The UN is abused by a collection of despotic states to condemn a member of the free world for "violations" that are primarily imaginary. The one deviation in the UN relationship with Israel was its surprising vote to recognize the Jewish State in 1948. Since then, all of the UN's Middle East activities have arisen because of Arab demands. Its committees and military personnel are nearly all comprised of Third World members sympathetic to the PLO.

EUROPEAN COMMUNITY

The European Union plays a constructive role in the pursuit of peace

The PA receives $3 billion in financial aid from the European Union. The West Bank and Gaza representative of the European Commission says that these funds go "to instill humanitarian principles, respect for human rights and the concept of a viable democracy." $280,000 is spent with the Middle East Center for Legal and Economic Research, allowing Palestinian refugees to make claims on the properties they abandoned in Israel in 1947-48. Another recipient of European money is the Applied Research Institute (ARIJ), which "aims at inspecting and scrutinizing Israeli colonizing activities in their different forms." ARIJ and the Land Research Center, another beneficiary of EU funds, use satellite images to monitor Israeli construction activity. $220,000 more is given to the International Committee on House Demolitions. The mission statement of this organization is to "resist all aspects of the occupation." More than $200,000 was given to Ir Shalem, a group that litigates Israelis who purchase houses in the Moslem Quarter of Jerusalem that were once Jewish owned.

The Europeans have condemned Israel for "excessive use of force" against Palestinians but have been silent about Arab terrorism against Israel. Israeli Prime Minister Ariel Sharon may be branded a war criminal in Belgium, as a result of a Palestinian who filed a complaint in public court blaming him for the Sabra and Shatilla refugee camp massacre, while Arafat, who murdered a Belgian diplomat in 1972, is received as a head of state. In July 2001, lawmakers in Denmark threatened to file a complaint against Israeli ambassador Carmi Gillon, who once served as the chief of Israel's security service, because he admitted in a recent interview that he authorized using torture on several Arab suspects.

PALESTINIAN VIOLENCE 2000-01

<u>i. Effect on Israel</u>

The Israeli economy is being brought to its knees by Palestinian violence.

With 4,000 high-tech companies, Israel is the most high-tech country in the world *per capita*; The Shekel was one of the strongest currencies in the world in 2000, appreciating 2.87% more than the US dollar and 11% more than the Euro. Exports rose in 2000 by 24.4%. Foreign reserves are at an all-time high. The Tel Aviv Stock Exchange was the 6th best performing market in the world. Israel had no inflation in 2000. Salomon Smith Barney and Moody's reaffirmed Israel's credit rating for 2001. The Bank of Israel estimates that the recent wave of Palestinian violence has cost Israel $2 billion, or 1% of GDP. Tourism has absorbed half of this loss, the construction industry has lost $750 million and there has been $250 million in lost trade with the PA. Despite this, Israel still maintains a *per capita* growth rate of 3.4% (*Arutz 7*, June 26, 2001).

Through June 2001, Israel experienced an economic slowdown. Compared to 2000, GDP dropped by 0.6% and unemployment rose. Tourism, construction, agriculture, and high-tech were most affected.

The latest Palestinian campaign of violence has caused worldwide Jewish support to weaken towards Israel

Since September 2000, more than 40,000 Jews have made *Aliyah* (immigration to Israel). Emigration from North America also rose in 2000. 5,000 Jews have visited the country on solidarity missions and 20,000 more Jewish students have come there to study. Tourism is down. Israel's hotel industry stands to lose $150 million in 2001. The violence has had an effect on people's travel plans. However, this is not a reflection of their support, because international Jewry remains fervently supportive of Israel.

Superior weaponry makes Israel immune to Palestinian violence; It makes living uncomfortable, but the Palestinians do not represent an existential threat

When you look at the balance of power in the Middle East, it is easy to conclude that Israel has the upper hand militarily. Even with Arab soldiers from various Arab countries outnumbering Israel by a ratio of approximately 25:2, Israel still possesses enough strength to have prevented an all-out war for the last 28 years. However, the Palestinians present a new complication for the IDF. If the Arabs were to launch a full-scale war by surprise, Israel would be required to mobilize its forces as quickly as possible before damage could be done. If it was not able to mobilize rapidly, it could lead to

Israel's defeat and ultimate destruction. Senior Israeli army officials are concerned about the role of armed Palestinians preventing Israel from mobilizing, for even a few hours delay could be costly. The Palestinians know Israel inside-out. They know where the major arteries are and the location of all army bases. They are armed sufficiently and have easy access to all of Israel. If Israel was mobilizing and faced with an orchestrated campaign of roadside bombings, shootings and other disruptions, it could provide invading Arab armies with the window of opportunity that they need to damage Israel irreparably before a defense could even be mounted. When Israel captured Orient House following the August suicide bombing in Jerusalem, it found detailed files on Israeli police and security forces, as well as a developed military strategy for attacking the Jewish communities of the West Bank and Gaza (*Arutz 7*, August 10, 12). Having Palestinians armed with mortars, grenades, anti-tank and anti-aircraft weapons, rocket-propelled grenades, Katyusha rockets and automatic weapons is an existential threat to Israel.

Israeli Arabs have stayed out of the conflict

The most recent wave of violence has had heavy encouragement from Israeli Arab leaders. Incitement has come from Israeli Arab Members of Knesset (MK) such as Azmi Bishara, who said on March 26, 1999: "The Jewish nation was a fiction with no right to exist" (*ICEJ News*).

Israeli Arab MK, Muhammad Baraka, encouraged Palestinian violence in this statement in *Al-Hayat Al-Jedida* (November 7, 1999): "...the Palestinian people cannot enter these negotiations on the basis of the [present] balance of power, because with this balance of power -- we [are sure] to lose...we must establish an active balance of power on the ground."

Taleb A-Sana, Israeli Arab MK, commented on a Palestinian who shot and killed Israelis outside the Israeli Defense Ministry building on August 5, 2001: "This is an attack of special quality because it was not against civilians but against soldiers in the very heart of Israel. The Israelis have to understand that if there is no security for Palestinians there will not be security for Israelis. There can be no guilt feelings in this case. This is the legitimate struggle *par excellence* of the Palestinian people."

Abdul Malik Dahamshe, Israeli Arab MK, on PA TV on September 1, 2000 stated: "We exaggerate when we say 'peace'...what we are speaking about is '*Hudna,*' a temporary cease-fire."

A suicide bomb attack in Nahariya on September 9, 2001 was carried out by a 48-year old Israeli Arab from the Western Galilee.

On September 5, 2001, Israel arrested a cell of 16-year olds from the Galilee that was carrying out terrorist acts for the Tanzim. These youths were responsible for a bomb attack at the Golani Junction a week before being apprehended. In March 2001, Israel uncovered a Hezbollah cell of Israeli Arabs in the Galilee that was being prepared to carry out abductions of Israeli soldiers. Reportedly, Hezbollah is running many other Israeli Arabs cells. As of July 2001, 30 Israeli Arabs were arrested on suspicion of belonging to terrorist organizations such as Hezbollah and Hamas.

ii. Dealing with it

Israeli border closures in the West Bank and Gaza have brought untold economic hardship on the Palestinians

The sole reason why the Israelis have limited Palestinian movement from the PA areas to Israel is that of security. With a cadre of Palestinians prepared to blow themselves up in the Israeli heartland, the IDF has been instructed to limit Palestinian travel within the Green Line. Although there are travel restrictions, exceptions for commercial goods, food, medicine, ambulances and medical crews apply. There is a clear correlation between Palestinian movement within Israel and the number of Israeli civilians killed and wounded. While Israel has suffered over $2 billion in damages from the recent wave of PA-controlled violence, so too have the Palestinians. However, percentage-wise the damage is much greater for the Palestinians. Alon Liel, the Director of Israel's Foreign Ministry, said on February 14, 2001: "...they themselves have ruined their economy. I would say with this wave of violence, the Palestinians have committed economic suicide...If they have these kinds of [suicide] attacks, we cannot remove the closure."

The Palestinian economy was growing before the PA spurned the peace process to foster violence. According to a UN report, the PA economy grew 7% in 1999. GDP grew 6% and GNP grew 7%. Labor flows rose 15% and planned construction rose 14%. Outstanding bank credit to private businesses also increased 32%. The report also indicated that unemployment dropped as well. Now, according to an April 2000 survey done by the Center for Palestine Research and Studies, there is 17% unemployment under the PA, 25% in Gaza. GDP has fallen more than 40% since September 2000.

The Middle East conflict can be resolved through Israelis compromising

Israel was ready to cede all of the Arab areas of East Jerusalem, the Temple Mount, all but a small handful of settlements, all of Gaza and more than 95% of the West Bank. For the territory in the West Bank that it would keep, Israel offered border modifications that would include ceding territory from within the Green Line to the Palestinians. Yassir Arafat rejected the offer. Hassan Nasrallah, the Secretary General of Hezbollah, was quoted on *Radio Nur*, March 31, 2001: "The Zionist entity is a cancerous entity and, therefore, there is no room for compromise with it."

Israel's assassination squads are a clear-cut example of state terrorism

Kofi Annan, the Secretary General of the UN, told the *Associated Press* on July 5, 2001: "[I am] deeply disturbed by the reported decision of the government of Israel to continue the practice of what have become known as 'targeted assassinations'...If Israel's practice...isn't halted, it is bound to further aggravate the crisis of confidence between the parties and make an already extremely fragile situation even more precarious." Is this statement accurate?

The PA has not fulfilled its obligation to arrest terrorists who have murdered Israelis. Its cooperation was part of several agreements that Arafat signed. The PA committed to apprehending terrorists in Oslo, Oslo-2, Wye, Camp David, the Mitchell Plan and the Tenet cease-fire. Since the *al-Aqsa* Intifada began, more than 250 convicted terrorists have been released from prison. They were responsible for suicide bombings, bus bombings, drive-by shootings and ambushes on civilians and military personnel. The planners of the Dolphinarium bombing that killed 21 Israeli youths were released by Arafat and never brought to justice. Israel acted against the planners of this operation, who had been responsible for many other suicide bombings in Israel and were planning many more. The following operations were planned at their headquarters in Shechem that Israel targeted on July 31, 2001:

June 1 - Tel Aviv, Suicide bomb attack at Dolphinarium night club, 21 killed, 84 wounded

May 18 - Netanya, Suicide bomb attack at the entrance to the Sharon Mall, 5 killed, 74 wounded

April 22 - Kfar Saba, Suicide bomb attack near a bus, 1 killed, 47 wounded

March 28 - Neveh Yamin, Suicide bomb attack in the parking lot at gas station, 2 killed, 4 wounded

March 27 - Jerusalem, Suicide bomb attack near a bus at the French Hill intersection, 12 wounded

March 4 - Netanya, Suicide bomb attack on Rehov Herzl, 3 killed, 60 wounded

March 1 - Suicide bomb attack at the Mei Ami intersection, 1 killed, 12 wounded

January 1 - Netanya, Suicide car bomb attack on Rehov Dizengoff and Rehov Herzl, 36 wounded

December 22, 2000 - Suicide bomb attack at the Mehola junction, 3 wounded

November 22 - Hadera, Car bomb explosion on Rehov Hanassi, 2 killed, 36 wounded

When Israel killed an Islamic Jihad activist on July 1, 2001, it was because of information received that he was planning to send out suicide bombers to targets in Israel. Israel asked the PA to arrest him, but was turned down outright. This terrorist, who was killed when his car was attacked by an IDF helicopter, was already responsible for at least 4 other bombings.

This Israeli policy is not a case of state terror, but preemptive self-defense that is responsible for saving human lives. Israel has no choice but to protect its citizens. Shimon Peres, Israel's Foreign Minister, explained: "Israel does not assassinate people. It goes after leaders who dispatch young men to blow themselves up in the midst of Israelis. Suicide bombers cannot be threatened by death. The only way to stop them is to intercept those who send them." Former U.S. Secretary of Defense Caspar Weinberger said: "If the targeting and killing of the leader or leaders [of aggressive warfare] can help to end a war quickly, and thus spare the lives of hundreds of thousands of combatants, it is hard to find any moral argument for not attempting to kill the leaders..." The US is now employing this exact policy against Osama Bin Laden.

A Time for Truth: Annan is wrong. A sovereign state cannot sit by idly and allow its civilian centers to become bombing galleries for fanatics wired with explosives.

Israelis are using excessive force against the Palestinians

Amnesty International condemned Israel for using too much force in its reprisals against the Palestinians.[10] UN Security Council Resolution 1322 was penned for the same reason. The only way to determine whether or not Israel has employed too much force is to compare its actions with others:

> 1) In 1998, when Osama Bin Laden attacked the American embassies in Kenya and Tanzania, the US ordered a cruise missile strike against his bases in Afghanistan.
> 2) President Reagan responded to the Libyan murder of two American servicemen in 1986 by bombing Moammar Qaddaffi's residence in Libya.
> 3) In Somalia, the UN brought in gunships to combat militants and in the process shot and killed hundreds of civilians. US troops in Somalia also used anti-tank missiles and 20 mm cannon against civilian demonstrators. The problem that the troops faced was that the armed militia was using civilians as human shields.
> 4) On May 4, 1970, the US National Guard killed 4 American students for throwing rocks in protest against the war in Vietnam at Kent State University.

---

[10] Only after this condemnation did they send out a fact-finding mission to investigate what actually occurred.

5) Over 4,000 Panamanians were killed when the US invaded in an attempt to depose President Noriega. Heavy ammunition was used against civilians in this theater. Never was there a threat to American existence or to its soil during this operation.

6) During the Haj season in Mecca, Saudi Arabian troops responded to disturbances by opening up their machine guns on unarmed Iranians. The Iranians claim that 600 were killed and 4,500 wounded.[11]

Neither the UN nor Amnesty ever condemned these events. Rather, Israel is scrutinized and held to an entirely different standard. Nevertheless, Israeli forces use rubber bullets to limit fatalities. They issue warnings well in advance of attacks, in order to prevent civilians from being harmed. During IDF Apache helicopter attacks, very few people were hurt because warnings were issued 3 hours before the attack and most people heeded them. The primary targets of these attacks were buildings that housed bomb factories or that were used to launch attacks against Israel. Because of the use of heavy weaponry, such as the missiles fired from the Apaches, in civilian areas, one would assume that there would be hundreds of casualties. This has not been the case. Just because Israel is using powerful weapons does not mean that it is using excessive force. Is excessive force only defined by the size of the gun? Which case do you think is the better example of excessive force: a suicide bomber detonating himself in a crowded pizza shop killing 15 people, mostly women and children, and wounding over 130, or when a tank shell levels an empty house?

Israel's response to the Jerusalem suicide bombing of August 9, 2001 was to seize Orient House, the PA's Jerusalem headquarters. They leveled a Jenin house used by the Islamic Jihad for planning suicide bombing operations. Nobody was killed or injured in either action.

iii. Why is it Happening?

Palestinian violence is understandable

Almost from the outset, Arabs in British Mandate Palestine opted for violence over peace. Long before the PLO was established and a defined Palestinian nation existed, the Arabs in Israel said "no" to partition of Palestine, "no" to Jewish immigration and "no" to a Jewish state.

In 1920, the Grand *Mufti* of Jerusalem, Hajj Amin al-Husseini, grandfather of Faisal, dictated local Arab politics. Husseini used his position to incite the Arab

---

[11] The Saudis put the death toll at 275.

masses to violence against the Jewish population of the *Yishuv*, the Jewish settlement. He never met with Jews and dissuaded others from doing so.

The Arabs of Palestine did not have a movement of independence. Even the first leader of the PLO, Ahmed Shukhairy, said that: "It is common knowledge that Palestine is nothing but Southern Syria." So too, Husseini never proposed establishing a state for the Arabs of Palestine. He was simply a virulent anti-Semite. His incitement was religious, not political, convincing the uneducated masses through baseless rumors that the Jews were destroying mosques in Jerusalem and carrying out widespread murder of Moslem worshippers.

In 1920, Arab riots in Jerusalem marked the beginning of a new relationship with the *Yishuv*. The local Arab newspaper, *Suria al-Jenubiyah*,[12] was calling for bloodshed and the masses responded with a three-day campaign of looting and murder. Another leader of the incitement was Jerusalem's mayor, Moussa Khazam Pasha. The local British forces prevented the Jews from defending themselves on this and many subsequent occasions, allowing the Arabs to carry out the massacre. Arab violence continued unabated in 1921 and left 47 Jews dead, 147 wounded and untold property destroyed throughout the country. Rather than punish the perpetrators, the British punished the victims. They limited Jewish immigration, arrested Jewish leaders who advocated self-defense, and, in 1922 reneged on the 1917 Balfour Declaration. Arab violence continued with the massacre of 133 Jews in Hebron in 1929. Leading the way was *Sheikh* Taleb Marka, a religious leader, crying "Slaughter the Jews, drink their blood. Today is the day of Islam, the day ordained by the prophet Allah and the Prophet calls upon you to avenge the blood of your Moslem brothers killed in Jerusalem." The ancient Hebron Jewish community was evacuated, ending a Jewish presence in the city that dated for centuries.

Similar to today, Arab policemen hired by the British to prevent this type of occurrence, were in the thick of the rioting and responsible for many of the murders. The incitement that led to this massacre occurred in mosques. False rumors of mass killings of Arabs were circulated to cause a frenzy in the Arab community. Husseini's incitement was met with a 15-year prison sentence that was given *in absentia*. Soon thereafter, he was not only pardoned by the British High Commissioner, but appointed *Mufti* in 1921, the highest Arab position of authority in British Mandate Palestine. Regardless of the violence that was subsequently carried out through incitement by Husseini, the British chose to cover it up or ignore it entirely. The similarity between Husseini and Arafat, both of whom were dismissed as murderers, installed as local leaders and had their virulent anti-Semitism ignored by the local

---

[12] "Suria" is Arabic for Syria. Even the title of the local Arab newspaper shows how the land was perceived by the Arabs of Palestine.

rulers is uncanny. It is not surprising that Arafat said at the Bandung Conference in 1985 that he takes "immense pride" in being the *Mufti*'s student, and said that the PLO is "continuing the path" set by the *Mufti*.

Finally, in 1937, Husseini was forced to flee because of his brazen violence against the Jews of Palestine. Nevertheless, he continued to direct operations from Lebanon. During World War II, he traveled to Europe to meet with Hitler, Eichmann and Himmler, volunteering to do his part in the Final Solution.

The Arab Higher Committee appointed Husseini its leader in 1945, despite testimony in the Nuremberg Trials from Eichmann's secretary proving that Husseini was a war criminal who collaborated with the Nazis and "had a part in the decision to liquidate the Jews of Europe."

Following the 1948 war, the UN created the Palestine Conciliation Committee to help the parties of the war negotiate a peace agreement. All Arab delegations voted against this committee and only an armistice that halted the war could be reached. Israel still accepted a two-state solution, even after a war that killed and wounded nearly 10% of its population.

After the 1967 war, Israel offered to withdraw from all captured territory in exchange for a full peace from its neighbors. The Arab leaders, meeting in Khartoum in 1967, adopted a policy that would define the Arab attitude towards Israel for the next three decades -- "no peace with Israel, no negotiations with Israel, no recognition of Israel."

A Time for Truth: The Palestinians have never strayed from the path of violence, which they adopted from the outset. For the last 80 years, they have resorted to violence against Israel. Even when they finally embarked on a track of negotiation at Oslo in 1993, it was spurned in favor of violence when they were unable to realize 100% of their demands.

This conflict is about land, not hatred

When a suicide bomber detonated himself on June 1, 2001 while standing amidst a crowd of young girls who were waiting for admittance to the Dolphinarium nightclub in Tel Aviv, he had been infected with Hepatitis B before embarking on his mission, according to the *New Yorker* (July 9, 2001). When his body exploded all over the area, pieces came into contact with several people who survived the attack, but who may have become infected with the disease.

Suicide bombers put shards of glass, bolts and nails into the bag in which their bomb is carried because they want to injure as many bystanders as possible, even if they are not killed by the blast.

In Hebron, a Palestinian sniper murdered Shalhevet Pass, a 10-month old girl. Ra'anan Gissen, the Spokesperson for Prime Minister Sharon, was quoted in the *New York Times* of March 27, 2001: "This was a premeditated murder in which a sniper put his cross hair on the head of a baby girl and blew it off." The *Voice of Palestine* broadcast the official PA reaction: "On the matter of the baby settler who was killed in Hebron...we already said that her death was a fishy action and there is information according to which this baby was retarded and it was her mother who killed her in order to get rid of her."[13]

Two 13 year-old boys, Koby Mandell and Yossi Ishran, were found dead in a cave near their hometown of Tekoa on May 9, 2001. They had to be identified by their dental records because their bodies and faces were bludgeoned to the point of non-recognition. They were apparently killed with stones, then repeatedly stabbed (*Arutz 7*).

Two Israeli IDF reservists, Yosef Avrahami and Vadim Norzitch, were driving to their military base and took a wrong turn into PA-controlled Ramallah. They were stopped by two Palestinian policemen, who took them into custody at the Ramallah police station. As presented in the case in Israeli court against the two Palestinian policemen, one of the PA policemen notified the participants of a funeral for an Arab who was killed while rioting against Israel the previous day, that if they came to the police station, he would turn the IDF prisoners over to them. Before the crowds arrived, other Arab officers inside the station got to the Israelis first, attacking them with metal pipes. By the time the two Israelis were dead, a frenzied mass had assembled outside the station. The dead bodies were then thrown out the second-story window to the cheering crowd below.

iv. Palestinian Tactics

Israeli soldiers target Palestinian children during riots

Children are being killed in alarmingly high numbers during the Intifada of 2000-01. About 20% of Palestinian injuries and fatalities are youths under 18. Why? The PA press says that Israeli soldiers are specifically shooting at children. Hanan Ashrawi was quoted in the *Jordan Times* of October 29, 2000: "The most blatantly racist slur is the Israeli theft of our humanity as parents. In an attempt to rob us of our most basic feelings, we are accused of sending our 'children out to die' for the sake of scoring 'media points'." The international media has mostly mirrored the PA point of view and also depicts IDF soldiers as child-killers. But are they justified in their conclusion?

---

[13]This case did not garner 1/100th the media attention that the killing of Mohammed al-Dura received.

When Palestinians riot against Israel they use very distinct combat formations. The mob is made up of groups of children throwing stones at Israeli soldiers. These children are bait, and are used by the Palestinian adults as human shields. Amid each circle of children is a Palestinian adult armed with an assault weapon, usually a Kalashnikov, shooting at Israelis. This practice contravenes every human rights convention imaginable. It is very difficult for the IDF to defend itself because, when its soldiers attempt to stop the source of fire, children could get hurt or even killed.

On May 8, 2001, Prime Minister Ariel Sharon, commenting on the tragedy of a young Palestinian schoolgirl's death, said: "The Palestinians quite often deploy their mortars by schools, then behind schools. They use mortars and then disappear immediately. It has happened several times, and that is what happened this time. The soldiers, after one of our communities was hit by mortar fire, reacted immediately to the place where the mortar was fired."

Palestinian children are being used as political pawns in Yassir Arafat's ongoing game of bringing international pressure on Israel for mounting casualties on the Palestinian side. The sight of dead Palestinian youths in newspapers across the world brings sympathy to the Palestinian cause and outrage against Israel. It is a non-issue to Yassir Arafat that he is sacrificing the lives of innocents to gain sympathy. The unfortunate part is that it works. The PA gains by abusing the human rights of its children.

The tragic event of Mohammed Al-Dura's death underscores this very issue. Who is at fault for a twelve-year-old being shot dead? What is a father doing with his son, several miles from his home, at a junction at the outskirts of town, near an Israeli military checkpoint? What do we think about a father who knowingly brings his little child to a scene where there is a live exchange of ammunition?

The answers to these questions show the value system of many of these families that allow their little children to attend riots where they are in mortal danger. Are these children innocent? Many surely are too young to know why they are there, or why they are throwing stones. Palestinian schoolbooks and board games are replete with anti-Semitic imagery. Very young children are taught that Israelis epitomize evil. Television shows inculcate them with the honor of martyrdom in the fight against Israel. TV ads encourage children to stop playing with toys and to pick up stones to fight the enemy. Yes, these children are innocent, and the responsibility for their deaths lie squarely on the shoulders of their parents, and religious and political leaders who never give them a chance to learn anything but hatred.

Leaders in the Palestinian Authority encourage the children to go out into the streets to combat Israel. The Tulkarm Women's Union has been about the only public Palestinian voice to express apprehension about this policy.

They wrote Arafat a letter asking him "to stop sending innocent children to their death." One woman told the Israeli press that PA security forces pick up children after school and transport them to riot sites. Because Israeli checkpoints are no longer inside Palestinian residential areas, rioters have to seek out Israelis in order to confront them.

The Tanzim

Officially part of Yassir Arafat's Fatah, Tanzim ("organization") is an armed grass-roots militia that oversees attacks on Israel in the streets of the West Bank and Gaza. Established in 1983, the Tanzim became a recognized group during the first Intifada by coordinating street riots and attacks on Israelis. The Tanzim run summer youth camps for the PA, where young children are indoctrinated about the conflict with Israel, are inculcated with hatred and taught how to kill.

The members of the Tanzim are all Palestinians who come from the cities and towns of the West Bank and Gaza, as opposed to the senior PA leadership, who mostly came from Tunisia with Arafat in 1993. The PA directly finances the Tanzim. Its two main leaders are Marwan Barghouti and Hussein Sheikh. Barghouti is also a veteran member of Fatah and the PA's legislative body.

The Tanzim were among the instigators of the Temple Mount riots in 1996 and the *Naqba* (Disaster, i.e. Israeli Independence) Day riots of 2000. Members of Tanzim are armed (even though the Oslo Accords only allow for the Palestinian police to carry weapons) and help procure weapons for Palestinians who want to shoot at Israelis. In the recent wave of violence, the Tanzim has been responsible for carrying out many of the hit-and-run drive-by shootings against Israeli civilian motorists. The Tanzim are renowned for engaging the IDF in gunfight battles using assault weapons while surrounded by groups of children.

Shabiba

The Shabiba is Fatah's youth division. It has a very close association with the Tanzim and is led by Barghouti and Sheikh.

Suicide bombers are also victims of this conflict

Elementary school children have been dressed up as suicide bombers and paraded through the streets of Gaza acting out imaginary scenes of suicide bombings. Saddam Hussein and the PA provide incentives for martyrdom of children by giving financial rewards to families who have had children killed while actively engaging Israel. While the PA rewards such families with $2,000, Iraq donates $10,000. Saddam also contributes $1,000 for serious injuries and $500 for minor injuries. When you consider that the *per capita* income in Gaza is only slightly more than $1,000, this kind of money garners permanent allegiance.

Martyrdom is very prestigious among Palestinians. Youngsters dream of fulfilling this role and feel that being a bomber and killing Israelis, especially civilians, will bring honor to their families. One youth, aged 14, who was shot during riots against an Israeli checkpoint, said that he wanted desperately to become a martyr: "When I become a martyr, give out cake" (*Al-Hayat Al-Jedida*, November 9, 2000). Another 12 year old, who also died on the streets during a riot, had been writing his own death announcements on the walls of his home (*Al-Hayat Al-Jedida*, November 30, 2000).

The Palestinian bomber who murdered 21 Israeli youths in June 2001 outside a Tel Aviv nightclub was feted by his family following his death. The family threw a party to celebrate their son's murders. "I am very proud of what my son did and, frankly, am a bit jealous," said the father on June 26, 2001, "My son has fulfilled the Prophet Mohammed's wishes. He has become a hero. Tell me what more could a father ask?"

A Time for Truth: Because Palestinian society glorifies martyrdom, many aspire to end their lives this way, even young children. Suicide bombers are simply mass murderers and are the worst perpetrators of this conflict, not its victims.

Arafat is doing all he can to curb the violence

In 1996, Arafat arrested the leaders of radical dissident groups operating in the areas under the PA's control as per the Oslo agreement. His policy was clear-cut and he implemented it. In 1998, after he signed the Wye Document, 200 Gazans belonging to Hamas were rounded up. Israeli Foreign Minister Shimon Peres told a group of European Ministers on June 4, 2001 that the first 24 hours of the cease-fire with the PA showed a marked reduction in violence, thus this "has shown that [Arafat] can control the situation." However, the next day, violence resumed once more. It seems clear that Arafat can control the violence. But does he want to?

According to the June 24, 2001 edition of German television program *Weltspiegel*, Arafat wrote a congratulatory letter to the family of the Tel Aviv Dolphinarium suicide bomber in which he wrote that the killer's self-sacrifice was worthy of admiration: "To turn one's body into a bomb is the best example of willingness to make a sacrifice." The letter was produced on the program with Arafat's signature. Arafat called the bomber a "wonderful example of a hero." When Israel presented Arafat with the names of two of the masterminds behind this suicide attack, Arafat acted on the information immediately. According to reports in the June 24 Israeli Press, the two men were summoned by PA security agents, where they admitted their involvement, promised not to carry out any more attacks and were released. This occurred just days after Arafat signed the Tenet agreement in which he committed to arrest all people directly responsible for terrorism.

In the 4 weeks following Arafat's acceptance of the June 2, 2001 cease-fire, there were 296 attacks on Israelis leaving 9 dead and 50 wounded. These attacks included rock-throwing, fire-bombings, mortar attacks and shootings. Here is an example of the events of one day, Wednesday June 27, 2001:

Shooting attack in Neve Dekalim, Israeli ambulance fired on
Shooting attack in Neve Dekalim, firefighting crew shot at
RPG attack in Neve Dekalim,
Mortar attack at Neve Dekalim,
Shooting attack in Yakinton, IDF outpost
Grenade attack in Rafiah, IDF outpost
Roadside bombing, Rafiah
Shooting attack in Einav, drive-by shooting
Shooting attack in Shechem, drive-by shooting
Firebomb attack in Hebron, soldiers attacked
Rock throwing attack in Bethlehem, IDF outpost
Firebomb and stone throwing attack in Hebron, IDF soldiers
Shooting attack in Modi'in, civilian woman shot at
Shooting attack in Ofra, IDF outpost
Firebomb attack in Yakir, civilians attacked

Looking at this list, one can understand Israeli Defense Minister Binyamin Ben-Eliezer's comment that, "I have never seen such a bloody and violent cease-fire." Arafat publicly declares that the cease-fire applies only to Area A, not Areas B and C, in direct contravention to the Mitchell Plan that he signed. Areas B and C contain the bulk of the Israeli West Bank settlements and are still under IDF control.

So is he in control of the violence or not? A vast majority of Palestinians feel that Arafat is in control. According to the Jerusalem Media Center's June 2001 poll, of surveyed Palestinians, 71.6% feel that Arafat has complete control over the violence.

Suicide bombers are just children; they don't really know what they're doing

Most bombers are in their young twenties; one was 48-years old. These are not children. Senior leaders take would-be bombers through the motions before their missions. A potential bomber is taken to a graveyard and told to lie down for hours between graves as part of the preparation. He is wrapped in a white burial shroud and hood. He then gets taken to a safe house where

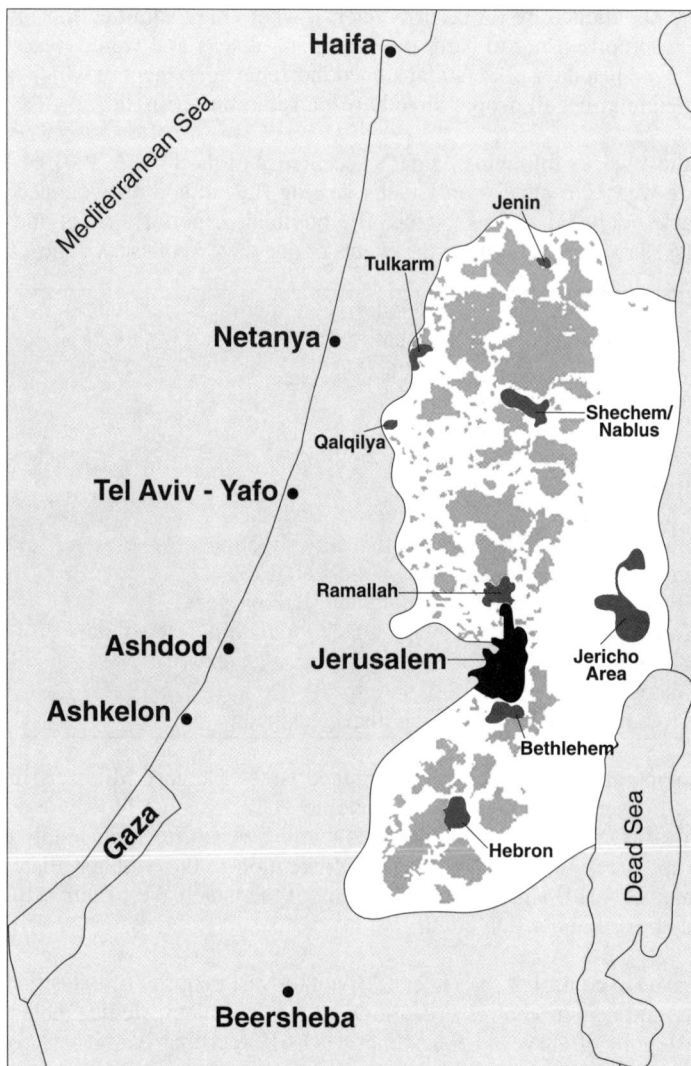

Haifa

Mediterranean Sea

Jenin

Tulkarm

Netanya

Shechem/
Nablus

Qalqilya

Tel Aviv - Yafo

Ramallah

Ashdod

Jerusalem

Jericho
Area

Ashkelon

Bethlehem

Dead Sea

Gaza

Hebron

Beersheba

AREA A - Full Palestinian Control

AREA B - Palestinian Administration,
Israeli Security

AREA C - Still to be Negotiated

Jerusalem - Still to be Negotiated

he gives full consent for his actions on videotape (*USA TODAY*, June 26, 2001). This whole routine is played out for the bomber. He knows what is going to happen to his victims and the time spent in the graveyard must convince him that he is about to end his own life. The families are never informed, but it is difficult to imagine that they would convince their sons to change their minds. As the father of the Dolphinarium bombing said: "I only wish I had 20 sons who would follow his path, I wouldn't try to stop them because with Jews there's no other way" (*Near East Report*, June 25, 2001).

Palestinians target only Israelis in the territories

Israel-proper has been the target of nearly all the suicide bombings. While the majority of rioting and sniping still occurs in the West Bank and Gaza, the Palestinian war to eliminate Israel has been brought to the core of the country.

Here is a brief list of bombings that occurred in the month of April alone:

> Kfar Saba -- April 4, 2001: Bomb discovered before it went off in the Yosefthal neighborhood
>
> Kfar Saba -- April 14, 2001: Bombs planted on the busiest street in town
>
> Kfar Saba -- April 14, 2001: Near a synagogue. The latter was meant to detonate as worshippers left the synagogue following Saturday night services
>
> Netanya -- April 29, 2001: Near Bank Ha-Poalim in the busiest commercial center
>
> Hod Hasharon -- April 30, 2001: A bomb exploded in a residential neighborhood

These are just 5 of many more bombings that occurred or were foiled by Israeli security forces since the Intifada was restarted. Israel determined that one gang of 6 Palestinians, several of whom belonged to Arafat's Fatah organization, carried out these particular 5 acts, and several more in the territories. They had planned many more attacks on Israel, including a suicide attack in Ra'ananah (*Israel Ministry of Foreign Affairs*, June 10, 2001).

On August 16, 2000, PA Communications Minister Imad Faluji commented on the Palestinian military readiness at a Palestinian funeral near Ramallah: "We are capable of blowing up Israeli cities. The Palestinians will not be satisfied with attacking military targets, but would strike at Israel's heart."

Because Palestinian population growth will lead to Palestinians outnumbering Israelis in the next ten years, according to a PA report, Jewish immigrants attract much attention for the PA. *Al-Hayat Al-Jedida* ran an article that called for terrorist attacks against new immigrants: "We must choose targets that will cause them death and fear...We long for the tears of the prostitutes of Tel Aviv who came from Russia and elsewhere, and that their mothers' hearts will burn." The June 2001 suicide bombing at the Dolphinarium in Tel Aviv that killed mostly Russian immigrants, certainly proves that these words are more than rhetoric.

Palestinians only target Israeli military personnel

Ahmed Yassin, the spiritual leader of Hamas, spoke with *Islam Online* on April 1, 2001. When asked about the objectives of suicide bombers, he replied "it is best to check the exact timing and location in order to cause a maximum number of [deaths to] soldiers and civilians of the Zionist enemy." Dr. Halabiya, a member of the PA *Fatwa* Council and Rector of Advanced Studies at the Islamic University in Gaza, spoke on PA TV on October 13, 2000: "The Jews are the Jews...They are all liars...They are terrorists. Therefore it is necessary to slaughter them and murder them, according to the words of Allah." The vast majority of deaths caused by suicide bombers are civilian. As of August 15, 2001, since the Intifada was restarted there have been 802 civilians injured within the Green Line -- mostly in bomb blasts -- whereas only 43 military personnel have sustained injuries in this period of time (*www.btselem.org*).

Here is a list of the events of just the third week in August 2001:
Saturday – Arabs open fire on an Israeli civilian car, killing two young men and one woman
Sunday – Israeli civilian shot and killed while buying cloth from a Palestinian merchant near Tulkarm
Monday – Palestinians shoot and fire mortars at Gilo from Beit Jala
Tuesday – Israeli civilian truck driver delivering gas to a Palestinian village is murdered
Thursday – Israeli is shot and killed at a Palestinian diner where he had been a regular customer
Thursday – Israeli forces apprehend 3 Arab men armed with rifles near Jerusalem
Friday – Bomb found in the Galilee before it was detonated

The al-Aqsa Intifada is another war of stones and knives

During the first Intifada in the 1980s, there was a clear order by the PLO and the local Palestinian leadership not to use weapons. This is no longer the case. In the first 6 weeks of the latest wave of violence, there were more than 1,300 armed attacks against Israelis. Now, the Palestinians engage the Israeli army at military outposts near Israeli civilian population centers with assault weapons, usually behind a cover of children. Armed Palestinians fire frequently on civilian Israeli vehicles in the West Bank and Gaza. Suicide bombers blow themselves up among crowds of Israeli civilians in Israel-proper. Mortars are launched from residential Arab homes, schools and mosques at Israeli towns in the Negev, Jerusalem and Gaza. Snipers fire on Jerusalem's Gilo neighborhood from Beit Jala, a neighboring Arab village.

The Palestinian Authority used the Oslo Accords as an excuse to establish a quasi-military presence in the West Bank and Gaza instead of a police force. These policemen and security personnel carry semi-automatic weapons and have been apprehended with rocket-propelled grenades (RPGs) and anti-tank missiles. They are said to possess land mines and anti-aircraft weapons as well. As of 1998, the PA had 35,000 automatic weapons for its police, almost double the allowance stated in the Oslo Accords.

Weapons of nearly every kind are being smuggled into the West Bank and Gaza to an extent where it is impossible for Israel to control the situation. The London-based *Foreign Report* wrote in 1998 that the PA was digging tunnels from Gaza to Egypt to smuggle in RPGs and SAM-7 anti-aircraft missiles. *Time Magazine* made similar reports as far back as 1996. In May 2001, Israelis captured a boat smuggling Katyusha rockets and anti-aircraft missiles that would have allowed Gaza-based assaults to reach Tel Aviv.

Ahmed Jibril, the leader of the Popular Front for the Liberation of Palestine - General Command, sent a ship loaded with weapons to Gaza which the Israeli Navy intercepted. Here is a list of the cargo as reported by the *Jerusalem Post* on May 7, 2001:

> 20 RPGs
> 9 RPG sights
> 100 PG-7 rockets
> 50 OG-7 rockets
> 150 RPG charges
> 120 RKG anti-tank grenades
> 4 SA-7 surface-to-air Strella missiles
> 2 60 mm mortar launchers
> 98 60 mm mortar shells
> 50 107 mm Katyusha rockets
> 70 anti-tank missiles
> 24 hand grenades
> 30 Hungarian Kalashnikov assault rifles
> 116 Kalashnikov ammunition magazines
> 13,000 rounds of 7.62 mm Kalashnikov ammunition

Every year the IDF discovers dozens of underground tunnels running from the Egyptian side of the border into Gaza. These passages are used for smuggling arms into the PA areas. In 1999, Israel found one tunnel that had lighting, a telephone system, air conditioning and a small rail line that ran from end to end. The task is made difficult for the IDF because the Palestinian border town of Rafiah runs on both the Israeli and Egyptian sides of the border, with only a narrow strip in between that the IDF patrols. The Palestinians circumvent the land patrols by digging underneath and passing weapons from the Egyptian side into Gaza.

In June, Israel apprehended Sa'id Ashi, who was manufacturing and producing mortar shells in a Gaza factory. The operation was overseen by Ghazi Jabali, the Chief of the PLO's Para-military Police. Jabali is high on the Israeli 'Wanted' list because of his involvement in terrorist attacks. Ashi was the owner of a metal factory in Gaza that received orders for 10,000 mortar shells and hand grenades. *Israel Radio* reported on May 23, 2001 that he told Israel that the clandestine operation involved doing some of his work at PA police headquarters. While Ashi cast the metal, Jabali was responsible for assembling them and filling them with explosives. In 1997, it was reported that the PA had established its own hand grenade manufacturing plant in Gaza as well.

Brigadier-General Yair Naveh of the IDF claims that the Gaza areas under PA control have become "the largest weapons storehouse in the Middle East." Israel says that Arafat and other PA VIPs have repeatedly used personal cars and Arafat's airplane to smuggle weapons into Gaza since at least 1997. Israeli newspapers reported in August 1999 that "the Palestinian naval commando unit purchased military equipment in Europe, Russia, and China, which was smuggled into the Gaza Strip through Egypt, using tunnels constructed under the Rafiah border area."

Palestinian police are armed with assault weapons that they have readily used against Israeli soldiers and civilians. Many of the civilian population, as well as members of youth and militant groups have access to similarly powerful arms. Tanzim, a wing of Arafat's Fatah, has authorized its members to fire on Israelis.

The IDF reports that from September 29, 2000 to April 30, 2001 there were close to 5,000 attacks on Israelis. 3,230 of these shooting incidents were directed at military facilities and more than 1,100 at civilian communities and vehicles. Over 350 bombs and grenades were detonated or found before they could explode. All this evidence makes absurd Fatah leader Marwan Barghouti's July 13, 2001 response to a question on the number of illegal weapons in the West Bank: "We're talking dozens [of weapons], not more."

v. Support for

The majority of Palestinians do not support suicide bombings

A recent poll conducted by the Palestinian Center for Public Opinion showed that 76% of all Palestinians support suicide bombings. Hassan Yousuf, spokesman for Hamas, addressed this finding by telling the *Palestine Report* (June 6, 2001) that: "People welcome these operations against Israelis as they would a wedding." Among the youth, there is 90% support according to a survey done by Bir Zeit University (*Kol Yisrael*, June 12, 2001). Immediately after the Jerusalem suicide bombing in August 2001, Arabs sang and danced in the streets of the West Bank, Gaza and Lebanon. Guns were fired in the air while cake and candy was passed out. A spokesman for Islamic Jihad said, "Even the animals in the fields are happy about this attack."

Bombings

1994:
April 6 – Afula, Car-bomb attack on a bus, 8 killed
April 13 – Hadera, Suicide bombing on a bus in the central bus station, 5 killed
October 19 – Tel Aviv, Suicide bombing on the No. 5 bus on Dizengoff Street, 22 killed.
November 11 – Netzarim, Gaza Strip, Palestinian riding a bicycle detonated explosives strapped to his body, 3 soldiers killed

1995:
January 22 – Netanya, Two consecutive Palestinian bombs exploded at the Beit Lid junction, 18 soldiers killed and one civilian
April 9 – Kfar Darom, Gaza Strip, A bus was hit by an explosives-laden Palestinian van, 8 killed
July 24 – Ramat Gan, Suicide bomb attack on a bus, 6 killed
August 21 – Jerusalem, Suicide bombing of a Jerusalem bus, 4 killed

1996:
February 25 – Jerusalem, Suicide bombing of bus No. 18 near the Central Bus Station, 26 killed (17 civilians and 9 soldiers)
February 25 – Ashkelon, Suicide bomber at a hitchhiking post, 1 killed
March 3 – Jerusalem, Suicide bombing of bus No. 18 on Jaffa Road, 19 killed (16 civilians and 3 soldiers).
March 4 – Tel Aviv, Outside Dizengoff Center, a suicide bomber detonated a 20-kilogram nail bomb, 13 killed (12 civilians and one soldier)

1997:
March 21 – Tel Aviv, Suicide bomber detonated a bomb on the terrace of a café, 3 Israelis were killed and 48 wounded
July 30 – Jerusalem, Two consecutive Palestinian suicide bombings in the Mahane Yehuda market, 16 killed and 178 wounded
September 4 – Jerusalem, Three Palestinian suicide bombings at the Ben Yehuda pedestrian mall, 5 killed and 181 wounded

1998:
October 29 – An explosives-laden car was driven into an Israeli army jeep escorting a bus with 40 elementary school students in the Gaza Strip, 1 soldier killed

2000:
November 22 – Hadera, Car bomb explosion on Rehov Hanassi, 2 killed, 36 wounded
December 22 – Suicide bomb attack at the Mehola junction, 3 wounded

2001:
January 1 – Netanya, Suicide car bomb attack at Rehov Dizengoff and Rehov Herzl, 36 wounded
March 1 – Suicide bomb attack at the Mei Ami intersection, 1 killed, 12 wounded
March 4 – Netanya, Suicide bomb attack on Rehov Herzl, 3 killed, 60 wounded
March 27 – Jerusalem, Suicide bomb attack near a bus at the French Hill intersection, 12 wounded
March 28 – Neveh Yamin, Suicide bomb attack in the parking lot at gas station, 2 killed, 4 wounded
April 22 – Kfar Saba, Suicide bomb attack near a bus, 1 killed, 47 wounded
May 18 – Netanya, Suicide bomb attack at the entrance to the Sharon Mall, 5 killed, 74 wounded
June 1 – Tel Aviv, Suicide bomb attack at Dolphinarium night club, 21 killed, 84 wounded

August 9 – Jerusalem, Suicide bomb attack at Sbarro restaurant, 15 killed, 132 wounded
August 12 – Kiryat Motzkin, Suicide bomb attack on restaurant patio, 21 wounded
August 21 – Jerusalem, Car Bomb attack in Russian Compound, 1 wounded
September 4 – Jerusalem, Suicide Bomb attack in downtown area, 21 wounded
September 9 – Nahariya, Suicide Bomb attack at train station, 3 killed, 90 wounded
October 6 – Kibbutz Sheluchot, Suicide Bomb attack against day-care center intercepted, 1 killed

Political and religious leaders have vocally supported and encouraged this inhumane practice. The Palestinian Council of Religious Leaders published a *"Fatwa"* (religious edict) in *Al-Ayyam* on May 6, 2001 that said of the suicide bombings: "These acts of sacrifice are legitimate, and their legitimacy is derived from the Koran and Islamic law." Khamad Almadavi, a preacher at the *al-Aqsa* mosque and the Chairman of the Islamic Appeals Court in Jerusalem, said in an interview in London that "the suicide attacks are commanded by the Koran and the command applies to every Moslem." *Sheikh* Ibrahim Madhi, in a June 8, 2001 sermon on PA TV a few days after Arafat accepted the cease-fire, avowed: "…Blessings to whoever put a belt of explosives on his body or on his son's and plunged into the midst of the Jews."

Yassir Arafat was quoted on Egyptian *Orbit TV* on April 18, 1998 as saying: "I would like to say that I envy the martyrs and I hope to become one of them."

Khalad Mashal of Hamas, quoted by *Reuters* in February 2001, said: "You (Jews) will never have security in this place, not even on a single centimeter of this land. This is a call for every Palestinian to turn into a time bomb -- to fight them with every means at your disposal." The chairwoman of the Hezbollah Women's Movement was quoted on *Al-Jezira* TV in December 2000: "I will push my child to participate in the resistance, and I pray that my son ends his life as a *shaheed* (martyr)."

"When I walk outside, young (Palestinian) children come up to me and say 'conduct another bombing to make us happy, *Sheikh*'" says Hassan Yousuf of Hamas, "I cannot disappoint them. They won't have to wait long." Yousuf says he has tens of thousands of youths ready to become suicide bombers, "We like to grow them, from kindergarten through college." Hamas kindergartens have signs that read: "The children of the kindergarten are the *shaheeds* of tomorrow" (*USA TODAY*, June 26, 2001).

Here are some random quotations from Palestinians, who represent the popular sentiment on the subject of children and martyrdom:
"If I had 20 children, I would send them all down (to fight), I wouldn't spare any of them. We're not scared of death." – 50-year old woman, resident of Nablus (*AP*)
I'm prepared to sacrifice my 6 children. I'm serious. I don't mind if I lose them if that brings back *al-Aqsa*." – Mother of one of the suicide bombers (*NBC News*)
"I will make my body a bomb that will blast the flesh of Zionists, the sons of pigs and monkeys." – 11 year old boy from Gaza City (*USA TODAY*, June 26, 2001)
"I'm happy to die for my country, as long as a couple of Israeli soldiers die too." – 12-year old boy
"My purpose is not to be wounded, but something more sublime - martyrdom." – 13-year old boy

Suicide bombers are the work of extreme elements in Palestinian society, not the PA

The PA avidly supports the bombers in their press, the *Al-Hayat Al-Jedida*. PA Minister of Supplies, Abd Al-Aziz Shahin, said on October 8, 2000: "We will turn ourselves into invisible bombs against [Israeli] soldiers. The blood will always defeat the sword. This is human history." Youssef Jamah, PA Minister of Holy Sites, stated in an April 29, 2001 interview on Egyptian TV "The suicide bombings are a legitimate means through which the Palestinians fight the enemy. Their aim is to serve Allah, and through them, they fight for Allah and for the Islamic faith and homeland. The attacks are the command of Allah." The PA gives full military funerals to suicide bombers, oftentimes with empty coffins because nothing remains of the bomber's corpse (*Jerusalem Report*, June 7, 2001).

The Middle East conflict is political, not religious

On three different occasions, PA TV broadcast *Hadiths* (Oral Laws, often attributed to Mohammed himself) calling for killing Jews: "The Day of Judgment will not come until you do battle against the Jews, until the last Jew hides behind some tree, and the stone and tree shall say: Moslem, servant of God, leave a Jew behind me, kill him." The *al-Aqsa* mosque has been used repeatedly to call for the murder of Jews and to affirm that anyone who concedes even an inch of the land to the Jews is "a revolting criminal who is doomed to go to hell." PA TV repeatedly broadcasts its clerics calling the conflict the eternal religious war of Islam. This is the will of Allah because the Jews are enemies of Allah and killing them is the decree of Allah.

June 8, 2001: *Sheikh* Ibrahim Madhi delivered the key Friday sermon from *Sheikh Ijlin* mosque in Gaza City that was broadcast on PA television. He said: "Blessings to whoever waged *jihad* for the sake of Allah; blessings to whoever raided for the sake of Allah; blessings to whoever put a belt of explosives on his body or on his son's and plunged into the midst of the Jews crying '*Allahu Akbar*, praise to Allah, there is no God but Allah and Mohammed is His messenger.'"

Arafat's appointed *Mufti* of Jerusalem and Palestine, *Sheikh* Ikrimi Sabri delivered a sermon from the Temple Mount's *al-Aqsa* mosque on May 25, 2001, in which he said: "Oh People, I swear by Allah, that the thing you hate [meaning death] is what you are going out to seek today: The *Shahada* [Martyrdom]...We tell them [Jews]: in as much as you love life -- the Moslem loves death and martyrdom. There is a great difference between he who loves the hereafter and he who loves this world. The Moslem loves death and strives for martyrdom."

Sheikh Abd Al-Halim Ayyash from Jerusalem explained that "a *Shaheed* [martyr] has a high rank and value in Islam, in both this world and the Hereafter. The strive for Martyrdom is a desired virtue in Islam, but not every soul is capable of it, because someone who strives for Martyrdom must have a high degree of faith, religious determination, devotion, and loyalty to supreme religious and national causes."

Islamic Jihad leader Ramadan Abdallah Shalah said in November 1996: "In the end Israel will disappear as the Koran states. From the standpoint of the Koran, there is no place for Israel and its existence is not justifiable."

A Hamas leader, Abdel-Aziz Rantisi, averred: "Islam does not permit giving up one inch of Palestine and states that Palestine belongs to the Moslems, belongs to the Palestinian people, not to the Jews. Bartering land is not liberation and is not permissible in Islam" (May 27, 1998).

Suicide bombers are recruited in religious centers. Hamas sends its religious leaders to look for devout youths in mosques. The Palestinian who carried out the June 1, 2001 suicide attack in Tel Aviv was recruited because he was very pious. Hamas promises the martyrs that their families will be financially compensated, their pictures posted in schools and mosques and that they will receive eternal heaven[14] (*USA TODAY*, June 26, 2001).

The name Fatah itself is religious. It means 'conquest' and is based on the 48th *Sura* of the Koran. The passage involves Allah promising Mohammed that if he returns to Mecca, the site of his earlier defeat, he will 'conquer' his enemies. The founders of Fatah thus chose this name because they saw the Palestinians returning to Palestine in the same way that Mohammed returned to Mecca -- the vanquished returning to wipe out the victors.

---

[14] with 72 "black-eyed" virgins for their pleasure, according to Islamic tradition.

122

Osama Bin Laden is anti-American, not anti-Western, which is why he has never attacked Israel

On June 1, 2000, the IDF arrested Nabil Ukal, who was illegally crossing the Egyptian border into Israel. Ukal was supposed to have entered Israel as Al Qaeda's first representative in the Gaza Strip and begin recruiting Israeli Arabs for terrorist acts against Israel.

Ukal had been in Gaza before embarking for Pakistan, where he made his way to Afghanistan for training in a Bin Laden camp. While in Gaza, he met with the leader of Hamas, Ahmed Yassin, and was given $10,000 in support of his activities. Just before Palestinian violence resumed in September 2000, ten members of the Bin Laden cell were arrested by Israeli forces (*Ha'aretz*, September 14, 2001).

vi. Responsibility for

Israel is responsible for the violence

By asking two questions, we can find the answer to this misconception: (1) If the Arabs stopped attacking Israel, what would happen? (2) If Israel stopped its military from fighting the Palestinians, what would happen? The answer to the first question is nothing would happen. There would be a complete cessation of violence. The Sharon government already tested the answer to the second question when it imposed a unilateral cease-fire in May 2001. The Israeli quiescence was met by an intensification of violence by the Palestinians.

vii. Settlements

Israeli settlements are an obstruction to peace

It is the settlement issue that illustrates what the Arab concept of peaceful coexistence is. If there will ever be peaceful coexistence between the Palestinians and Israelis, it will be done on the basis of sharing the land. The Palestinian insistence on sharing Israel, but making its sovereign territory '*Judenrein*' (free of Jews) is a red flag towards true intentions. Tanzim leader Marwan Barghouti says unequivocally: "The settlers need to be evacuated." This opinion follows the model of all the Arab countries since 1948. After these countries compelled their Jewish populations to flee or be killed, their stance towards the Jewish State was purely hostile for more than half a century. Even the countries without pre-war Jewish populations, such as Jordan and Saudi Arabia, have been virulently anti-Israel and anti-Semitic. The 1967 and 1973 wars that brought the West Bank, Sinai, Golan Heights and Gaza Strip under Israeli rule did not cause any change to Arab foreign policy. They wanted to rid the land of Jews before the wars and so too afterward.

The Israeli acquisition of territory and establishment of settlements does not effect the Arab position. Every Jewish city, village and town in Israel is considered a settlement that has to be destroyed.

A large number of these Jewish settlements on "Arab lands" were Jewish towns and villages that were wiped out by the invading Arab armies in 1947-48. There was a substantial Jewish population in the Gush Etzion region, south of Jerusalem, that was annihilated by the Jordanian and Iraqi armies. Massuot Yitzchak, Ein Tzurim and Revadim suffered similar fates. In Gaza there were settlements that existed before 1948 that were wiped off the map by the Egyptian army. Kfar Darom was one such village that was infamous, in 1948, for Egyptian soldiers blowing off the legs of three siblings. There is no reason why the 7 Arab armies that invaded Israel, even before it declared itself a state, should be awarded a victory and that these lands should be considered 'Arab' possessions.

Does the PA say that Jewish residents of the West Bank and Gaza should be incorporated into a Palestinian state? Do they say that Israel has 1.2 million Arab citizens, so why cannot Palestine have 200,000 Jewish citizens? No. It demands complete withdrawal of every Jew from the West Bank and Gaza while insisting on resettling millions of Arabs within Israel. Former US President Ronald Reagan said that "All people -- Moslems, Jews and Christians -- are entitled to live on the West Bank." He is right in thinking that sharing the land on both sides of the equation is necessary for coexistence. This shows the hypocrisy of the Palestinian position on peace. There can be no coexistence, only liquidation of any and every Jewish presence until there is no one left.

The expansion of Israeli settlements does not threaten peace, nor does it contravene any agreements entered into with the Palestinians. Both parties agreed in 1993 that the status of the West Bank and Gaza should be left unchanged until final status talks have begun. The argument that Israeli expansion of settlements contravenes this is untrue. Certainly Israeli expansion for natural growth is not as threatening to the status of the areas as Arafat having brought 90,000 Palestinian "refugees" from other countries into these areas since Oslo. One family that moved from Jordan to the West Bank City of Qalqilya in 1999, produced the suicide bomber that killed 21 Jewish youths in Tel Aviv in June 2001. They came to the PA-controlled area because it offered more economic opportunity than Jordan (*USA TODAY*, June 26, 2001). The Palestinian demand for Israel halting settlement expansion for natural growth is tantamount to Israel prohibiting Israeli Arabs from renting new apartments in Haifa, Jaffa and Ramle.

Under Prime Minister Yitzchak Rabin, a complete settlement freeze existed. Ehud Barak offered to dismantle the vast majority of settlements in exchange for peace. This was met with a new wave of violence that has left dozens dead. Are settlements the issue? US Senator George Mitchell would have you think so, equating Israeli construction with Arab violence and murder. First, is building a house the equivalent of a suicide bomber who blows himself up in a crowd of civilians? Second, if the settlements were an obstruction, would it not follow that the Palestinians would want them dismantled, which is precisely what was offered by Prime Minster Barak? Therefore, the settlement issue reveals the true Palestinian intention, and is not the stumbling block to peace.

A June 2001 Jerusalem Media Center poll found that 67.1% of Palestinians are in favor of continuing the violence against Israel even if the Israelis instituted a settlement freeze. A paltry 25.1% said that the Intifada should be stopped if Israel halts "the Jewish settlement."

The Israelis are building up the West Bank and Gaza to create irreversible facts on the ground that will prevent peace from ever being reached

Since 1993, over 400,000 Arabs have moved into the areas under the PA, in violation of the Oslo Accords. This is more than double the 200,000 Israelis who moved to the West Bank and Gaza since the early 1970s. In that same period of time, the Arabs have built 261 new settlements in the West Bank, far outnumbering the 144 Israeli settlements. Most of these new Arab settlements have been built in direct contravention of the Oslo Accords. Many Arab day workers come over the Allenby Bridge or the Rafiah border into Israel and never leave. Thus, not only are these Arab settlements illegal, but Arab settlers are entering into the area under illegal pretexts and staying, creating new facts on the ground (*worldnetdaily.com*, April 25, 2001).

Israeli settlements in the West Bank and Gaza have displaced thousands of Arabs from their land

The vast majority of Israeli settlers live in areas that have been placed away from Arab population centers. These communities either straddle the Green Line and serve as satellite communities for Israel's major cities or are situated in the Jordan Valley desert. The Israeli Supreme Court prevented the establishment of a settlement on privately owned Arab land in 1979 because it did not fulfill any security purpose. The various governments of Israel have purchased lands in the West Bank and Gaza from absentee landlords. In 1975, the Jewish National Fund purchased $7 million of West Bank property in this fashion.

viii. Comparative

Palestinian suicide bombers are identical to the Japanese kamikaze fighters of WWII

The only two similarities between the kamikazes and the suicide bombers are that both ended up dead and usually both took enemy lives in their act of dying. That is where the similarities end. The kamikaze fighters were military pilots who struck ONLY at military targets -- almost always American naval ships. Palestinian suicide bombers almost never attack military targets, choosing to insert themselves clandestinely into crowded civilian areas where they then detonate their explosives. In fact, the goal of the suicide bomber is to kill as many civilians as possible.

Since the 1993 Oslo Accords there have been over 30 suicide bombings that have killed more than 200 Israelis. These bombers are religious fanatics who are promised eternal heaven for their murderous deeds by Moslem clerics. According to their religious leaders, killing civilians is identical to killing soldiers because all Jews are the enemies of their people and faith. The Japanese were committing acts of loyalty for their nation and Emperor, trying to disable the enemy military by their acts, not killing defenseless human beings.

A Time for Truth: The Intifada was launched because of the Palestinian leadership's inability to accept coexistence with the Jewish people. The PA is still focused on destroying Israel and feels that only violence can achieve this goal. All of Palestinian society is being incited to violence and the number of volunteers for suicide bombings is overflowing. The issues are not the West Bank and Gaza, Israeli settlements or how much force the IDF uses, but what the intent of the Palestinians is. The Palestinian objective remains that of ridding the land of all Jews.

JERUSALEM

Jerusalem should be internationalized because it belongs to all people, not Israel

There are four reasons why Jerusalem should not be internationalized. First, internationalization has not worked in any place it has been tried. The model of post-World War II Berlin does not provide much hope for internationalization to succeed because Berlin became the symbol of the Cold War between the Soviets and Americans and remained divided for more than 40 years. Second, it is merely an excuse to take the capital of the Jewish State out of Jewish hands. There was never a call for sharing the city when it was under Turkish, British or Jordanian rule. The pressure began only when Israel took it over.

Third, the city has never been more openly free in its history than at present. There is complete freedom of worship in Jerusalem for all faiths. Mosques, churches and synagogues abound in the city and there are no restrictions placed on worship -- unless these religious sites are being used to foment violence, which the Moslem sites all too often are. The Palestinian religious clerics frequently deliver sermons at the Temple Mount mosques to incite their people to violence against Israel. Several riots have occurred on the Temple Mount following Friday services. In the name of tolerance, Israel allowed the Moslem *Waqf* to administer the Arab areas of the Temple Mount after the IDF captured the Old City in 1967. When the city was under Jordanian rule, Jews were not given access to their holiest site, the Western Wall. The Jordanians destroyed 58 synagogues. They desecrated cemeteries on the Mount of Olives. Latrines and slum dwellings were erected beside the Western Wall. Under Israel's rule there has never been a campaign to destroy places of worship. Mosques in Israel are controlled by the *Waqf*, not by Israel.

Last of all, Jerusalem should belong to its majority population. Jews have been the majority in Jerusalem since the late 1870s-early 1880s. They have been the largest ethnic group in the city since the 1840s -- well before modern day immigration began.

The Arabs accept the internationalization of Jerusalem

The UN concept for making Jerusalem an international city was accepted by the Jewish Agency in 1947 because it saw that the Arabs wanted war and it wanted to spare this holy city from conflict. The Arabs rejected internationalization and the Partition Plan. Only in the aftermath of the 1948 war, because there was a sovereign Jewish presence in half of the city, did the Arab countries start to call for internationalizing the city. All but one – Jordan. The Jordanians ruled the other half of the city and refused to permit any UN supervision in their part of the city until they lost it in the 1967 war that they helped initiate. Then they began calling for internationalization as well.

Israel exploits Jerusalem in Jewish history for political purposes

In June 2001, the official PA web-page for Jerusalem holy sites read: "*Al-Boraq* Wall: It is part of the exterior facade of the western wall of *al-Aqsa* mosque...Some Orthodox religious Jews consider it a holy place for them, and claim that the wall is part of their temple which all historic studies and archaeological excavations have failed to find any proof for such a claim. In order to undermine the foundations of *al-Aqsa* mosque, the Israeli government has converted it into a religious shrine for Jews, prohibiting non-Jews to enter it, except for a limited number of tourists."

King David conquered Jerusalem and made it the capital of Israel 3,000 years ago. His son, Solomon, erected the First Temple on Mount Moriah, in the heart of Jerusalem. Mount Moriah was central to the Jewish faith well before King David captured the city from the Jebusites. Abraham was said to have performed the *Akedah*, the binding of Isaac, on this very site. According to the biblical tradition, Isaac's son Jacob wrestled with an angel on this same holy site. Jerusalem was the center of Judaism until it was sacked and destroyed by the Romans in 70 CE and the people were exiled from the land. Yet, Jerusalem remained in the prayers and thoughts of all Jews, no matter how far they were from the land of their people.

The Koran, however, has no mention of Jerusalem explicitly or implicitly. Mohammed, in his failed attempt to win the Jews over, instructed his followers to pray towards Jerusalem as the Jews of Saudi Arabia did. When Mohammed came to the conclusion that the Jews would not convert to his new faith, he ceased this custom and wiped out the entire Jewish community. It was then that Mecca became the sole city of importance to Islam. The Haj, Moslem pilgrimage, is made only to Mecca -- nowhere else. Even when the Arabs conquered Jerusalem, on their way to capturing Damascus -- a city deemed much more important to them -- no major mosque was built on the Temple Mount for close to 60 years. It was only much later, towards the end of the 7th century, that a passage in the Koran, referring to Mohammed traveling to a "further mosque," '*al-Masjid al-Aqsa,*' was interpreted as Jerusalem and hence the name of the present day Temple Mount mosque. This entire campaign on the part of later Moslem thinkers was done in order to elevate Islam above Judaism and Christianity, and prove that Abraham, Moses and all the other key biblical figures were really Moslems. Later Islamic interpretations went on to include Mohammed visiting Mount Sinai, Hebron, Bethlehem and other key places from the two major world religions.

Ehud Barak put Jerusalem on the negotiating table. He offered to divide the city and relinquish rights to all of the visible Temple Mount for sake of peaceful resolution of the conflict. His effort was met with Arafat's latest campaign of choreographed violence, ironically entitled the "*al-Aqsa* Intifada.*"*

Historically, Jerusalem has always been an Arab city

At no time in history was Jerusalem ever an Arab capital. When Jordan occupied Jerusalem between 1948-1967 there was never an attempt to make Jerusalem its capital. Amman, a city of limited historical importance, remained capital over Jerusalem. Jerusalem only became prominent to the Arabs once Israel captured it from the Jordanians in 1967. Jerusalem is touted as the third most important city in Islam but, when it was under Jordanian control for 19 years, not one of the *Imams* or *Muftis* from Saudi Arabia is known to have visited the Moslem Shrines of Jerusalem.

Moslems pray towards Mecca; Jews pray towards Jerusalem. Jerusalem is mentioned over 700 times in Jewish Scripture yet is unmentioned in the Koran. There have been more Jews than Moslems in Jerusalem since the 1840s. While under Jordanian rule, though there was never an attempt to make Jerusalem an Arab city, there was definitely an effort to eradicate the city of its Jewish heritage. In the 19 years of Jordanian reign, 58 synagogues were destroyed and Jewish access to remaining sites was forbidden. Jews were even barred entry to the Western Wall and Temple Mount during this period. The ancient Jewish cemetery on the Mount of Olives was also desecrated. There has been a continuous Jewish presence in Jerusalem since recorded time. Jerusalem has been a center of Jewish life throughout the millennia. Jewish religious schools have always thrived in Jerusalem, some having been there for centuries. No Islamic school of any importance has ever been located in Jerusalem. The city was not even a provincial capital during centuries of Moslem rule.

Teddy Kollek, former Mayor of Jerusalem, summed up the importance of Jerusalem: "For three thousand years, Jerusalem has been the center of Jewish hope and longing. No other city has played such a dominant role, as has Jerusalem in the history, culture, religion and consciousness of a people…if you want one simple word to symbolize all of Jewish history, the word would be Jerusalem."

All the famous personalities associated with Jerusalem, such as King David, King Solomon, Jesus, Herod, Hezekiah, Isaiah and Jeremiah, are either Christian or Jewish. None is Moslem.

When Israel seized Jerusalem, it was an act of aggression

On the second day of the Six-Day War, the Jordanians ignored Israeli appeals to stay out of the war and opened a third front against Israel on the cease-fire lines that divided Jerusalem. It sent its army across the No Man's Land into Israeli territory. Israel responded to this act of war and three days later, the city was conquered and unified under Israeli control. One of the very first acts taken by Israel was to open the Western Wall to Jewish visitors, a privilege denied by the previous Jordanian rulers. The Knesset enacted a law on June 27, 1967 guaranteeing free access to religious places of all faiths. This remains a vital part of Israel's policy of tolerance and religious freedom. Arab propaganda from Beirut, Cairo and Damascus accused Israel of intentionally targeting Moslem shrines during the fighting. Despite intense hand-to-hand combat in the streets of Jerusalem, Moslem shrines that were hit had minimal damage because Israel, out of respect for the holy sites, consciously avoided using artillery or aerial bombing in its defense of Jerusalem against Jordanian aggression.

The only way to bring peace is for Israel to recognize that Jerusalem needs to be divided and shared

Prime Minister Barak offered to divide Jerusalem into two separate capital cities, one for Palestinians and one for Israelis. Arafat rejected the offer. Despite Barak's overture, which went further than any Israeli proposal had ever gone before, the concept of sharing the city is simply not enough for the Palestinians. Arab East Jerusalem as a capital of Palestine and full rights to the visible Temple Mount are not enough for the Palestinians. And it is not just the PA, the alternatives to the PA are Islamic Jihad and Hamas who overtly call for the removal of all Jews from the land. By rejecting Barak, the PA has shown its hand and it looks identical to Hamas and Islamic Jihad. Barak's offer was met with a massive wave of orchestrated violence that has cost dozens of lives on both sides.

All the foreign embassies are located in Tel Aviv because no country recognizes Jerusalem as Israel's capital

There were 13 different countries with embassies in Jerusalem until the Arabs began a campaign of economic blackmail against them in the early 1980s. Iraq and Saudi Arabia led this crusade by threatening to cut off oil supplies, and economic and diplomatic ties to any country with an embassy in Jerusalem. Bolivia, Chile, Columbia, Costa Rica, Dominican Republic, Ecuador, El Salvador, Guatemala, Haiti, the Netherlands, Panama, Uruguay and Venezuela all moved out.

By 1983, Costa Rica rethought its position and moved back to Jerusalem, where it still remains today. El Salvador followed suit one year later and then the Ivory Coast moved its embassy to Jerusalem while establishing full diplomatic relations with Israel, unusual for an African country. It came under intense pressure from the Arab World and it reconsidered its position, quickly moving back to Tel Aviv.

Under the Clinton Administration, the US said it was moving its Embassy to Jerusalem. The Jerusalem Embassy Act was passed by Congress and approved by Clinton towards the end of his second term. However, President Bush invoked a waiver that prevents the US from breaking ground on this approved Jerusalem embassy because of "national security interests."

Israeli excavations have threatened the Moslem holy shrines

Israel came under severe criticism for excavating the outer wall area of the Temple Mount in the 1970s. This area has been developed into a plaza where tourists of many faiths now visit to better appreciate the life and times of the Second Temple period. Israel was again criticized in 1996 for digging a tunnel directly underneath the *al-Aqsa* mosque. This allegation was presented as front-page news across the world. The Arabs were 'enraged' and started throwing stones down from the heights of the Temple Mount mosque area onto Jewish worshippers praying below at the Western Wall. This holiest of Jewish sites had to be evacuated and cordoned off on the eve of one of Judaism's major holy days. The tunnel that was opened is thousands of years old, and dates from Hasmonean times. It runs outside the Temple walls, never coming more than several hundred yards from the southern wall of the Temple Mount, where the *al-Aqsa* mosque stands. Additionally, the tunnel was not being dug; rather it had been there for centuries. Israel simply opened a new exit that was at the base of the Arab shouk in the Moslem Quarter, nowhere near any of the mosques.

According to Hershel Shanks, editor and publisher of *Biblical Archaeological Review*, the Palestinians are destroying unexcavated Jewish remains on the Mount and throwing them out. The *Waqf* has been cited for 35 different violations of Israeli Antiquities Law including rebuilding Solomon's Stables, dating from the First Temple, as a mosque. 6,000 tons of earth were dug up and dumped into rivers and landfills. Independent archaeologists lament the fact that they saw foundation stones that will never be studied and their direct importance and placement never known because of this reckless abuse of a holy site.

The Israeli government covertly supports Jewish fringe parties trying to blow up the Temple Mount mosques

There are groups in Israel that advocate building the Third Temple on the Temple Mount. The most renowned of these groups is called the Temple Mount Faithful. They are a very small group that tries to gain access to the

Mount twice a year, on specific dates, but always has access blocked by the Israeli police. They have not inflicted any damage whatsoever on any Moslem shrine in Israel.

A Time for Truth: Jerusalem is the subject of a great Arab myth that began when Israel gained possession of the city in 1967. When Jerusalem was under Jordanian control, Jewish sites were vandalized, destroyed or converted into garbage heaps. Under Jordanian authority, Jews were denied access to all their holy sites. During this time, the Arab holy sites were well kept, but not the subject of any great attention in the Moslem World. In fact, they were largely ignored. Amman, the capital of Jordan, was considered more important to Jordan than Jerusalem. This Arab myth underscores the whole attitude of the Islamic World towards Israel, that wherever the Jews are in this land, they will be attacked physically, politically -- and even historically.

TERRITORY

As evidenced by early Zionist meetings, the Jewish people could have picked a homeland anywhere. There is nothing special about Israel in Jewish history

Many of the early Zionists saw the writing on the wall in Europe and the dire need to find a place -- any place -- that could be used to shelter Jews from violent anti-Semitism. Zionist leaders from Eastern Europe and Russia considered Argentina, Madagascar and Kenya because of a fear of pogroms, which were becoming more frequent and harsh. However, even before the leaders of the political movement were contemplating these options, immigration to Palestine was moving at its own pace. Irrespective of political decisions, Jews had begun to move back to Palestine in the 19th century from Yemen, Morocco, Iraq and Turkey, as well as Russia and Europe. The political leaders could have debated the merits of any country in the world to serve as a haven, but the Jewish people were making the decision for them by going to the one place that Jewish history, prayer and culture dictated -- the Land of Israel.

The West Bank and Gaza Strip are occupied territories

In 1948, when the British evacuated Palestine, the Arab armies launched an all-out assault on the Jewish *Yishuv*. The Egyptians captured the Gaza Strip and the Jordanian army seized the West Bank, and a portion of Jerusalem including all but a tiny enclave of the Old City. According to international law, capturing territory in an offensive war is illegal. When Israel defeated Egypt, Syria and Jordan during the Six-Day War of 1967, it was a defensive war and the land it captured is not considered occupied under international law.

Israel's demand to keep the West Bank and Golan Heights as buffer zones is unrealistic. Iraq proved this when it attacked Israel during the Gulf War with SCUD missiles

The US-led coalition against Iraq thought that its air campaign had brought Saddam Hussein to his knees, but in fact it hardly even set back his weapons production industry. His army and Republican Guard are as powerful as ever. Iraq's missile attacks against Israel did not achieve any military results, but rather caused much damage. Aerial attacks can kill people, but not defeat a nation. This case was also proven in England during the Nazi *Blitzkrieg* and in North Vietnam. In 1983, the US Joint Chiefs of Staff said that, "From a strictly military point of view, Israel would require the retention of some captured territory in order to provide militarily defensible borders." Control of the ground is still the most vital aspect of deciding the outcome of a war.

Haifa

Mediterranean Sea

21 miles
35 km

Netanya   9 miles
15 km

Samaria

Tel Aviv - Yafo   11 miles
18 km

Jordan River

Ashdod   22 miles
36 km   Jerusalem

Ashkelon

7 miles
11 km

Gaza

Judea

Dead Sea

10 miles
16 km

Beersheba

Under Jordanian Rule Until 1967

Under Egyptian Rule Until 1967

In October 1973, when the Syrian and Egyptian armies attacked Israel by surprise, had Israel not possessed the Golan Heights and the Gaza Strip, Syrian and Egyptian tanks could have reached Tel Aviv. Had that occurred, Israel might not have been able to fight back. Certainly without this buffer zone, the Arab armies' missiles would have hit population centers rather than military positions.

Israel controls the Middle East's water resources

Israel is presently considering importing 200 million cubic meters of water from Turkey. The Kinneret (Sea of Galilee) has fallen below its danger-line. It is more than five meters below its full point and present use is outdistancing the rate of replenishment. The drought in the Middle East is effecting Israel. Israel is still subject to Syria and Lebanon cutting off the headwaters of the Yarmouk that provide the Kinneret with its water. Israel had a deficit of 500 million cubic meters of water in the summer of 2001. If this pace continues, damages to the ecosystem could render Israel's major water source undrinkable.

Even though the terms for water under the Israel-Jordan peace treaty have concluded, Israel is still providing arid Jordan with 40 million cubic meters of water in 2001, despite its own heavy deficit and severe needs.

Israel has no need for the water sources of the West Bank

60% of Israel's freshwater lies in the West Bank. Ceding these sources to the PA could prove disastrous to the future of Israel, especially considering that the level of the Kinneret has fallen below its danger-line.

A Time for Truth: Israel is a tiny country that holds great historical and religious meaning for the Jewish people. The Jewish State could not have been founded elsewhere. Jews have been focused on returning to Israel for thousands of years, since the Romans destroyed the Second Temple and carried the Jews into exile. The Jewish Bible and the Talmud are filled with references to Tiberias, Hebron, Shechem, Bethlehem, Beer Sheva and Jerusalem, the cities of the Land of the Jewish People. There is no such place as the West Bank in the Bible, just a land west of the Jordan River called Israel.

PLO

Arafat and the PLO gained notoriety because of the justness of its cause

Much of the PLO's international success is due to the UN. The Arab nations have used the UN as a forum to isolate Israel diplomatically and legitimize the PLO. The UN blindly accepted the PLO in the 1970s. It helped promote its cause without ever extracting a price of moderation for joining the community of nations. At the time, the Egyptian government said that recognition of the PLO would cause it to moderate, leading to peace and an abatement of terrorism. There were never any preconditions to the acceptance of the PLO into the UN; thus its campaign of terror increased and it became even more extreme. In the years 1970-74 before the UN rolled out the red carpet for Arafat, the number of incidents of PLO terror outside of Israel stood at 116. Following Arafat's speech to the General Assembly, this number remained even at 119 between 1975-79 and then increased to 181 between 1980-86.

The UN sanctioned the PLO's uninhibited use of terrorism by giving it unconditional access to all its committees and sessions. The UN was founded to promote peace and security around the world, but has been used by its Arab members to foster war and hatred. When one Arab member, Egypt, pursued peace with Israel, the Arab nations used the UN General Assembly to repeatedly attack Egypt for negotiating peace. Even the ICAO, the International Civil Aviation Organization, which suffered the most from PLO skyjackings, invited the PLO to its conferences on how to combat aerial piracy. The UN has a rich track record of denying Israel the equal protection that its members are guaranteed. It has helped promote the PLO armed struggle against Israel.

Fatah gained its appeal among Palestinians due to successful propaganda about violence against Israel. In 1968, a battle took place at Karameh, Jordan. Fatah fought with Jordanian soldiers against the IDF and killed 28 Israelis in the protracted shootout. At least 200 Arabs were killed. Fatah claimed victory and publicized a slaughter of 400 Israelis. Thousands flocked to join Fatah to get a chance to kill Israelis. Still the PLO remained largely unpopular except with the Palestinians in Lebanon. But the more violence was carried out against the world, the more the PLO became recognized as a force with which to be reckoned. The first Intifada in 1987 was not begun with the complicity of the PLO. It was planned and coordinated by Palestinians living in the West Bank and Gaza. The PLO moved in and adopted it as its own doing, trying to run it from its headquarters in Tunis. Despite garnering an international reputation because of its access to the UN, the PLO did not officially assume the role of Palestinian leadership until the early 1990s.

The PLO was legally in Lebanon, thus making the Israeli invasion illegal

In 1969, the PLO signed the Cairo Agreement stating that it would not operate bases in southern Lebanon, conduct military training in refugee camps or shell Israel from Lebanese territory. In the Malkert Agreement of 1973, the PLO promised to remove heavy weapons from refugee camps, end terrorist activity in Lebanon and cease using refugee camps as training bases. By 1975, Arafat had tanks, anti-aircraft guns and 15,000 troops under his command. In 1977, the Shtaura Agreement was meant to restore sovereignty to Lebanon throughout its borders, have the PLO relinquish control of the refugee camps, cease importing arms and ammunition and stop all military training. By 1982, when Israel invaded, the PLO had a full army with 5 divisions under its command.

The autonomy of the PLO in Lebanon grew following the PLO's expulsion from Jordan. Many of these newcomers had been radicalized by the PLO in Jordan and were committed to armed struggle against Israel. Because of the PLO, the lives of the Lebanese in the southern portion of the country turned anarchic -- characterized by kidnappings, carjackings, arbitrary land appropriations and evictions.

There are two reasons why Israel was not in contravention of any international law when it invaded Lebanon: first, Lebanese sovereignty was not violated because the IDF operation was not against Lebanon but the PLO; and second, Article 51 of the UN Charter allows countries the right to self-defense, and Israel invaded to stop PLO attacks into northern Israel. However, when Syria invaded Lebanon in 1976, it did violate Lebanese sovereignty because it established itself as the rulers of the country.

The PLO no longer supports terrorism

E-Kihan, the official newspaper of the Iranian government, claims that Arafat was involved in planning the bombing of the World Trade Center in 1993. Israeli intelligence reached the same conlcusion through its sources. Arafat maintains a training facility in Sudan to this day where Fatah trains with Sudanians and Iranians (*Arutz 7*, September 12, 2001).

On May 25, 2001, the *Mufti* of Jerusalem and Palestine, speaking from the *al-Aqsa* mosque during his Friday sermon said: "...you have brothers wrongly and aggressively jailed in America. They have been forgotten. They were charged with false claims about the bombing of the World Trade [Center] in New York. We, from the *al-Aqsa* mosque and on your behalf, demand the release of these prisoners."

The PLO includes many members who are still on the US State Department list of terror organizations. The Palestine Liberation Front-Abu Abbas Faction (PLF) and the Popular Front for the Liberation of Palestine (PFLP) are members of the PLO. The Democratic Front for the Liberation of Palestine (DFLP) was recently dropped from the list. Fatah has a close relationship with three other members of this list: Hamas, Hezbollah and the Islamic Jihad.

The PLO was always miscast as a terrorist organization, it really was a group of freedom fighters

Arab terrorists were responsible for 45 hijackings of civilian airplanes. Here is a brief list of some of the more renowned skyjackings:

February 1970: Swissair - 47 killed in mid-air
May 30, 1972: Lod, Israel - 26 killed
February 10, 1973: Munich, Germany - 1 killed
August 5, 1973: Athens, Greece - 5 killed
December 17, 1973: Rome, Italy - 31 killed
August 11, 1976: Istanbul, Turkey - 4 killed
June 19, 1985: Beirut, Lebanon - 1 killed
November 23, 1985: Malta - 67 killed
December 3, 1985: Rome, Italy - 13 killed
December 27, 1985: Vienna, Austria - 3 killed
September 5, 1986: Karachi, Pakistan - 21 killed
April 1988: Cyprus - 2 killed

On the ground they were just as lethal. Here is a sample of some PLO terrorism against the international community in 1972. The PLO:

1) blew up a West German electricity plant
2) blew up a Dutch gas plant
3) blew up an oil refinery in Trieste, Italy
4) murdered 24 at Israel's Lod airport in conjunction with the Japanese Red Army
5) murdered 11 Israeli athletes at the Munich Olympics

Palestinian terrorists entered Israel from Lebanon on several occasions in 1974 and killed 52 Israelis, mainly women and children in Ma'alot, Kiryat Shemona, Shamir and Nahariya. Ayatollah Khomeini's first official visitor, after he overthrew the Shah of Iran, was Yassir Arafat because of the PLO assistance to the Iranian *mujahiddin* (fighters) in bringing down the Shah. The PLO has worked closely with Idi Amin of Uganda, the Nicaraguan Sandinistas and nearly every major terrorist group in the world, the IRA, Baader-Meinhoff Gang, the Red Brigades, the Japanese Red Army and Abu Nidal.

In 1985, Mohammed Abbas, a member of the PLO Executive Council, hijacked an ocean liner, the *Achille Lauro*, and shot and killed a wheelchair-bound American Jew, who was then dumped overboard.

A Time for Truth: The PLO was founded upon a program of terrorism and destruction. It claims that it has evolved into an organization committed to statesmanship. There is no evidence to support this claim. The PLO is now the Palestinian Authority that rules its own people despotically, embezzling money and denying basic freedoms to its people while it continues to attack Israeli civilians through terrorist actions.

WARS

The Deir Yassin massacre shows that Israelis have no moral high ground, they also murder innocent people

When the 1948 War of Independence was being fought against invading Arab forces, the Jews had several different militias rather than a cohesive army. Initially the Arabs were able to put Jerusalem under siege and nearly cut its Jewish population off from the rest of the country, making it difficult for them to receive water or supplies. Israeli forces were able to keep one road into Jerusalem open. Arab forces entered into two villages, Deir Yassin and Castel, overlooking this vital road to try to complete the siege. Iraqi, Syrian and Jordanian soldiers moved in as well without evacuating the local population, but rather using them as cover. The Jewish armies responded. The *Haganah* captured Castel after several intense battle with heavy casualties on both sides.

Deir Yassin, only 700 meters from Givat Shaul, a Jewish Jerusalem neighborhood, was used as a post for the constant harassing of Israeli convoys trying to enter Jerusalem and incessant sniping at Jewish neighborhoods. On the same day that Castel was captured, the *Irgun* and Stern Group attempted to capture Deir Yassin. Knowing there were civilians still in the village, the Jewish forces forfeited the element of surprise in order to make a public call to the villagers to evacuate. The General Secretariat of the Arab League corroborated this fact: "On the night of 9 April 1948, the peaceful Arab village of Deir Yassin, on the outskirts of Jerusalem, was surprised by loudspeakers calling for the inhabitants of the village to evacuate it immediately." About 200 civilians evacuated, the remainder stayed. Street by street, the Israelis advanced under intense gunfire emanating from civilian homes. Of the 120 Jewish fighters, 5 were killed and 36 wounded, a high percentage of casualties. Of the 800-1000 residents of the village, 116 were killed according to the British *Guardian*. Once the village was taken, contrary to Arab propaganda, there was no slaughter. The death of women and children was a function of their not having evacuated. One can only wonder if they willingly chose to remain in the battle zone or if they were forced to stay by the Arab soldiers who were using them as human shields.

Israel started the 1956 Sinai War and showed that it is an expansionist State by seizing the entire Sinai Peninsula

In 1956, Egypt illegally blocked the Suez Canal, armed Sharm el-Sheikh, at the southern tip of the Sinai Peninsula, with artillery and closed the Straits of Tiran. In the Gaza Strip between 1949-1956 there were 1,843 cases of armed robbery, 1,339 armed clashes with Egyptian soldiers, 435 cross-border incursions and 172 cases of sabotage that left 364 Israelis wounded and 101 dead, mostly civilian. Egypt struck a deal in 1955 to import Soviet arms through Czechoslovakia, nationalized the Suez Canal and unified military commands with Syria and Jordan for the declared purpose of attacking Israel. In Sinai, by 1956, Egypt had amassed 45,000 troops, mostly in the Gaza region. Israel won the war and captured all of the Sinai. In 1957, Israel withdrew from the entire Sinai -- unconditionally.

Israel ganged up with France and England to surprise Egypt in 1956

Israel fought by itself in the Sinai War of 1956. French and British promises to open up separate fronts to liberate the Egyptian-nationalized Suez Canal were broken, leaving Israel to fight alone against a larger, better equipped and mobilized Egyptian army. The war began on October 29, 1956. The French and British bombed some token sites along the Canal and the Nile Delta region on October 31, but only sent its paratroopers into the Sinai on November 5, well after the war had been decided by the Israeli Defense Forces.

Israel launched the 1967 Six-Day War on unprepared Arab armies

When Israel launched a surprise attack against Egypt's airfields on June 5, 1967, leveling its air force in one fell swoop, it was in response to *cassus belli* by Egypt and Syria. Egyptian President Gamal Abdel Nasser had mobilized his army and had moved extra planes to airfields in close proximity to Israel. 1,000 tanks were brought into Sinai in the middle of May when Egypt declared a state of emergency. 100,000 troops, representing 7 divisions, marched into Sinai as well.

On May 16, the Egyptian government demanded that the UN Emergency Force withdraw from its position along the Israel-Egypt border. UN troops guarding the Straits of Tiran were told to leave, which they promptly did on May 22. Then Egypt imposed a blockade on the Gulf of Aqaba and closed the Straits of Tiran to Israeli shipping. These are all considered acts of war in international law. *Radio Cairo* was broadcasting calls of war against the Zionist enemy.

The Soviets were pumping military equipment into Egypt and Syria and encouraging them to go to war. Ultrasonic MiG-21 planes, the most modern T-55 tanks, the newest Soviet artillery and ground-to-air missiles were shipped into Egypt. Under the brand new Ba'ath regime, Syria was continuously shelling Israel's northern towns with its artillery, causing the residents of towns such as Metulla and Kiryat Shemona to live in emergency shelters.

Arab terrorists attacked Israel 35 times in 1965, 41 times in 1966 and 37 times in the first few months of 1967. In April, Syrian tanks and mortars were fired at Israeli farms on the Sea of Galilee leading to a further escalation of tension. Syria's *Radio Damascus* was calling for all-out war against Israel.

King Hussein of Jordan, despite Israeli requests to stay out of the impending war, traveled to Cairo on May 30 to sign a five-year mutual defense pact with Egypt. Now Egypt had defense pacts with Syria, Iraq and Jordan. Other Arab states sent expeditionary forces to Egypt so they could participate in the impending war. The combined Arab forces mobilized to fight Israel numbered 250,000 troops, 2,000 tanks, and 700 fighter and bomber planes.

Israel did not really have to attack the Arabs in 1967. It could have used diplomatic channels to resolve the conflict and avoid war

Why did Israel not attack the Arab armies on May 30 or 31 after Egypt mobilized its army? Before launching its attack, Israel tried to calm the atmosphere by having the United States contact Egypt. Israel and the US agreed on a few days leeway to try to convince the Arab leaders to avert the impending war. This plan was to no avail. It was only then, when diplomatic resolution was clearly no longer an option, that Israel launched a preemptive strike against Egypt.

Israel used the 1967 war as a pretext for an unprovoked land grab of the Sinai, Golan Heights, West Bank and Gaza

Prior to the war, Syria was using the strategic advantage of the Heights to lob artillery shells at Israel's northern settlements and towns, which were completely exposed at the base of the mountains of the Golan. Similarly, the coastal plain of the Sharon Valley, where Tel Aviv is located and the heart of Israel's population resides, was vulnerable to attacks from the hills of Judea and Samaria, where Arab cities, such as Qalqilya and Tulkarm, were used by Jordanian forces to bombard Israel. With nine miles to the coast, these hill positions gave Arab artillery access to the vast majority of Israeli citizens. The Gaza Strip was taken as a buffer against an Egyptian invasion. It is merely 30 miles from Gaza to Tel Aviv. Had Israel not controlled these lands during the 1973 Arab surprise attack on Yom Kippur, the fate of Israel might have been very different. Instead of fending off Syrian attacks in the Golan, these battles might have been waged in the streets of Carmiel, Tiberias and Zefat. If not for the buffer zone of the West Bank, Jordan could easily have penetrated through to Kfar Saba, Tel Aviv, Rishon LeZion and Jerusalem. On the Egyptian front, the Sinai and Gaza protected Israel from Egyptian tanks rolling up the coast through Ashdod and Ashkelon right into Jaffa and Tel Aviv.

After the war, Israel felt that the Arabs would finally realize that Israel was a *fait accompli* and enter into peace negotiations. Israel was willing to give back all the land it had captured in exchange for a true and lasting peace. The infamous meeting of Arab leaders in Khartoum put a dash to these hopes. The three "Nos" of Khartoum stood as Arab policy for years. The policy was no peace, no negotiation and no recognition.

UN Security Council Resolution 242 calls for Israel to withdraw from all occupied territories

---

RESOLUTION 242

Expressing its continuing concern with the grave situation in the Middle East,

Emphasizing the inadmissibility of the acquisition of territory by war and the need to work for a just and lasting peace in which every State in the area can live in security,

Emphasizing further that all Member States in their acceptance of the Charter of the United Nations have undertaken a commitment to act in accordance with Article 2 of the Charter,

1) Affirms that the fulfillment of Charter principles requires the establishment of a just and lasting peace in the Middle East which should include the application of both the following principles:

Withdrawal of Israeli armed forces from territories occupied in the recent conflict;

Termination of all claims or states of belligerency and respect for and acknowledgement of the sovereignty, territorial integrity and political independence of every State in the area and their right to live in peace within secure and recognized boundaries free from threats or acts of force;

2) Affirms further the necessity

For guaranteeing freedom of navigation through international waterways in the area;

For achieving a just settlement of the refugee problem;

For guaranteeing the territorial inviolability and political independence of every State in the area, through measures including the establishment of demilitarized zones;

3) Requests the Secretary General to designate a Special Representative to proceed to the Middle East to establish and maintain contacts with the States concerned in order to promote agreement and assist efforts to achieve a peaceful and accepted settlement in accordance with the provisions and principles in this resolution;

4) Requests the Secretary-General to report to the Security Council on the progress of the efforts of the Special Representative as soon as possible.

Arthur J. Goldberg, the US Ambassador to the UN during the Six-Day War, drafted the text of Resolution 242. He rejected the assertion that the resolution calls for a complete Israeli withdrawal from the territories it captured. He wrote: "Resolution 242 simply endorses the principle of withdrawal of Israel's armed forces from territories occupied in the recent conflict and interrelates this with the principle that every state in the area is entitled to live in peace within secure and recognizable boundaries."

Goldberg specifically did not write the words *the* or *all the* territories in the text (see our underline above). Withdrawal is also premised on security and peace; it is not unconditional.

Former US Under Secretary of State for Political Affairs Eugene Rostow said that Resolution "242 establishes three principles: 1) Israel can occupy and administer the territories it occupied during the Six-Day War until the Arabs make peace, 2) When peace agreements are reached, they should delineate 'secure and recognized' boundaries to which Israel would withdraw, 3) Those boundaries could differ from the Armistice Demarcation Lines of 1949."

Israel started the War of Attrition in 1969

In April 1969, President Nasser of Egypt violated the UN cease-fire that ended the Six-Day War of 1967 by firing artillery across the Suez Canal at Israeli positions. This war, in which aircraft, missiles and artillery were used, lasted 16 months. Israel suffered 200 fatalities during this sustained campaign by Egyptian forces. In 1970, the first actual Super Power involvement in the region occurred when a team of Soviet pilots engaged Israel in MiG-21s. The Israeli Air Force shot down 5 of them without any losses. Shortly thereafter, Egypt agreed to a cease-fire that held until it invaded Israel in the Yom Kippur War of 1973.

The Arabs only attacked in 1973 to liberate territory lost in 1967

If the Arabs merely wanted to liberate lost territory, they would have accepted Israel's offer to return all captured lands in 1967. Syria's Assad and Egypt's Sadat were very candid on *Radio Damascus* and *Radio Cairo*. Both men were calling for a complete liberation of Palestine and the eradication of the Jewish State. They were stirring the Arab World into a frenzy and the response was overwhelming. The entire Arab World was rallying to wipe Israel off the map. Iraq, Jordan, Sudan, Morocco, Tunisia, Kuwait, Saudi Arabia, Algeria and Libya all sent troops to Egypt or Syria to help defeat the "Zionist enemy." Lebanon did not participate, but allowed Arab troops unlimited use of its land. Egypt received a few pilots from Pakistan, some surface-to-air missile (SAM) technicians from North Vietnam and some tank officers and artillery gunners from Cuba.

Israel signed the peace treaty with Egypt only to eliminate the possibility of a united Arab front

Were Israel simply content to have peace with Egypt, then why bother to offer territorial compromises with the Palestinians, Syrians, Lebanese and Jordanians? According to this theory, once peace with Egypt was concluded, Israel should have been in the driver's seat because it could no longer be threatened on all of its borders simultaneously. While the strategic implications of the peace treaty with Egypt were immense for Israel, it was not the ideal solution. In fact, the peace treaty itself does not propose to be the end of the regional conflict, but rather a step towards ending it. A major clause in the agreement calls for the cessation of Israeli military rule in the West Bank and Gaza, and the establishment of Palestinian autonomy (See Appendix II). Israel also hoped that the peace treaty with Egypt would be a blueprint for agreements with its other neighbors.

Israel's 1982 invasion of Lebanon is another clear example of its expansionist designs.

After several unsuccessful forays over the border to try and put an end to PLO aggression, Israel invaded Lebanon. Continuous missile launching and terrorist incursion by the PLO and many of the other Arab groups hostile to Israel, such as Amal, Hezbollah and Islamic Jihad, forced Israel's northern population to live in bunkers. In the decade that preceded the full-scale Israeli reprisal, there were more than 3,000 rocket attacks that caused over 300 civilian casualties in Kiryat Shemona alone.

The PLO entered Lebanon in 1969 and immediately began attacking Israel with everything at its disposal. By 1982, the PLO army had swelled to over 15,000. The PLO was using high-grade Soviet equipment and receiving assistance from the Syrian Air Force. As a result of Palestinian attacks between 1965-82, 689 Israelis were killed and 3,799 wounded.

Because the PLO had established itself as a permanent hostile force in southern Lebanon, Israel launched the Litani Operation against the PLO. The PLO was powerful, operated autonomously and did not take orders from the Lebanese government. Initially the IDF succeeded in halting attacks, but when it withdrew its forces from Lebanon, the PLO reappeared in the area.

When Philip Habib, President Reagan's special envoy to the Middle East, proposed a cease-fire in 1981, the PLO and Israel accepted. The PLO violated this cease-fire 148 times. While the IDF abided by the agreement, the PLO used this period of calm to stockpile enough arms to equip 5 full infantry brigades.

When Shlomo Argov, Israel's ambassador to Great Britain was gunned down on June 3, 1982 by the PLO, Israel bombed two PLO bases in Lebanon. Then the PLO unleashed everything it had at Israel, firing more than 1,000 shells at 23 northern Israeli settlements over a 24-hour period. The IDF mounted Operation Peace for the Galilee to put an end, once-and-for-all, to the intolerable situation on its border with Lebanon. Israel tried diplomacy and the cease-fire did not hold; it tried armed conflict, but every time it withdrew its forces, the PLO resumed hostilities. Therefore, it invaded with the intention of ridding Lebanon of the PLO altogether.

Following Israel's successful banishment of the PLO from Lebanon, Iran started funneling arms to local groups, training and radicalizing them for continuing the fight against Israel. Had Israel withdrawn from its security zone, the situation would have gone back to the way it was pre-1982. Israel continued to battle these Iranian-backed Islamic Fundamentalist groups until it withdrew from its security zone in 2000.

Israel's Sabra and Shattila massacre: One of the modern world's biggest slaughters

In the Palestinian refugee camps of Sabra and Shatilla in Lebanon the Phalangists killed 460, including 15 women and 20 children in 1982. Many of the slain were armed combatants. After a national investigation, Israel took indirect responsibility even though it had not participated in any way. This massacre does not begin to measure up to the ruthless slaughtering of civilians by the modern Arab rulers. The following is a brief sampling:

Hafez Assad, Syria, 1982: 20,000-30,000 civilians killed in the leveling of the city of Hamah
King Hussein, Jordan, 1970: 5,000 Palestinians killed while putting down a coup against his regime
King Fahd, Saudi Arabia, 1987: 300-600 unarmed Iranian pilgrims killed in one day, 4,500 wounded
Ahmad Hassan al-Bakr, Iraq, 1974: 15 towns and 205 Kurdish villages razed to the ground. Hundreds of thousands fled as refugees, tens of thousands killed by napalm and air force bombings
Saddam Hussein, Iraq, 1987: Iraqi air force drops poison gas on Kurdish city of Halabja, killing 5,000
Yassir Arafat, Lebanon, 1976: Christian city of Damour overrun by PLO; 582 people killed; bodies were found mutilated and dismembered. Operation led by as-Saiqa leader Zuhayr Mushin
Iran-Iraq War, 1980s: Over 1,000,000 killed, including children sent out to the battlefront to fight; poison gas used by Iraq against Iranian positions

A Time for Truth: Israel has been involved in many wars, all of which have been defensive. Charges of Israeli violations are mostly Arab propaganda, created to make Israel look like it plays by the same rules as the Arabs in warfare. The IDF has a different standard. It has never been involved in the kind of conduct that has led Arab armies to murder thousands in one fell swoop. As for expansionism, Israel conquered territory that was used to assault the Jewish State repeatedly, to the point where the citizens of Israel could no longer live in peace. The heights of the Golan and the West Bank were used for these purposes. Gaza was a center for Egyptian and Palestinian terrorism against Israel and the Sinai was used by Nasser to impose a naval blockade on Israel. Over the years, Israel has offered to return all of these areas to the Arab nations in exchange for peace. Only Egypt has taken Israel up on the offer.

UNITED STATES

Israel has the United States in its back pocket

The United States and Israel have a friendly relationship based on common values. They are both democracies, enjoy freedom of speech, due process for the accused, checks and balances on government and a free press.

From the outset, the US was neither an advocate nor a close ally of Israel. During the Arab invasion of 1948, the US imposed an arms embargo on Israel that hindered the newfound State's ability to defend itself. On numerous occasions the US has been reluctant to condemn the Arabs or take action when they breach international law with acts of war. The closing of the Suez Canal and the Tiran Straits in 1956 and 1967 were not met with any US action and both times led to war against Israel. In fact, President Eisenhower was against the British, French and Israeli campaign against Egypt in 1956 and compelled Israel to withdraw unconditionally from the entire Sinai, a territory larger than all of Israel. The US has never taken an active role in trying to help resettle the Arab refugees from 1948 and this issue remains at the fore of the Middle East conflict.

When Israel annexed the Golan Heights in 1981, President Reagan suspended a strategic cooperation agreement with Israel and delayed delivery of fighter planes because of disenchantment over Israeli reprisals against the PLO in Lebanon.

The Bush I Administration was constantly at odds with Likud Prime Minister Yitzhak Shamir, issuing ultimatums that threatened the friendship between the two countries. Secretary of State James Baker tried to delay humanitarian aid in loan guarantees to Israel for settling Soviet and Ethiopian Jews unless Israel would cancel its settlement policy in the West Bank and Gaza. During the Gulf War, the US warned Israel not to respond to Iraqi SCUD missile attacks for fear of enflaming the Arab countries that participated in the US coalition in the Persian Gulf. Though Israel was hit with 39 SCUDs that left 4,000 Israelis homeless, it never responded to these Iraqi acts of war.

As of October 2001, Bush II is denying $800 million in US aid for the Israeli withdrawal from Lebanon. The US had promised Israel this financial assistance to build new fences and military posts along the border with Lebanon.

US arms are responsible for Israel's existence

The Israeli-American arms relationship did not began until 1962. Until then Israel was primarily dependent on French weapons. The Soviets began supplying the Arab World with its top-grade weaponry in 1955, commencing the arms race in the Middle East. In 1962 President Kennedy approved the *sale* of Hawk anti-aircraft missiles to Israel. When the Arabs invaded Israel in 1948, it fought without any support from the US.

The US now considers the PLO a friend and ally

Not long ago, US Congressional Law considered the PLO a terrorist organization. According to Section 5201 of the US Code on Foreign Relations and Intercourse, "The PLO was directly responsible for the murder of an American citizen on the *Achille Lauro* cruise liner in 1985, and a member of the PLO's Executive Committee is under indictment in the United States for the murder of that American citizen." Furthermore, "The head of the PLO has been implicated in the murder of a United States Ambassador overseas," and, "The PLO and its constituent groups have taken credit for and been implicated in, the murders of dozens of American citizens abroad."

US Congressional Law determined that "the PLO and its affiliates are a terrorist organization and a threat to the interests of the United States." All of these laws were shelved in 1993 because the Clinton Administration was trying to make a peacemaker out of Arafat. Former US Ambassador to Israel Martin Indyk told the *Jerusalem Post* on July 8, 2001 that "The Clinton Administration came in at a moment of a great sense of opportunity. There was a sense in which it was felt that peace could be achieved on all fronts." Now that this window has been slammed shut by Arafat, the US is once again considering the redesignation of the PLO as a terrorist organization.

During the Gulf War, Yassir Arafat, the PLO and all the Palestinian organizations supported Saddam Hussein in his war against the American-led coalition.

The present feeling towards the US in Palestinian circles is summed up by one of Arafat's close friends and Member of the PA *Fatwa* Council, Dr. Halabiya: "Wherever you are, kill those Jews and those Americans who are like them and those who stand by them. They are all in one trench, against the Arabs and the Moslems because they established Israel here...They wanted the Jews to be their spearhead."

On July 3, 2001, Marwan Barghouti, leader of the Tanzim, said: "For us, the US is a partner in the aggression and the occupation and the party that offers political cover, and complete military, financial and economic assistance to Israel."

Presently, the US Congress is discussing whether or not to penalize the PLO for not living up to its commitment to fight terror. The penalty would be the closure of the Palestinian Information Office in Washington, the designation of the PLO as a terrorist organization and a limitation of humanitarian assistance, (much of which ends up in Arafat's personal coffers).

The Mitchell Report favored Israel

The May 2001 US fact-finding mission led by Senator George Mitchell, gained Arafat's 100% acceptance. Ariel Sharon objected to the conclusions. Israel felt that the Mitchell Committee whitewashed Palestinian violence. Since Sharon won the Israeli election, he has insisted that Arafat halt the violence as a precondition for negotiations. Arafat has increased the violence. The Mitchell Committee, in its attempt to be evenhanded, apportioned equal blame to both parties, equating Israel's settlement campaign with Arab suicide bombings, mortar launching and rampant shooting at Israeli population centers, such as Gilo, a Jerusalem neighborhood. In doing this, the Committee sanctioned Arafat's use of violence. The Mitchell document suggested that Israel consider unilaterally ceasing settlement construction. Arafat began the latest wave of violence after rejecting PM Barak's peace offer, which included eliminating the vast majority of the settlements. The construction of a house and the blowing up of a pizza shop filled with children are not equal actions. This report says that Palestinian terror tactics are legitimate and should be responded to with Israeli concessions. However, this is precisely what Israel was doing when Arafat unleashed the guns, bombs, mortars and stones.

President Clinton played favorites, favoring Israel

In April 2001, former President Clinton, speaking in Philadelphia, told the audience that he was ready to cancel the White House ceremony, where the infamous "Golden Handshake" between Prime Minister Rabin and Arafat took place, because Arafat insisted on wearing his pistol during the event. Despite Arafat's having been invited to the White House during the Clinton Administration more than any other leader in the world, the US could not get him to buy into the peace process. When the process collapsed, Clinton blamed Arafat. Having a US President publicly lay blame on a foreign politician can only indicate one thing -- Arafat truly was at fault.

With Clinton putting his reputation on the line to try to resolve the conflict, it was frustrating to deal with Arafat, who funneled American and international money into personal bank accounts and contravened every agreement he signed. Yet, under the Clinton Administration, the Palestinians could have achieved statehood in more than 95% of the West Bank, all of Gaza, with East Jerusalem as their capital, sovereignty over the visible portion of the Temple Mount and a dismantling of nearly all Jewish settlements. This could have been attained while securing a peace treaty with Israel and full international recognition. Under President Clinton's supervision, the Palestinians could have gained more through negotiations than ever before.

The US favors Israel at the expense of the Arab World

The US and Israel enjoy a favorable relationship, due mostly to their shared value system of democracy and freedom. Israel is the largest recipient of US aid. It receives nearly $3 billion annually. The second largest recipient is Egypt, who receives $2 billion annually as part of a $52 billion US aid package, which included an annulment of its $7.1 billion national debt a few years ago.

Egyptian life has been markedly improved by US money. Their military is stocked with top-grade US equipment such as M1-A1 tanks and F-16 warplanes. US advisers and consultants help devise strategy for the Egyptian army. The Egyptian army is now considered the second strongest in the Middle East. US money has been used to build mosques, schools, roads, sewage systems and a telecommunications system. Since the US became involved with Egypt, *per capita* income has risen 30% and the gross domestic product has grown 5% annually. All of this aid was given for one reason -- Egypt's taking the steps to end its role in warmongering. When it made peace with Israel, it helped create the kind of regional stability that the US is trying to achieve on all fronts. Because of the importance of peace in this oil-filled region, the US made it even more worthwhile for Egypt to sign a deal with Israel. Besides getting the entire Sinai Peninsula from Israel, Egypt, through US aid, has greatly improved the lives of thousands of its citizens.

Jordan is seeking to reap the benefits of its peace treaty with Israel by entering into a free trade agreement with the United States. In April 2001, President Bush said that this agreement was one of the White House's top trade priorities. President Clinton had been urging Jordan's lenders to ease the burden on its $7 billion debt and gave $300 million in financial assistance to the Hashemite Kingdom. Jordan already receives $225 million in US economic and military aid annually.

Since the Gulf War coalition with Islamic states, the US has removed all Arab parties from the terrorism list

Syria, Iraq and Iran remain on the list of state sponsors. At present, there are debates in the US Congress as to whether or not to reinsert the PLO onto this list. It was removed in September 1993. Still on the list are a host of Arab groups, two of which (*italics*) are in the PLO: the Popular Front for the Liberation of Palestine-General Command (PFLP-GC); Abu Nidal Organization (ANO), Hamas (Islamic Resistance Movement), Hezbollah (Party of God), Palestine Islamic Jihad-Shaqaqi Faction (PIJ), *Palestine Liberation Front-Abu Abbas Faction* (PLF), and the *Popular Front for the Liberation of Palestine* (PFLP). The *Democratic Front for the Liberation of Palestine* (DFLP) was dropped off the list very recently.

Jordan

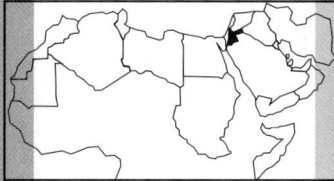

Area:	89,213 sq. km
Population:	5.0 Million
Date of Independence:	May 25, 1946
Head of State:	King Abdallah
GDP per capita:	$4,800
Defense Budget:	$488 Million
Active Military:	103,880
Tanks:	1,246
Combat Aircraft:	106
Artillery:	544

Arab Republic of Egypt

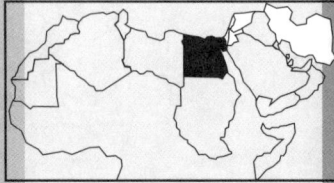

Area:	1 Million sq. km
Population:	68.3 Million
Date of Independence:	Feb. 28, 1922
Head of State:	Hosni Mubarak
GDP per capita:	$4,400
Defense Budget:	$2.5 Billion
Active Military:	448,500
Tanks:	3,960
Combat Aircraft:	583
Artillery:	1,378

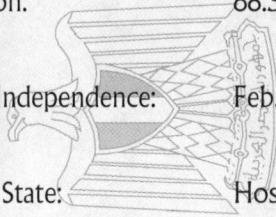

Kingdom of Saudi Arabia

Area: 1.96 Million sq. km

Population: 22.0 Million

Date of Independence: Sept. 23, 1932

Head of State: King Fahd

GDP per capita: $10,300

Defense Budget: $18.4 Billion

Active Military: 162,500

Tanks: 1,055

CombatAircraft: 432

Artillery: 568

Colin Powell's hands off approach benefits Israel

Since the US mediated the Oslo Process that led to Arafat assuming control of parts of the West Bank and Gaza, Arafat has used the grace period to establish a heavily armed terrorist state. Arafat now possesses a 20,000-man Republican Guard divided into 9 battalions. It is equipped with anti-tank and hand-held anti-aircraft weapons, machine guns and armored vehicles. As the key mediator of all these PA-violated agreements, the US has a responsibility to help prevent more bloodshed. Treating the PA with kid gloves is not a method that has worked well at all. Every time the US makes an evenhanded remark that equates Israeli settlements with Palestinian terrorism, the US is sending Arafat a clear signal that he is unhindered in his violence and that it may continue.

The US needs the Arabs for their oil

Two decades ago, the US imported 32% of its oil from the Middle East. Today the situation is different. Less than 20% comes from Middle East sources. Venezuela is now the largest supplier to the US, accounting for about 20% of the US market. Saudi Arabia only supplies approximately 15%, down from 21% in 1979. The US now imports about half of its oil from Western Hemisphere countries like Venezuela, Canada, and Mexico. US exploration in the Gulf of Mexico may lead to the availability of more domestic reserves and further lessen dependence on Middle East resources.

A Time for Truth: The US and Israel enjoy a healthy relationship that is rooted in shared values of freedom and democracy. It is not without its problems, but overall the differences do not overcome the foundation of commonality. There is a balance in US policy between oil politics and supporting democracy that is a source of tension between the US and Israel at times, but the relationship is on solid ground, despite the continuous change in political leaders.

AFTERSHOCK: SEPTEMBER 11, 2001

The reason for the September 11, 2001 attacks against the US is its Middle East policy and support of Israel

Newsweek (October 1, 2001) reports that 58% of Americans believe that the US was attacked because of its support for Israel. The US was not attacked on September 11, 2001 because of its foreign policy. It was attacked because of its ideals and way of life. It was attacked because of its free-market, equal rights, freedom of speech, democratic government and regard for human rights. The very things for which Americans stand and which it has gone to war to protect are the cause of these attacks. These attacks would have happened irrespective of whether America had a different foreign policy, President or relationship with Israel. Those who believe that the Middle East would be quiescent if Israel did not exist ignore the decade-long war between Iran and Iraq in the 1980s, border wars between Libya and Chad, civil wars in Lebanon and Sudan, Iraq's invasion of Kuwait and two decades of Syrian military-rule over Lebanon. The Arab war against Israel is not just a war against the Jewish people, but also an Islamic war against Western values.

Israel does not belong in an anti-terror coalition

The US has declared that it is at war against the terrorists who perpetrated the September 11, 2001 attacks on the World Trade Center and Pentagon. One of the first US acts in this war was to try to create an international anti-terror coalition. The reason the terrorists struck at the US is because they are opposed to the American way of life. They are against the freedoms that distinguish the Western way of life. The only Middle East country that adheres to this same way of life is democratic Israel. American allies were contacted in an attempt to create a united front against the Osama Bin Laden network. The Moslem countries in this group immediately said that they would not be involved in a coalition that included Israel, and Saudi Arabia denied the US access to launch operations from its territory against Moslem Afghanistan. This statement says very clearly that the Saudis put Moslem brotherhood ahead of its alliance with America.

The US was said to be considering the inclusion of Syria, Sudan, Iran and the Palestinian Authority in this coalition (*Washington Post*, September 25, 2001; *AP*, October 8, 2001). Not only do these entities train and harbor terrorists, but they may all have direct involvement with Al Qaeda (*AP*, October 6, 2001; *Boston Herald*, October 7, 2001).

Terrorists operate in networks. Al Qaeda could not exist without state support and relationships with other terrorist organizations. It is likely that the bombers of the World Trade Center in 1993 trained with Yassir Arafat's Fatah organization in Sudanese training camps (*Jerusalem Post*, September 13, 2001; *Arutz 7*, September 12, 2001). It is also probable that Hezbollah has trained with Al Qaeda personnel (*Baltimore Sun*, September 19, 2001). It is most likely that training has been financed by or coordinated with Iraq, Syria, Sudan and Iran at different times (*Washington Post*, October 12, 2001).

A Time for Truth: Israel is the front-line fighter in the war against terrorism and belongs on the US team. If the US coalition against terror becomes a reunion of terrorists and its supporters, the coalition, in the words of former Israeli PM Bibi Netanyahu, "will preclude possibility of overall victory," and "will melt down because of its own internal contradictions" (*Jerusalem Post*, September 21, 2001).

The US has taken a stance against all terror organizations

The US has frozen funding from a myriad of terrorist organizations, but has omitted Hamas, Islamic Jihad, Fatah and Hezbollah from this list. All these organizations have been responsible for recent deaths of American citizens. Next to Al Qaeda, Hezbollah has murdered more Americans than any other group on the US State Department list of terrorist organizations. Hezbollah's omission is most curious since three individuals on the most recent FBI 'Most-Wanted List' are its members (*AP*, October 10, 2001). However, Mohammed Abbas, the chief of the Palestine Liberation Front (a PLO faction), who carried out the murder of an American Jew on the *Achille Lauro* cruise-ship in 1985, was omitted from the list.

The war against terrorism will fail unless Israel is pushed to resolve its conflict with the Palestinians

The US is pushing Israel to make concessions with Arafat as a means of making the Arab countries more receptive to the American campaign against worldwide terrorism. US foreign-policymakers have yet to draw the conclusions that the Palestinian plight is an anti-Western fight. The Arab world equates Israel with America and the agenda of Palestinian suicide and roadside bombers is the destruction of the Middle Eastern representative of Western mores and values - Israel. The Palestinian suicide bombers target Western sites, such as discotheques and American chain restaurants, not synagogues or Jewish religious schools. According to Efraim Eytam, a retired Israeli brigadier-general, "those who attacked the Tel Aviv Dolphinarium and New York's Twin Towers share the same cultural roots an aims" (*Jerusalem Report*, October 8, 2001).

Prominent Palestinians have commented on the US war against terrorism. Israeli Arab MK Abdul Malik Dahamshe said: "The US never proved Bin Laden's connection to the September 11 attacks." Mohammed Kenaan, one of Dahamshe's colleagues, said: "The US simply decided that it wants to liquidate Islam and the Moslems." Israeli Arab MK Muhammad Baraka concurred: "[The US] fans the flames of terrorism, hits innocent people...The US wants to stabilize its power and the distribution of world wealth in an unjust manner" (*Arutz 7*, October 5, 2001). Islamic Jihad leader Abdullah Shami said: "What happened in the US made us extremely happy, even if we were not responsible for it" (*Jerusalem Post*, September 16, 2001). When the attacks on the World Trade Center and Pentagon occurred, Palestinians celebrated widely. When the US attacked Afghanistan on October 7, 2001, thousands of Palestinians demonstrated in the West Bank against the US action, including Tanzim leader Marwan Barghouti and other senior Fatah leaders (*Ha'aretz*, October 12, 2001).

The US is against targeted assassinations

The US still claims (*CNN*, October 15, 2001) that it is against the Israeli policy of killing terrorist leaders who are planning operations against Israeli civilians. However, the US is targeting Osama Bin Laden and has sent forces to Afghanistan to try to assassinate him.

A Time for Truth: The war against Israel is merely the center-stage for the war against the West. Pushing Israel into making concessions will only convince the anti-Western forces that the West is weak and vulnerable to more attacks.

CONCLUSION

Arafat and the PA seem to be planning for an all-out war against Israel, but any astute observer knows that the Palestinians are no match for Israel in a war. So what is really going on in the Middle East?

Arafat knows that in order to defeat Israel, two interdependent things have to occur: first, Israel has to launch a massive retaliation against Arab terrorism that would draw the Arab countries into war; and second, the Arab armies have to simultaneously open up all fronts against Israel.

Palestinian suicide bombings and sensational killings are meant to bait Israel into a full-scale reaction. Until now, Israel has not taken the bait, but is trying to neutralize the PA policy of suicide bombings, mortar launching and sniping by preempting the killings and assassinating the planners of these operations. Arafat is using Hamas and the Islamic Jihad in the same way that the Arab States used the PLO in the 1970s and 1980s -- to harass Israel without direct accountability. If Israel were to use excessive force by bombing a West Bank or Gaza Strip city, killing hundreds, that might cause the Arab countries to mobilize forces against Israel. If Israel were to blow up one or both of the Temple Mount mosques, that could also enrage the Arab World to the point of launching an assault on the Jewish State.

Arafat knows that he lacks support. Iraq is behind the Palestinian leader and could either attack Israel with SCUD missiles, which could be loaded with chemical or biological warheads, or send its army and air force to fight. Jordan is at peace with Israel, but because of its large Palestinian majority, it could be convinced to either enter a war, or, more likely, turn the other cheek to an Iraqi use of its airspace and terrain to attack Israel. King Abdallah would be more likely to follow the tide in the Arab World rather than risk a civil war or a potential coup.

As hostile as Syria is to Israel, it also despises Yassir Arafat. However, it seems certain that if Israel violated Moslem religious sites or committed a significant reprisal against the Palestinians, with heavy Palestinian casualties, Syria would mobilize its forces and attack Israel under the banner of being the savior of the Palestinian people -- not the Palestinian Authority.

Even with Syria, Iraq and Jordan committed to a war, the Arabs know that the chances of winning would be slim and would refrain from launching an attack unless Egypt was involved. Egypt has observed a cold peace with Israel for more than two decades. Egypt has nothing to gain and everything to lose from entering a war against Israel. Since it entered into peace with Israel, the US has brought untold benefits to Egypt. President Hosni Mubarak knows the importance of American money to his country. If Egypt broke the Camp David peace treaty, the relationship with the US would be put at risk. However, if Israel launched a massive operation against the Palestinians, even if Mubarak balked at opening up a front against Israel – and he might not, he could be overthrown by a popular political or military coup, launched by leaders who want to take Egypt into war. While Mubarak's regime is presently strong, it should be recalled that Egyptian radicals assassinated President Anwar Sadat because he made peace with Israel.

A Time for Truth: The noise level in the Middle East is deafening. The rhetoric emanating from the Arab media is as loud as it has ever been. Upon reading and watching the news, you would believe that war is imminent. It is certain that the PA is doing all it can to make war a reality, but right now the Arab countries are too pragmatic and frightened to commit to Arafat's agenda.

APPENDIX I: PLO Charter

Article 1: Palestine is the homeland of the Arab Palestinian people; it is an indivisible part of the Arab homeland, and the Palestinian people are an integral part of the Arab nation.

Article 2: Palestine, with the boundaries it had during the British Mandate, is an indivisible territorial unit.

Article 3: The Palestinian Arab people possess the legal right to their homeland and have the right to determine their destiny after achieving the liberation of their country in accordance with their wishes and entirely of their own accord and will.

Article 4: The Palestinian identity is a genuine, essential, and inherent characteristic; it is transmitted from parents to children. The Zionist occupation and the dispersal of the Palestinian Arab people, through the disasters which befell them, do not make them lose their Palestinian identity and their membership in the Palestinian community, nor do they negate them.

Article 5: The Palestinians are those Arab nationals who, until 1947, normally resided in Palestine regardless of whether they were evicted from it or have stayed there. Anyone born, after that date, of a Palestinian father - whether inside Palestine or outside it - is also a Palestinian.

Article 6: The Jews who had normally resided in Palestine until the beginning of the Zionist invasion will be considered Palestinians.

Article 7: That there is a Palestinian community and that it has material, spiritual, and historical connection with Palestine are indisputable facts. It is a national duty to bring up individual Palestinians in an Arab revolutionary manner. All means of information and education must be adopted in order to acquaint the Palestinian with his country in the most profound manner, both spiritual and material, that is possible. He must be prepared for the armed struggle and ready to sacrifice his wealth and his life in order to win back his homeland and bring about its liberation.

Article 8: The phase in their history, through which the Palestinian people are now living, is that of national (*watani*) struggle for the liberation of Palestine. Thus the conflicts among the Palestinian national forces are secondary, and should be ended for the sake of the basic conflict that exists between the forces of Zionism and of imperialism on the one hand, and the Palestinian Arab people on the other. On this basis the Palestinian masses, regardless of whether they are residing in the national homeland or in diaspora (*mahajir*) constitute - both their organizations and the individuals - one national front working for the retrieval of Palestine and its liberation through armed struggle.

Article 9: Armed struggle is the only way to liberate Palestine. Thus it is the overall strategy, not merely a tactical phase. The Palestinian Arab people assert their absolute determination and firm resolution to continue their armed struggle and to work for an armed popular revolution for the liberation of their country and their return to it. They also assert their right to normal life in Palestine and to exercise their right to self-determination and sovereignty over it.

Article 10: Commando action constitutes the nucleus of the Palestinian popular liberation war. This requires its escalation, comprehensiveness, and the mobilization of all the Palestinian popular and educational efforts and their organization and involvement in the armed Palestinian revolution. It also requires the achieving of unity for the national (*watani*) struggle among the different groupings of the Palestinian people, and between the Palestinian people and the Arab masses, so as to secure the continuation of the revolution, its escalation, and victory.

Article 11: The Palestinians will have three mottos: national (*wataniyya*) unity, national (*qawmiyya*) mobilization, and liberation.

Article 12: The Palestinian people believe in Arab unity. In order to contribute their share toward the attainment of that objective, however, they must, at the present stage of their struggle, safeguard their Palestinian identity and develop their consciousness of that identity, and oppose any plan that may dissolve or impair it.

Article 13: Arab unity and the liberation of Palestine are two complementary objectives, the attainment of either of which facilitates the attainment of the other. Thus, Arab unity leads to the liberation of Palestine, the liberation of Palestine leads to Arab unity; and work toward the realization of one objective proceeds side by side with work toward the realization of the other.

Article 14: The destiny of the Arab nation, and indeed Arab existence itself, depend upon the destiny of the Palestine cause. From this interdependence springs the Arab nation's pursuit of, and striving for, the liberation of Palestine. The people of Palestine play the role of the vanguard in the realization of this sacred (*qawmi*) goal.

Article 15: The liberation of Palestine, from an Arab viewpoint, is a national (*qawmi*) duty and it attempts to repel the Zionist and imperialist aggression against the Arab homeland, and aims at the elimination of Zionism in Palestine. Absolute responsibility for this falls upon the Arab nation - peoples and governments - with the Arab people of Palestine in the vanguard. Accordingly, the Arab nation must mobilize all its military, human, moral, and spiritual capabilities to participate actively with the Palestinian people in the liberation of Palestine. It must, particularly in the phase of the armed Palestinian revolution, offer and furnish the Palestinian people with all possible help, and material and human support, and make available to them the means and opportunities that will enable them to continue to carry out their leading role in the armed revolution, until they liberate their homeland.

Article 16: The liberation of Palestine, from a spiritual point of view, will provide the Holy Land with an atmosphere of safety and tranquility, which in turn will safeguard the country's religious sanctuaries and guarantee freedom of worship and of visit to all, without discrimination of race, color, language, or religion. Accordingly, the people of Palestine look to all spiritual forces in the world for support.

Article 17: The liberation of Palestine, from a human point of view, will restore to the Palestinian individual his dignity, pride, and freedom. Accordingly the Palestinian Arab people look forward to the support of all those who believe in the dignity of man and his freedom in the world.

Article 18: The liberation of Palestine, from an international point of view, is a defensive action necessitated by the demands of self-defense. Accordingly the Palestinian people, desirous as they are of the friendship of all people, look to freedom-loving, and peace-loving states for support in order to restore their legitimate rights in Palestine, to re-establish peace and security in the country, and to enable its people to exercise national sovereignty and freedom.

Article 19: The partition of Palestine in 1947 and the establishment of the state of Israel are entirely illegal, regardless of the passage of time, because they were contrary to the will of the Palestinian people and to their natural right in their homeland, and inconsistent with the principles embodied in the Charter of the United Nations, particularly the right to self-determination.

Article 20: The Balfour Declaration, the Mandate for Palestine, and everything that has been based upon them, are deemed null and void. Claims of historical or religious ties of Jews with Palestine are incompatible with the facts of history and the true conception of what constitutes statehood. Judaism, being a religion, is not an independent nationality. Nor do Jews constitute a single nation with an identity of its own; they are citizens of the states to which they belong.

Article 21: The Arab Palestinian people, expressing themselves by the armed Palestinian revolution, reject all solutions which are substitutes for the total liberation of Palestine and reject all proposals aiming at the liquidation of the Palestinian problem, or its internationalization.

Article 22: Zionism is a political movement organically associated with international imperialism and antagonistic to all action for liberation and to progressive movements in the world. It is racist and fanatic in its nature, aggressive, expansionist, and colonial in its aims, and fascist in its methods. Israel is the instrument of the Zionist movement, and geographical base for world imperialism placed strategically in the midst of the Arab homeland to combat the hopes of the Arab nation for liberation, unity, and progress. Israel is a constant source of threat vis-à-vis peace in the Middle East and the whole world. Since the liberation of Palestine will destroy the Zionist and imperialist presence and will contribute to the establishment of peace in the Middle East, the Palestinian people look for the support of all the progressive and peaceful forces and urge them all, irrespective of their affiliations and beliefs, to offer the Palestinian people all aid and support in their just struggle for the liberation of their homeland.

Article 23: The demand of security and peace, as well as the demand of right and justice, require all states to consider Zionism an illegitimate movement, to outlaw its existence, and to ban its operations, in order that friendly relations among peoples may be preserved, and the loyalty of citizens to their respective homelands safeguarded.

Article 24: The Palestinian people believe in the principles of justice, freedom, sovereignty, self-determination, human dignity, and in the right of all peoples to exercise them.

Article 25: For the realization of the goals of this Charter and its principles, the Palestine Liberation Organization will perform its role in the liberation of Palestine in accordance with the Constitution of this Organization.

Article 26: The Palestine Liberation Organization, representative of the Palestinian revolutionary forces, is responsible for the Palestinian Arab people's movement in its struggle - to retrieve its homeland, liberate and return to it and exercise the right to self-determination in it - in all military, political, and financial fields and also for whatever may be required by the Palestine case on the inter-Arab and international levels.

Article 27: The Palestine Liberation Organization shall cooperate with all Arab states, each according to its potentialities; and will adopt a neutral policy among them in the light of the requirements of the war of liberation; and on this basis it shall not interfere in the internal affairs of any Arab state.

Article 28: The Palestinian Arab people assert the genuineness and independence of their national (*wataniyya*) revolution and reject all forms of intervention, trusteeship, and subordination.

Article 29: The Palestinian people possess the fundamental and genuine legal right to liberate and retrieve their homeland. The Palestinian people determine their attitude toward all states and forces on the basis of the stands they adopt vis-à-vis to the Palestinian revolution to fulfill the aims of the Palestinian people.

Article 30: Fighters and carriers of arms in the war of liberation are the nucleus of the popular army which will be the protective force for the gains of the Palestinian Arab people.

Article 31: The Organization shall have a flag, an oath of allegiance, and an anthem. All this shall be decided upon in accordance with a special regulation.

Article 32: Regulations, which shall be known as the Constitution of the Palestinian Liberation Organization, shall be annexed to this Charter. It will lay down the manner in which the Organization, and its organs and institutions, shall be constituted; the respective competence of each; and the requirements of its obligation under the Charter.

Article 33: This Charter shall not be amended save by [vote of] a majority of two-thirds of the total membership of the National Congress of the Palestine Liberation Organization [taken] at a special session convened for that purpose.

APPENDIX II: The Camp David Accords
September 17, 1978

The Framework for Peace in the Middle East

Muhammad Anwar al-Sadat, President of the Arab Republic of Egypt, and Menachem Begin, Prime Minister of Israel, met with Jimmy Carter, President of the United States of America, at Camp David from September 5 to September 17, 1978, and have agreed on the following framework for peace in the Middle East. They invite other parties to the Arab-Israel conflict to adhere to it.

Preamble:

The search for peace in the Middle East must be guided by the following:

The agreed basis for a peaceful settlement of the conflict between Israel and its neighbors is United Nations Security Council Resolution 242, in all its parts.

After four wars during 30 years, despite intensive human efforts, the Middle East, which is the cradle of civilization and the birthplace of three great religions, does not enjoy the blessings of peace. The people of the Middle East yearn for peace so that the vast human and natural resources of the region can be turned to the pursuits of peace and so that this area can become a model for coexistence and cooperation among nations.

The historic initiative of President Sadat in visiting Jerusalem and the reception accorded to him by the parliament, government and people of Israel, and the reciprocal visit of Prime Minister Begin to Ismailia, the peace proposals made by both leaders, as well as the warm reception of these missions by the peoples of both countries, have created an unprecedented opportunity for peace which must not be lost if this generation and future generations are to be spared the tragedies of war.

The provisions of the Charter of the United Nations and the other accepted norms of international law and legitimacy now provide accepted standards for the conduct of relations among all states.
To achieve a relationship of peace, in the spirit of Article 2 of the United Nations Charter, future negotiations between Israel and any neighbor prepared to negotiate peace and security with it are necessary for the purpose of carrying out all the provisions and principles of Resolutions 242 and 338.

Peace requires respect for the sovereignty, territorial integrity and political independence of every state in the area and their right to live in peace within secure and recognized boundaries free from threats or acts of force.

Progress toward that goal can accelerate movement toward a new era of reconciliation in the Middle East marked by cooperation in promoting economic development, in maintaining stability and in assuring security.

Security is enhanced by a relationship of peace and by cooperation between nations which enjoy normal relations. In addition, under the terms of peace treaties, the parties can, on the basis of reciprocity, agree to special security arrangements such as demilitarized zones, limited armaments areas, early warning stations, the presence of international forces, liaison, agreed measures for monitoring and other arrangements that they agree are useful.

Framework:

Taking these factors into account, the parties are determined to reach a just, comprehensive, and durable settlement of the Middle East conflict through the conclusion of peace treaties based on Security Council resolutions 242 and 338 in all their parts. Their purpose is to achieve peace and good neighborly relations. They recognize that for peace to endure, it must involve all those who have been most deeply affected by the conflict. They therefore agree that this framework, as appropriate, is intended by them to constitute a basis for peace not only between Egypt and Israel, but also between Israel and each of its other neighbors which is prepared to negotiate peace with Israel on this basis.

With that objective in mind, they have agreed to proceed as follows:

A. West Bank and Gaza
1. Egypt, Israel, Jordan and the representatives of the Palestinian people should participate in negotiations on the resolution of the Palestinian problem in all its aspects. To achieve that objective, negotiations relating to the West Bank and Gaza should proceed in three stages:

> a. Egypt and Israel agree that, in order to ensure a peaceful and orderly transfer of authority, and taking into account the security concerns of all the parties, there should be transitional arrangements for the West Bank and Gaza for a period not exceeding five years. In order to provide full autonomy to the inhabitants, under these arrangements the Israeli military government and its civilian administration will be withdrawn as soon as a self-governing authority has been freely elected by the inhabitants of these areas to replace the existing military government. To negotiate the details of a transitional arrangement, Jordan will be invited to join the negotiations on the basis of this framework. These new arrangements should give due consideration both to the principle of self-government by the inhabitants of these territories and to the legitimate security concerns of the parties involved.

b. Egypt, Israel, and Jordan will agree on the modalities for establishing elected self-governing authority in the West Bank and Gaza. The delegations of Egypt and Jordan may include Palestinians from the West Bank and Gaza or other Palestinians as mutually agreed. The parties will negotiate an agreement which will define the powers and responsibilities of the self-governing authority to be exercised in the West Bank and Gaza. A withdrawal of Israeli armed forces will take place and there will be a redeployment of the remaining Israeli forces into specified security locations. The agreement will also include arrangements for assuring internal and external security and public order. A strong local police force will be established, which may include Jordanian citizens. In addition, Israeli and Jordanian forces will participate in joint patrols and in the manning of control posts to assure the security of the borders.

c. When the self-governing authority (administrative council) in the West Bank and Gaza is established and inaugurated, the transitional period of five years will begin. As soon as possible, but not later than the third year after the beginning of the transitional period, negotiations will take place to determine the final status of the West Bank and Gaza and its relationship with its neighbors and to conclude a peace treaty between Israel and Jordan by the end of the transitional period. These negotiations will be conducted among Egypt, Israel, Jordan and he elected representatives of the inhabitants of the West Bank and Gaza. Two separate but related committees will be convened, one committee, consisting of representatives of the four parties which will negotiate and agree on the final status of the West Bank and Gaza, and its relationship with its neighbors, and the second committee, consisting of representatives of Israel and representatives of Jordan to be joined by the elected representatives of the inhabitants of the West Bank and Gaza, to negotiate the peace treaty between Israel and Jordan, taking into account the agreement reached in the final status of the West Bank and Gaza. The negotiations shall be based on all the provisions and principles of UN Security Council Resolution 242. The negotiations will resolve, among other matters, the location of the boundaries and the nature of the security arrangements. The solution from the negotiations must also recognize the legitimate right of the Palestinian peoples and their just requirements. In this way, the Palestinians will participate in the determination of their own future through:

i.The negotiations among Egypt, Israel, Jordan and the representatives of the inhabitants of the West Bank and Gaza to agree on the final status of the West Bank and Gaza and other outstanding issues by the end of the transitional period.
ii.Submitting their agreements to a vote by the elected representatives of the inhabitants of the West Bank and Gaza.

iii.Providing for the elected representatives of the inhabitants of the West Bank and Gaza to decide how they shall govern themselves consistent with the provisions of their agreement.

iv.Participating as stated above in the work of the committee negotiating the peace treaty between Israel and Jordan.

d. All necessary measures will be taken and provisions made to assure the security of Israel and its neighbors during the transitional period and beyond. To assist in providing such security, a strong local police force will be constituted by the self-governing authority. It will be composed of inhabitants of the West Bank and Gaza. The police will maintain liaison on internal security matters with the designated Israeli, Jordanian, and Egyptian officers.

e. During the transitional period, representatives of Egypt, Israel, Jordan, and the self-governing authority will constitute a continuing committee to decide by agreement on the modalities of admission of persons displaced from the West Bank and Gaza in 1967, together with necessary measures to prevent disruption and disorder. Other matters of common concern may also be dealt with by this committee.

f. Egypt and Israel will work with each other and with other interested parties to establish agreed procedures for a prompt, just and permanent implementation of the resolution of the refugee problem.

B. Egypt-Israel
1.Egypt-Israel undertake not to resort to the threat or the use of force to settle disputes. Any disputes shall be settled by peaceful means in accordance with the provisions of Article 33 of the U.N. Charter.
2. In order to achieve peace between them, the parties agree to negotiate in good faith with a goal of concluding within three months from the signing of the Framework a peace treaty between them while inviting the other parties to the conflict to proceed simultaneously to negotiate and conclude similar Peace treaties with a view the achieving a comprehensive peace in the area. The Framework for the Conclusion of a Peace Treaty between Egypt and Israel will govern the peace negotiations between them. The parties will agree on the modalities and the timetable for the implementation of their obligations under the treaty.
C.Associated Principles

1.Egypt and Israel state that the principles and provisions described below should apply to peace treaties between Israel and each of its neighbors - Egypt, Jordan, Syria and Lebanon.

2. Signatories shall establish among themselves relationships normal to states at peace with one another.

To this end, they should undertake to abide by all the provisions of the U.N. Charter. Steps to be taken in this respect include:
  a.full recognition;
  b.abolishing economic boycotts;
  c.guaranteeing that under their jurisdiction the citizens of the other parties shall enjoy the protection of the due process of law.

3.Signatories should explore possibilities for economic development in the context of final peace treaties,with the objective of contributing to the atmosphere of peace, cooperation and friendship which is their common goal.

4.Claims commissions may be established for the mutual settlement of all financial claims.

5.The United States shall be invited to participated in the talks on matters related to the modalities of the implementation of the agreements and working out the timetable for the carrying out of the obligations of the parties.

6.The United Nations Security Council shall be requested to endorse the peace treaties and ensure that their provisions shall not be violated. The permanent members of the Security Council shall be requested to underwrite the peace treaties and ensure respect or the provisions. They shall be requested to conform their policies an actions with the undertaking contained in this Framework.

For the Government of Israel: Menachem Begin
For the Government of the Arab Republic of Egypt: Muhammed Anwar al-Sadat
Witnessed by Jimmy Carter, President of the United States of America

Framework for the Conclusion of a Peace Treaty Between Egypt and Israel

In order to achieve peace between them, Israel and Egypt agree to negotiate in good faith with a goal of concluding within three months of the signing of this framework a peace treaty between them:
It is agreed that:
The site of the negotiations will be under a United Nations flag at a location or locations to be mutually agreed.

All of the principles of U.N. Resolution 242 will apply in this resolution of the dispute between Israel and Egypt.
Unless otherwise mutually agreed, terms of the peace treaty will be implemented between two and three years after the peace treaty is signed.

The following matters are agreed between the parties:

1. the full exercise of Egyptian sovereignty up to the internationally recognized border between Egypt and mandated Palestine;

2. the withdrawal of Israeli armed forces from the Sinai;

3. the use of airfields left by the Israelis near al-Arish, Rafah, Ras en-Naqb, and Sharm el-Sheikh for civilian purposes only, including possible commercial use only by all nations;

4. the right of free passage by ships of Israel through the Gulf of Suez and the Suez Canal on the basis of the Constantinople Convention of 1888 applying to all nations; the Strait of Tiran and Gulf of Aqaba are international waterways to be open to all nations for unimpeded and nonsuspendable freedom of navigation and overflight;

5. the construction of a highway between the Sinai and Jordan near Eilat with guaranteed free and peaceful passage by Egypt and Jordan; and

6. the stationing of military forces listed below.

Stationing of Forces:

No more than one division (mechanized or infantry) of Egyptian armed forces will be stationed within an area lying approximately 50 km. (30 miles) east of the Gulf of Suez and the Suez Canal.

Only United Nations forces and civil police equipped with light weapons to perform normal police functions will be stationed within an area lying west of the international border and the Gulf of Aqaba, varying in width from 20 km. (12 miles) to 40 km. (24 miles).

In the area within 3 km. (1.8 miles) east of the international border there will be Israeli limited military forces not to exceed four infantry battalions and United Nations observers.

Border patrol units not to exceed three battalions will supplement the civil police in maintaining order in the area not included above.
The exact demarcation of the above areas will be as decided during the peace negotiations.

Early warning stations may exist to insure compliance with the terms of the agreement.

United Nations forces will be stationed:

1. in part of the area in the Sinai lying within about 20 km. of the Mediterranean Sea and adjacent to the international border, and
2. in the Sharm el-Sheikh area to insure freedom of passage through the Strait of Tiran; and these forces will not be removed unless such removal is approved by the Security Council of the United Nations with a unanimous vote of the five permanent members.

After a peace treaty is signed, and after the interim withdrawal is complete, normal relations will be established between Egypt and Israel, including full recognition, including diplomatic, economic and cultural relations; termination of economic boycotts and barriers to the free movement of goods and people; and mutual protection of citizens by the due process of law.

Interim Withdrawal:

Between three months and nine months after the signing of the peace treaty, all Israeli forces will withdraw east of a line extending from a point east of El-Arish to Ras Muhammad, the exact location of this line to be determined by mutual agreement.

For the Government of the Arab Republic of Egypt: Muhammed Anwar al-Sadat
For the Government of Israel: Menachem Begin
Witnessed by: Jimmy Carter, President of the United States of America

APPENDIX III: Declaration of Principles on Interim Self-Government Arrangements
September 13, 1993

The Government of the State of Israel and the P.L.O. team (in the Jordanian-Palestinian delegation to the Middle East Peace Conference) (the "Palestinian Delegation"), representing the Palestinian people, agree that it is time to put an end to decades of confrontation and conflict, recognize their mutual legitimate and political rights, and strive to live in peaceful coexistence and mutual dignity and security and achieve a just, lasting and comprehensive peace settlement and historic reconciliation through the agreed political process. Accordingly, the, two sides agree to the following principles:

ARTICLE I
AIM OF THE NEGOTIATIONS

The aim of the Israeli-Palestinian negotiations within the current Middle East peace process is, among other things, to establish a Palestinian Interim Self-Government Authority, the elected Council (the "Council"), for the Palestinian people in the West Bank and the Gaza Strip, for a transitional period not exceeding five years, leading to a permanent settlement based on Security Council Resolutions 242 and 338.

It is understood that the interim arrangements are an integral part of the whole peace process and that the negotiations on the permanent status will lead to the implementation of Security Council Resolutions 242 and 338.

ARTICLE II
FRAMEWORK FOR THE INTERIM PERIOD

The agreed framework for the interim period is set forth in this Declaration of Principles.

ARTICLE III
ELECTIONS

1. In order that the Palestinian people in the West Bank and Gaza Strip may govern themselves according to democratic principles, direct, free and general political elections will be held for the Council under agreed supervision and international observation, while the Palestinian police will ensure public order.

2. An agreement will be concluded on the exact mode and conditions of the elections in accordance with the protocol attached as Annex I, with the goal of holding the elections not later than nine months after the entry into force of this Declaration of Principles.

3. These elections will constitute a significant interim preparatory step toward the realization of the legitimate rights of the Palestinian people and their just requirements.

ARTICLE IV
JURISDICTION

Jurisdiction of the Council will cover West Bank and Gaza Strip territory, except for issues that will be negotiated in the permanent status negotiations. The two sides view the West Bank and the Gaza Strip as a single territorial unit, whose integrity will be preserved during the interim period.

ARTICLE V
TRANSITIONAL PERIOD AND PERMANENT STATUS NEGOTIA-
TIONS

1. The five-year transitional period will begin upon the withdrawal from the Gaza Strip and Jericho area.

2. Permanent status negotiations will commence as soon as possible, but not later than the beginning of the third year of the interim period, between the Government of Israel and the Palestinian people representatives.

3. It is understood that these negotiations shall cover remaining issues, including: Jerusalem, refugees, settlements, security arrangements, borders, relations and cooperation with other neighbors, and other issues of common interest.

4. The two parties agree that the outcome of the permanent status negotiations should not be prejudiced or preempted by agreements reached for the interim period.

ARTICLE VI
PREPARATORY TRANSFER OF POWERS AND RESPONSIBILITIES

1. Upon the entry into force of this Declaration of Principles and the with-drawal from the Gaza Strip and the Jericho area, a transfer of authority from the Israeli military government and its Civil Administration to the authorized Palestinians for this task, as detailed herein, will commence. This transfer of authority will be of a preparatory nature until the inauguration of the Council.

2. Immediately after the entry into force of this Declaration of Principles and the withdrawal from the Gaza Strip and Jericho area, with the view to promoting economic development in the West Bank and Gaza Strip, authority will be transferred to the Palestinians on the following spheres: education and culture, health, social welfare, direct taxation, and tourism. The Palestinian side will commence in building the Palestinian police force, as agreed upon. Pending the inauguration of the Council, the two parties may negotiate the transfer of additional powers and responsibilities, as agreed upon.

ARTICLE VII
INTERIM AGREEMENT

1. The Israeli and Palestinian delegations will negotiate an agreement on the interim period (the "Interim Agreement")

2. The Interim Agreement shall specify, among other things, the structure of the Council, the number of its members, and the transfer of powers and responsibilities from the Israeli military government and its Civil Administration to the Council. The Interim Agreement shall also specify the Council's executive authority, legislative authority in accordance with Article IX below, and the independent Palestinian judicial organs.

3. The Interim Agreement shall include arrangements, to be implemented upon the inauguration of the Council, for the assumption by the Council of all of the powers and responsibilities transferred previously in accordance with Article VI above.

4. In order to enable the Council to promote economic growth, upon its inauguration, the Council will establish, among other things, a Palestinian Electricity Authority, a Gaza Sea Port Authority, a Palestinian Development Bank, a Palestinian Export Promotion Board, a Palestinian Environmental Authority, a Palestinian Land Authority and a Palestinian Water Administration Authority, and any other Authorities agreed upon, in accordance with the Interim Agreement that will specify their powers and responsibilities.

5. After the inauguration of the Council, the Civil Administration will be dissolved, and the Israeli military government will be withdrawn.

ARTICLE VIII
PUBLIC ORDER AND SECURITY

In order to guarantee public order and internal security for the Palestinians of the West Bank and the Gaza Strip, the Council will establish a strong police force, while Israel will continue to carry the responsibility for defending against external threats, as well as the responsibility for overall security of Israelis for the purpose of safeguarding their internal security and public order.

ARTICLE IX
LAWS AND MILITARY ORDERS

1. The Council will be empowered to legislate, in accordance with the Interim Agreement, within all authorities transferred to it.

2. Both parties will review jointly laws and military orders presently in force in remaining spheres.

ARTICLE X
JOINT ISRAELI-PALESTINIAN LIAISON COMMITTEE

In order to provide for a smooth implementation of this Declaration of Principles and any subsequent agreements pertaining to the interim period, upon the entry into force of this Declaration of Principles, a Joint Israeli-Palestinian Liaison Committee will be established in order to deal with issues requiring coordination, other issues of common interest, and disputes.

ARTICLE XI
ISRAELI-PALESTINIAN COOPERATION IN ECONOMIC FIELDS

Recognizing the mutual benefit of cooperation in promoting the development of the West Bank, the Gaza Strip and Israel, upon the entry into force of this Declaration of Principles, an Israeli-Palestinian Economic Cooperation Committee will be established in order to develop and implement in a cooperative manner the programs identified in the protocols attached as Annex III and Annex IV .

ARTICLE XII
LIAISON AND COOPERATION WITH JORDAN AND EGYPT

The two parties will invite the Governments of Jordan and Egypt to participate in establishing further liaison and cooperation arrangements between the Government of Israel and the Palestinian representatives, on the one hand, and the Governments of Jordan and Egypt, on the other hand, to promote cooperation between them. These arrangements will include the constitution of a Continuing Committee that will decide by agreement on the modalities of admission of persons displaced from the West Bank and Gaza Strip in 1967, together with necessary measures to prevent disruption and disorder. Other matters of common concern will be dealt with by this Committee.

ARTICLE XIII
REDEPLOYMENT OF ISRAELI FORCES

1. After the entry into force of this Declaration of Principles, and not later

than the eve of elections for the Council, a redeployment of Israeli military forces in the West Bank and the Gaza Strip will take place, in addition to withdrawal of Israeli forces carried out in accordance with Article XIV.

2. In redeploying its military forces, Israel will be guided by the principle that its military forces should be redeployed outside populated areas.

3. Further redeployments to specified locations will be gradually implemented commensurate with the assumption of responsibility for public order and internal security by the Palestinian police force pursuant to Article VIII above.

ARTICLE XIV
ISRAELI WITHDRAWAL FROM THE GAZA STRIP AND JERICHO AREA

Israel will withdraw from the Gaza Strip and Jericho area, as detailed in the protocol attached as Annex II.

ARTICLE XV
RESOLUTION OF DISPUTES

1. Disputes arising out of the application or interpretation of this Declaration of Principles. or any subsequent agreements pertaining to the interim period, shall be resolved by negotiations through the Joint Liaison Committee to be established pursuant to Article X above.

2. Disputes which cannot be settled by negotiations may be resolved by a mechanism of conciliation to be agreed upon by the parties.

3. The parties may agree to submit to arbitration disputes relating to the interim period, which cannot be settled through conciliation. To this end, upon the agreement of both parties, the parties will establish an Arbitration Committee.

ARTICLE XVI
ISRAELI-PALESTINIAN COOPERATION CONCERNING REGIONAL PROGRAMS

Both parties view the multilateral working groups as an appropriate instrument for promoting a "Marshall Plan", the regional programs and other programs, including special programs for the West Bank and Gaza Strip, as indicated in the protocol attached as Annex IV.

ARTICLE XVII
MISCELLANEOUS PROVISIONS

1. This Declaration of Principles will enter into force one month after its signing.
2. All protocols annexed to this Declaration of Principles and Agreed Minutes pertaining thereto shall be regarded as an integral part hereof.

Done at Washington, D.C., this thirteenth day of September, 1993.

ANNEX I
PROTOCOL ON THE MODE AND CONDITIONS OF ELECTIONS

1. Palestinians of Jerusalem who live there will have the right to participate in the election process, according to an agreement between the two sides.
2. In addition, the election agreement should cover, among other things, the following issues:
    a. The system of elections;
    b. The mode of the agreed supervision and international observation and their personal composition; and
    c. Rules and regulations regarding election campaign, including agreed arrangements for the organizing of mass media, and the possibility of licensing a broadcasting and TV station.

3. The future status of displaced Palestinians who were registered on 4th June 1967 will not be prejudiced because they are unable to participate in the election process due to practical reasons.

ANNEX II
PROTOCOL ON WITHDRAWAL OF ISRAELI FORCES FROM THE GAZA STRIP AND JERICHO AREA

1. The two sides will conclude and sign within two months from the date of entry into force of this Declaration of Principles, an agreement on the withdrawal of Israeli military forces from the Gaza Strip and Jericho area. This agreement will include comprehensive arrangements to apply in the Gaza Strip and the Jericho area subsequent to the Israeli withdrawal.

2. Israel will implement an accelerated and scheduled withdrawal of Israeli military forces from the Gaza Strip and Jericho area, beginning immediately with the signing of the agreement on the Gaza Strip and Jericho area and to be completed within a period not exceeding four months after the signing

of this agreement.

3. The above agreement will include, among other things:

a. Arrangements for a smooth and peaceful transfer of authority from the Israeli military government and its Civil Administration to the Palestinian representatives.

b. Structure, powers and responsibilities of the Palestinian authority in these areas, except: external security, settlements, Israelis, foreign relations, and other mutually agreed matters.

c. Arrangements for the assumption of internal security and public order by the Palestinian police force consisting of police officers recruited locally and from abroad holding Jordanian passports and Palestinian documents issued by Egypt). Those who will participate in the Palestinian police force coming from abroad should be trained as police and police officers.

d. A temporary international or foreign presence, as agreed upon.

e. Establishment of a joint Palestinian-Israeli Coordination and Cooperation Committee for mutual security purposes.

f. An economic development and stabilization program, including the establishment of an Emergency Fund, to encourage foreign investment, and financial and economic support. Both sides will coordinate and cooperate jointly and unilaterally with regional and international parties to support these aims.

g. Arrangements for a safe passage for persons and transportation between the Gaza Strip and Jericho area.

4. The above agreement will include arrangements for coordination between both parties regarding passages:

a. Gaza - Egypt; and

b. Jericho - Jordan.

5. The offices responsible for carrying out the powers and responsibilities of the Palestinian authority under this Annex II and
Article VI of the Declaration of Principles will be located in the Gaza Strip and in the Jericho area pending the inauguration of the Council.

6. Other than these agreed arrangements, the status of the Gaza Strip and Jericho area will continue to be an integral part of the West Bank and Gaza Strip, and will not be changed in the interim period.

ANNEX III
PROTOCOL ON ISRAELI-PALESTINIAN COOPERATION IN ECO-
NOMIC AND DEVELOPMENT PROGRAMS

The two sides agree to establish an Israeli-Palestinian continuing Committee for Economic Cooperation, focusing, among other things, on the following:

1. Cooperation in the field of water, including a Water Development Program prepared by experts from both sides, which will also specify the mode of cooperation in the management of water resources in the West Bank

and Gaza Strip, and will include proposals for studies and plans on water rights of each party, as well as on the equitable utilization of joint water resources for implementation in and beyond the interim period.

2. Cooperation in the field of electricity, including an Electricity Development Program, which will also specify the mode of cooperation for the production, maintenance, purchase and sale of electricity resources.

3. Cooperation in the field of energy, including an Energy Development Program, which will provide for the exploitation of oil and gas for industrial purposes, particularly in the Gaza Strip and in the Negev, and will encourage further joint exploitation of other energy resources. This Program may also provide for the construction of a Petrochemical industrial complex in the Gaza Strip and the construction of oil and gas pipelines.

4. Cooperation in the field of finance, including a Financial Development and Action Program for the encouragement of international investment in the West Bank and the Gaza Strip, and in Israel, as well as the establishment of a Palestinian Development Bank.

5. Cooperation in the field of transport and communications, including a Program, which will define guidelines for the establishment of a Gaza Sea Port Area, and will provide for the establishing of transport and communications lines to and from the West Bank and the Gaza Strip to Israel and to other countries. In addition, this Program will provide for carrying out the necessary construction of roads, railways, communications lines, etc.

6. Cooperation in the field of trade, including studies, and Trade Promotion Programs, which will encourage local, regional and inter-regional trade, as well as a feasibility study of creating free trade zones in the Gaza Strip and in Israel, mutual access to these zones, and cooperation in other areas related to trade and commerce.

7. Cooperation in the field of industry, including Industrial Development Programs, which will provide for the establishment of joint Israeli-Palestinian Industrial Research and Development Centers, will promote Palestinian-Israeli joint ventures, and provide guidelines for cooperation in the textile, food, pharmaceutical, electronics, diamonds, computer and science-based industries.

8. A program for cooperation in, and regulation of, labor relations and cooperation in social welfare issues.

9. A Human Resources Development and Cooperation Plan, providing for joint Israeli-Palestinian workshops and seminars, and for the establishment of joint vocational training centers, research institutes and data banks.

10. An Environmental Protection Plan, providing for joint and/or coordinated measures in this sphere.

11. A program for developing coordination and cooperation in the field of communication and media.
12. Any other programs of mutual interest.

ANNEX IV
PROTOCOL ON ISRAELI-PALESTINIAN COOPERATION CONCERNING REGIONAL DEVELOPMENT PROGRAMS

1. The two sides will cooperate in the context of the multilateral peace efforts in promoting a Development Program for the region, including the West Bank and the Gaza Strip, to be initiated by the G-7. The parties will request the G-7 to seek the participation in this program of other interested states, such as members of the Organisation for Economic Cooperation and Development, regional Arab states and institutions, as well as members of the private sector.
2. The Development Program will consist of two elements:
    a. an Economic Development Program for the 'West Bank and the Gaza Strip.
    b. a Regional Economic Development Program.

A. The Economic Development Program for the West Bank and the Gaza strip will consist of the following elements:

1. A Social Rehabilitation Program, including a Housing and Construction Program.
2. A Small and Medium Business Development Plan.
3. An Infrastructure Development Program (water, electricity, transportation and communications, etc.)
4. A Human Resources Plan.
5. Other programs.

B. The Regional Economic Development Program may consist of the following elements:

1. The establishment of a Middle East Development Fund, as a first step, and a Middle East Development Bank, as a second step.
2. The development of a joint Israeli-Palestinian-Jordanian Plan for coordinated exploitation of the Dead Sea area.
3. The Mediterranean Sea (Gaza) - Dead Sea Canal.
4. Regional Desalinization and other water development projects.
5. A regional plan for agricultural development, including a coordinated regional effort for the prevention of desertification.
6. Interconnection of electricity grids.
7. Regional cooperation for the transfer, distribution and industrial exploitation of gas, oil and other energy resources.

8. A Regional Tourism, Transportation and Telecommunications Development Plan.
9. Regional cooperation in other spheres.

3. The two sides will encourage the multilateral working groups, and will coordinate towards their success. The two parties will encourage intersessional activities, as well as pre-feasibility and feasibility studies, within the various multilateral working groups.

AGREED MINUTES TO THE DECLARATION OF PRINCIPLES ON INTERIM SELF-GOVERNMENT ARRANGEMENTS

A. GENERAL UNDERSTANDINGS AND AGREEMENTS

Any powers and responsibilities transferred to the Palestinians pursuant to the Declaration of Principles prior to the inauguration of the Council will be subject to the same principles pertaining to Article IV, as set out in these Agreed Minutes below.

B. SPECIFIC UNDERSTANDINGS AND AGREEMENTS

Article IV
It is understood that:
1. Jurisdiction of the Council will cover West Bank and Gaza Strip territory, except for issues that will be negotiated in the permanent status negotiations: Jerusalem, settlements, military locations, and Israelis.

2. The Council's jurisdiction will apply with regard to the agreed powers, responsibilities, spheres and authorities transferred to it.

Article VI (2)
It is agreed that the transfer of authority will be as follows:
1. The Palestinian side will inform the Israeli side of the names of theauthorised Palestinians who will assume the powers, authorities and responsibilities that will be transferred to the Palestinians according to the Declaration of Principles in the following fields: education and culture, health, social welfare, direct taxation, tourism, and any other authorities agreed upon.
2. It is understood that the rights and obligations of these offices will not be affected.
3. Each of the spheres described above will continue to enjoy existing budgetary allocations in accordance with arrangements to be mutually agreed upon. These arrangements also will provide for the necessary adjustments required in order to take into account the taxes collected by the direct taxation office.

4. Upon the execution of the Declaration of Principles, the Israeli and Palestinian delegations will immediately commence negotiations on a

detailed plan for the transfer of authority on the above offices in accordance with the above understandings.

Article VII (2)

The Interim Agreement will also include arrangements for coordination and cooperation.

Article VII (5)

The withdrawal of the military government will not prevent Israel from exercising the powers and responsibilities not transferred to the Council.

Article VIII

It is understood that the Interim Agreement will include arrangements for cooperation and coordination between the two parties in this regard. It is also agreed that the transfer of powers and responsibilities to the Palestinian police will be accomplished in a phased manner, as agreed in the Interim Agreement.

Article X

It is agreed that, upon the entry into force of the Declaration of Principles, the Israeli and Palestinian delegations will exchange the names of the individuals designated by them as members of the Joint Israeli-Palestinian Liaison Committee.

It is further agreed that each side will have an equal number of members in the Joint Committee. The Joint Committee will reach decisions by agreement. The Joint Committee may add other technicians and experts, as necessary. The Joint Committee will decide on the frequency and place or places of its meetings.

Annex II

It is understood that, subsequent to the Israeli withdrawal, Israel will continue to be responsible for external security, and for internal security and public order of settlements and Israelis. Israeli military forces and civilians may continue to use roads freely within the Gaza Strip and the Jericho area.

APPENDIX IV: The Wye River Memorandum
October 23, 1998

The following are steps to facilitate implementation of the Interim Agreement on the West Bank and Gaza Strip of September 28, 1995 (the "Interim Agreement") and other related agreements including the Note for the Record of January 17, 1997 (hereinafter referred to as "the prior agreements") so that the Israeli and Palestinian sides can more effectively carry out their reciprocal responsibilities, including those relating to further redeployments and security respectively. These steps are to be carried out in a parallel phased approach in accordance with this Memorandum and the attached time line. They are subject to the relevant terms and conditions of the prior agreements and do not supersede their other requirements.

I. FURTHER REDEPLOYMENTS
A. Phase One and Two Further Redeployments
1. Pursuant to the Interim Agreement and subsequent agreements, the Israeli side's implementation of the first and second F.R.D. will consist of the transfer to the Palestinian side of 13% from Area C as follows:
1% to Area (A)
12% to Area (B)

The Palestinian side has informed that it will allocate an area/areas amounting to 3% from the above Area (B) to be designated as Green Areas and/or Nature Reserves. The Palestinian side has further informed that they will act according to the established scientific standards, and that therefore there will be no changes in the status of these areas, without prejudice to the rights of the existing inhabitants in these areas including Bedouins; while these standards do not allow new construction in these areas, existing roads and buildings may be maintained.

The Israeli side will retain in these Green Areas/Nature Reserves the overriding security responsibility for the purpose of protecting Israelis and confronting the threat of terrorism. Activities and movements of the Palestinian Police forces may be carried out after coordination and confirmation; the Israeli side will respond to such requests expeditiously.

2. As part of the foregoing implementation of the first and second F.R.D., 14.2% from Area (B) will become Area (A).

B. Third Phase of Further Redeployments
With regard to the terms of the Interim Agreement and of Secretary Christopher's letters to the two sides of January 17, 1997 relating to the further redeployment process, there will be a committee to address this question. The United States will be briefed regularly.

II. SECURITY

In the provisions on security arrangements of the Interim Agreement, the Palestinian side agreed to take all measures necessary in order to prevent acts of terrorism, crime and hostilities directed against the Israeli side, against individuals falling under the Israeli side's authority and against their property, just as the Israeli side agreed to take all measures necessary in order to prevent acts of terrorism, crime and hostilities directed against the Palestinian side, against individuals falling under the Palestinian side's authority and against their property. The two sides also agreed to take legal measures against offenders within their jurisdiction and to prevent incitement against each other by any organizations, groups or individuals within their jurisdiction.

Both sides recognize that it is in their vital interests to combat terrorism and fight violence in accordance with Annex I of the Interim Agreement and the Note for the Record. They also recognize that the struggle against terror and violence must be comprehensive in that it deals with terrorists, the terror support structure, and the environment conducive to the support of terror. It must be continuous and constant over a long-term, in that there can be no pauses in the work against terrorists and their structure. It must be cooperative in that no effort can be fully effective without Israeli-Palestinian cooperation and the continuous exchange of information, concepts, and actions.

Pursuant to the prior agreements, the Palestinian side's implementation of its responsibilities for security, security cooperation, and other issues will be as detailed below during the time periods specified in the attached time line:

A. Security Actions

1. Outlawing and Combating Terrorist Organizations

a. The Palestinian side will make known its policy of zero tolerance for terror and violence against both sides.

b. A work plan developed by the Palestinian side will be shared with the U.S. and thereafter implementation will begin immediately to ensure the systematic and effective combat of terrorist organizations and their infrastructure.

c. In addition to the bilateral Israeli-Palestinian security cooperation, a U.S.-Palestinian committee will meet biweekly to review the steps being taken to eliminate terrorist cells and the support structure that plans, finances, supplies and abets terror. In these meetings, the Palestinian side will inform the U.S. fully of the actions it has taken to outlaw all organizations (or wings of organizations, as appropriate) of a military, terrorist or violent character and their support structure and to prevent them from operating in areas under its jurisdiction.

d. The Palestinian side will apprehend the specific individuals suspected of perpetrating acts of violence and terror for the purpose of further investigation, and prosecution and punishment of all persons involved in acts of violence and terror.

e. A U.S.-Palestinian committee will meet to review and evaluate information pertinent to the decisions on prosecution, punishment or other legal measures which affect the status of individuals suspected of abetting or perpetrating acts of violence and terror.

2. Prohibiting Illegal Weapons
a. The Palestinian side will ensure an effective legal framework is in place to criminalize, in conformity with the prior agreements, any importation, manufacturing or unlicensed sale, acquisition or possession of firearms, ammunition or weapons in areas under Palestinian jurisdiction.
b. In addition, the Palestinian side will establish and vigorously and continuously implement a systematic program for the collection and appropriate handling of all such illegal items in accordance with the prior agreements. The U.S. has agreed to assist in carrying out this program.
c. A U.S.-Palestinian-Israeli committee will be established to assist and enhance cooperation in preventing the smuggling or other unauthorized introduction of weapons or explosive materials into areas under Palestinian jurisdiction.

3. Preventing Incitement
a. Drawing on relevant international practice and pursuant to Article XXII (1) of the Interim Agreement and the Note for the Record, the Palestinian side will issue a decree prohibiting all forms of incitement to violence or terror, and establishing mechanisms for acting systematically against all expressions or threats of violence or terror. This decree will be comparable to the existing Israeli legislation which deals with the same subject.
b. A U.S.-Palestinian-Israeli committee will meet on a regular basis to monitor cases of possible incitement to violence or terror and to make recommendations and reports on how to prevent such incitement. The Israeli, Palestinian and U.S. sides will each appoint a media specialist, a law enforcement representative, an educational specialist and a current or former elected official to the committee.

B. Security Cooperation
The two sides agree that their security cooperation will be based on a spirit of partnership and will include, among other things, the following steps:
1. Bilateral Cooperation
There will be full bilateral security cooperation between the two sides which will be continuous, intensive and comprehensive.
2. Forensic Cooperation
There will be an exchange of forensic expertise, training, and other assistance.
3. Trilateral Committee
In addition to the bilateral Israeli-Palestinian security cooperation, a high-

ranking U.S.-Palestinian-Israeli committee will meet as required and not less than biweekly to assess current threats, deal with any impediments to effective security cooperation and coordination and address the steps being taken to combat terror and terrorist organizations.

The committee will also serve as a forum to address the issue of external support for terror. In these meetings, the Palestinian side will fully inform the members of the committee of the results of its investigations concerning terrorist suspects already in custody and the participants will exchange additional relevant information The committee will report regularly to the leaders of the two sides on the status of cooperation, the results of the meetings and its recommendations.

C. Other Issues
1. Palestinian Police Force
a. The Palestinian side will provide a list of its policemen to the Israeli side in conformity with the prior agreements.
b. Should the Palestinian side request technical assistance, the U.S. has indicated its willingness to help meet these needs in cooperation with other donors.
c. The Monitoring and Steering Committee will, as part of its functions, monitor the implementation of this provision and brief the U.S.

2. PLO Charter

The Executive Committee of the Palestine Liberation Organization and the Palestinian Central Council will reaffirm the letter of 22 January 1998 from PLO Chairman Yasir Arafat to President Clinton concerning the nullification of the Palestinian National Charter provisions that are inconsistent with the letters exchanged between the PLO and the Government of Israel on 9/10 September 1993. PLO Chairman Arafat, the Speaker of the Palestine National Council, and the Speaker of the Palestinian Council will invite the members of the PNC, as well as the members of the Central Council, the Council, and the Palestinian Heads of Ministries to a meeting to be addressed by President Clinton to reaffirm their support for the peace process and the aforementioned decisions of the Executive Committee and the Central Council.

3. Legal Assistance in Criminal Matters

Among other forms of legal assistance in criminal matters, the requests for arrest and transfer of suspects and defendants pursuant to Article II(7) of Annex IV of the Interim Agreement will be submitted (or resubmitted) through the mechanism of the Joint Israeli-Palestinian Legal Committee and will be responded to in conformity with Article II (7) (f) of Annex IV of the Interim Agreement within the twelve week period.

Requests submitted after the eighth week will be responded to in conformity with Article II (7) (f) within four weeks of their submission. The U.S. has
been requested by the sides to report on a regular basis on the steps being
taken to respond to the above requests.
4. Human Rights and the Rule of Law

Pursuant to Article XI (1) of Annex I of the Interim Agreement, and without
derogating from the above, the Palestinian Police will exercise powers and
responsibilities to implement this Memorandum with due regard to internationally accepted norms of human rights and the rule of law, and will be
guided by the need to protect the public, respect human dignity, and avoid
harassment.

III. INTERIM COMMITTEES AND ECONOMIC ISSUES

1. The Israeli and Palestinian sides reaffirm their commitment to enhancing
their relationship and agree on the need actively to promote economic development in the West Bank and Gaza. In this regard, the parties agree to continue or to reactivate all standing committees established by the Interim
Agreement, including the Monitoring and Steering Committee, the Joint
Economic Committee (JEC), the Civil Affairs Committee (CAC), the Legal
Committee, and the Standing Cooperation Committee.

2. The Israeli and Palestinian sides have agreed on arrangements which will
permit the timely opening of the Gaza Industrial Estate. They also have concluded a "Protocol Regarding the Establishment and Operation of the
International Airport in the Gaza Strip During the Interim Period."

3. Both sides will renew negotiations on Safe Passage immediately. As
regards the southern route, the sides will make best efforts to conclude the
agreement within a week of the entry into force of this Memorandum.
Operation of the southern route will start as soon as possible thereafter. As
regards the northern route, negotiations will continue with the goal of reaching agreement as soon as possible. Implementation will take place expeditiously thereafter.

4. The Israeli and Palestinian sides acknowledge the great importance of the
Port of Gaza for the development of the Palestinian economy, and the expansion of Palestinian trade. They commit themselves to proceeding without
delay to conclude an agreement to allow the construction and operation of
the port in accordance with the prior agreements. The Israeli-Palestinian
Committee will reactivate its work immediately with a goal of concluding
the protocol within sixty days, which will allow commencement of the construction of the port.
5. The two sides recognize that unresolved legal issues adversely affect the
relationship between the two peoples. They therefore will accelerate efforts

through the Legal Committee to address outstanding legal issues and to implement solutions to these issues in the shortest possible period.

The Palestinian side will provide to the Israeli side copies of all of its laws in effect.
6. The Israeli and Palestinian sides also will launch a strategic economic dialogue to enhance their economic relationship. They will establish within the framework of the JEC an Ad Hoc Committee for this purpose. The committee will review the following four issues: (1) Israeli purchase taxes; (2) cooperation in combating vehicle theft; (3) dealing with unpaid Palestinian debts; and (4) the impact of Israeli standards as barriers to trade and the expansion of the A1 and A2 lists. The committee will submit an interim report within three weeks of the entry into force of this Memorandum, and within six weeks will submit its conclusions and recommendations to be implemented.

7. The two sides agree on the importance of continued international donor assistance to facilitate implementation by both sides of agreements reached. They also recognize the need for enhanced donor support for economic development in the West Bank and Gaza. They agree to jointly approach the donor community to organize a Ministerial Conference before the end of 1998 to seek pledges for enhanced levels of assistance.

IV. PERMANENT STATUS NEGOTIATIONS
The two sides will immediately resume permanent status negotiations on an accelerated basis and will make a determined effort to achieve the mutual goal of reaching an agreement by May 4, 1999. The negotiations will be continuous and without interruption. The U.S. has expressed its willingness to facilitate these negotiations.

V. UNILATERAL ACTIONS
Recognizing the necessity to create a positive environment for the negotiations, neither side shall initiate or take any step that will change the status of the West Bank and the Gaza Strip in accordance with the Interim Agreement.

ATTACHMENT: Time Line

This Memorandum will enter into force ten days from the date of signature.

TIME LINE

Note: Parenthetical references below are to paragraphs in "The Wye River Memorandum" to which this time line is an integral attachment. Topics not included in the time line follow the schedule provided for in the text of the Memorandum.

1. Upon Entry into Force of the Memorandum:
Third further redeployment committee starts (I (B)) Palestinian security work plan shared with the U.S. (II (A) (1) (b)) Full bilateral security cooperation (II (B) (1)) Trilateral security cooperation committee starts (II (B) (3)) Interim committees resume and continue; Ad Hoc Economic Committee starts (III) Accelerated permanent status negotiations start (IV)

2. Entry into Force - Week 2:

Security work plan implementation begins (II (A) (1) (b)); (II (A) (1) (c)) committee starts Illegal weapons framework in place (II (A) (2) (a)); Palestinian implementation report (II (A) (2) (b)) Anti-incitement committee starts (II (A) (3) (b)); decree issued (II (A) (3) (a)) PLO Executive Committee reaffirms Charter letter (II (C) (2)) Stage 1 of F.R.D. implementation: 2% C to B, 7.1% B to A. Israeli officials acquaint their Palestinian counterparts as required with areas; F.R.D. carried out; report on F.R.D. implementation (I(A))

3. Week 2-6:
Palestinian Central Council reaffirms Charter letter (weeks two to four) (II (C) (2)) PNC and other PLO organizations reaffirm Charter letter (weeks four to six) (II (C) (2)) Establishment of weapons collection program (II (A) (2) (b)) and collection stage (II (A) (2) (c)); committee starts and reports on activities. Anti-incitement committee report (II (A) (3) (b)) Ad Hoc Economic Committee: interim report at week three; final report at week six (III) Policemen list (II (C) (1) (a)); Monitoring and Steering Committee review starts (II (C) (1) (c) Stage 2 of F.R.D. implementation: 5% C to B. Israeli officials acquaint their Palestinian counterparts as required with areas; F.R.D. carried out; report on F.R.D. implementation (I (A))

4. Week 6-12:
Weapons collection stage II (A) (2) (b); II (A) (2) (c) committee report on its activities. Anti-incitement committee report (II (A) (3) (b)) Monitoring and Steering Committee briefs U.S. on policemen list (II (C) (1) (c)) Stage 3 of F.R.D. implementation: 5% C to B, 1% C to A, 7.1% B to A. Israeli officials acquaint Palestinian counterparts as required with areas; F.R.D. carried out; report on F.R.D. implementation (I(A))

5. After Week 12:
Activities described in the Memorandum continue as appropriate and if necessary, including: Trilateral security cooperation committee (II (B)(3)) (II (A) (1) (c)) committee (II (A) (1) (e)) committee Anti-incitement committee (II (A) (3) (b)) Third Phase F.R.D. Committee (I (B)) Interim Committees (III) Accelerated permanent status negotiations (IV)

INDEX: